THE POSTCOLONIAL SUBJECT

This book places the lens on postcolonial agency and resistance in a social and geopolitical context that has witnessed great transformations in international politics. What does postcolonial politics mean in a late modern context of interventions that seek to govern postcolonial populations? Drawing on historic and contemporary articulations of agency and resistance and highlighting voices from the postcolonial world, the book explores the transition from colonial modernity to the late modern postcolonial era. It shows that at each moment wherein the claim to politics is made, the postcolonial subject comes face to face with global operations of power that seek to control and govern. As seen in the Middle East and elsewhere, these operations have variously drawn on war, policing, as well as pedagogical practices geared at governing the political aspirations of target societies. The book provides a conceptualisation of postcolonial political subjectivity, discusses moments of its emergence, and exposes the security agendas that seek to govern it.

Engaging with political thought, from Hannah Arendt, to Frantz Fanon, Michel Foucault, and Edward Said, among other critical and postcolonial theorists, and drawing on art, literature, and film from the postcolonial world, this work will be of great interest to students and scholars of critical international relations, postcolonial theory, and political theory.

Vivienne Jabri is Professor of International Politics in the Department of War Studies, King's College London.

Interventions

Edited by:
Jenny Edkins, Aberystwyth University and
Nick Vaughan-Williams, University of Warwick

'As Michel Foucault has famously stated, "knowledge is not made for understanding; it is made for cutting". In this spirit The Edkins–Vaughan-Williams Interventions series solicits cutting edge, critical works that challenge mainstream understandings in international relations. It is the best place to contribute post-disciplinary works that think rather than merely recognize and affirm the world recycled in IR's traditional geopolitical imaginary.'
Michael J. Shapiro, University of Hawai'i at Mānoa, USA

The series aims to advance understanding of the key areas in which scholars working within broad critical post-structural and post-colonial traditions have chosen to make their interventions, and to present innovative analyses of important topics.

Titles in the series engage with critical thinkers in philosophy, sociology, politics and other disciplines and provide situated historical, empirical and textual studies in international politics.

Critical Theorists and International Relations
Edited by Jenny Edkins and Nick Vaughan-Williams

Ethics as Foreign Policy
Britain, the EU and the other
Dan Bulley

Universality, Ethics and International Relations
A grammatical reading
Véronique Pin-Fat

The Time of the City
Politics, philosophy, and genre
Michael J. Shapiro

Governing Sustainable Development
Partnership, protest and power at the world summit
Carl Death

Insuring Security
Biopolitics, security and risk
Luis Lobo-Guerrero

Foucault and International Relations
New critical engagements
Edited by Nicholas J. Kiersey and Doug Stokes

International Relations and Non-Western Thought
Imperialism, colonialism and investigations of global modernity
Edited by Robbie Shilliam

Autobiographical International Relations
I, IR
Edited by Naeem Inayatullah

War and Rape
Law, memory and justice
Nicola Henry

Madness in International Relations
Psychology, security and the global governance of mental health
Alison Howell

Spatiality, Sovereignty and Carl Schmitt
Geographies of the nomos
Edited by Stephen Legg

Politics of Urbanism
Seeing like a city
Warren Magnusson

Beyond Biopolitics
Theory, violence and horror in world politics
François Debrix and Alexander D. Barder

The Politics of Speed
Capitalism, the state and war in an accelerating world
Simon Glezos

Politics and the Art of Commemoration
Memorials to struggle in Latin America and Spain
Katherine Hite

Indian Foreign Policy
The politics of postcolonial identity
Priya Chacko

Politics of the Event
Time, movement, becoming
Tom Lundborg

Theorising Post-Conflict Reconciliation
Agonism, restitution and repair
Edited by Alexander Keller Hirsch

Europe's Encounter with Islam
The secular and the postsecular
Luca Mavelli

Re-Thinking International Relations Theory via Deconstruction
Badredine Arfi

The New Violent Cartography
Geo-analysis after the aesthetic turn
Edited by Sam Okoth Opondo and Michael J. Shapiro

Insuring War
Sovereignty, security and risk
Luis Lobo-Guerrero

International Relations, Meaning and Mimesis
Necati Polat

The Postcolonial Subject
Claiming politics/governing others in late modernity
Vivienne Jabri

Foucault and the Politics of Hearing
Lauri Siisiäinen

THE POSTCOLONIAL SUBJECT

Claiming politics/governing others in late modernity

Vivienne Jabri

Routledge
Taylor & Francis Group

LONDON AND NEW YORK

First published 2013 by Routledge
2 Park Square, Milton Park, Abingdon, Oxon, OX14 4RN

Simultaneously published in the USA and Canada
by Routledge
711 Third Avenue, New York, NY 10017

Routledge is an imprint of the Taylor & Francis Group, an informa business

British Library Cataloguing in Publication Data
A catalogue record for this book is available from the British Library

Library of Congress Cataloging in Publication Data
Jabri, Vivienne, 1958-
The postcolonial subject : claiming politics/governing others in late modernity / Vivienne Jabri.
p. cm. -- (Interventions)
Includes bibliographical references and index.
1. International relations. 2. Postcolonialism. I. Title.
JZ1251.J33 2012
325'.32--dc23
2011052217

ISBN: 978-0-415-68210-7 (hbk)
ISBN: 978-0-415-68211-4 (pbk)
ISBN: 978-0-203-11225-0 (ebk)

Typeset in Bembo by Saxon Graphics Ltd, Derby

CONTENTS

PREFACE

Two events frame the writing of this book. The first, the invasion of Iraq, made a lasting imprint, and indeed took me back to the spaces and locations that seemed to be in the distant past. Hatred of a tyrannical regime now went hand in hand with anger at the unleashing of violence and abuse by the world's strongest and largest military machine against an already abused population. This first event was the driver behind my last book, dedicated to exploring the subject of war and war's place in the transformation of the modern international, the terrain that had made the 'post' in the postcolonial meaningful. This first event remains with me now in the writing of this book, dedicated as it is to the postcolonial subject, she or he who remains the target of such war, seemingly vulnerable to global legislating practices authored elsewhere.

However, there emerged another 'event' during the writing of this book, once more in the Middle East, and one that again propelled me and others back to the region and the streets that were now being claimed by its populations. The resounding call was for a democratic future, one where the state could be reclaimed in the service of populations and not the oligarchical regimes that had been in place throughout the postcolonial era. The so-called Arab Spring was suggestive of a 'new' phenomenon and yet there had been other attempts at rebellion, other efforts at dissent, other calls for the right to politics. What seemed beyond dispute, and indeed continues to be so as I write this, is that, regardless of its outcomes, this was a significant, distinctly political moment, one that somehow, at least for this author, placed the lens on the postcolonial condition and the postcolonial subject.

The two events seem to represent two poles: on the one hand global power, and on the other the articulation of resistance. However, what is of greater interest is that the two events, or moments, could not be related in a uniform, linear causal relationship. That resistance against occupation had emerged and took many forms in the context of a fragmented, divided Iraq was not in doubt. However, what was of profound interest in relation to the uprisings of the Arab world was that resistance was being articulated against the local regimes, long sustained and reinforced by external powers. Populations that had long been subjected to an orientalist discursive framing, complicit in their depoliticiation, had now risen to claim politics, to assert a presence in political space and time.

Where the first event, the invasion of Iraq, represented the articulation of power, now globally rendered, and whose edict was and continues to be the government of others, the second brought forth the postcolonial subject's claim to politics. Where the first sought to depoliticise, and through such, to discipline and govern, the second sought to assert political agency. Where the first reacted with fear and trepidation against the potential of democracy in the Middle East, the second seemed to suggest a different imaginary, one that sought the conditions of possibility for politics and hence political contestation without fragmentation.

The two dynamics continue to be at play, generating tension within this moment of transformation. The imperatives of a global apparatus of security are all too present amidst calls for freedom, as are forces that seek to shape the future to come. The tensions are not just apparent in the dynamic between 'government' and 'politics', the imperative to govern the revolutionary moment and this moment's imaginary of a moment to come, but also in the local frames of meaning through which this latter moment is constituted. When placed in the context of late modernity, we might say that these tensions negotiate the lines of a cosmopolitan socio-political terrain that produces at one and the same time a cosmopolitanism of government that targets its machinery at the shaping of societies in accordance with a script authored elsewhere, and a cosmopolitanism of politics that seeks solidarity in a distinctly late-modern articulation of self-determination, and hence of politics.

The question that animates this project revolves around what it means to be a postcolonial subject in late modernity, how this subject is formed and shaped in an era wherein the colonial legacy is not just borne as an imprint, but seems to be resurgent, and how, despite the odds, this subject comes to articulate political agency. These are all interrelated questions and their complexity is multiplied by the sheer diversity that defines the postcolonial world, the experiences of its populations, and the socio-economic and political trajectories that position different parts of this world in relation to the international and its structural continuities. At the same time, to refer to a postcolonial subject immediately implies a focus on the 'post' in the postcolonial, so that the space and time of such a designation come to have profound significance. To ask the question 'what does it mean to be a postcolonial subject in late modernity?' is also to ask what does the modern international mean for this subject, how are the two constituted, and what role does the postcolonial subject have in relation to the international as a distinct location of politics? As will become apparent, there is no way in which these questions can be investigated without the acknowledgement of history and the constitutive role that the colonial legacy and its place in modernity play in the formation of the subject of politics in postcoloniality.

ACKNOWLEDGEMENTS

Any author can only do her work with a network of support. I am, as ever, grateful to my network of colleagues, friends, and family.

This book could not have been written without the generous sabbatical leave provided by King's College London. I am grateful to King's and to Professor Mervyn Frost and Professor Denise Lievesly for their support.

I have benefitted enormously from invaluable discussions I have had with a number of colleagues. The foothills of this project saw their first outing at the International Studies Association Convention in 2009 in San Francisco. I am grateful to Rosemary Shinko and Beate Jahn for their panel on the subject of cosmopolitanism, where my work on the cosmopolitan and the postcolonial was presented. I am especially grateful to Rose Shinko for a panel she organised devoted to my book project at the ISA North East Convention held in Baltimore in 2010. All on this panel, Rose herself, Christine Sylvester, Anna Agathangelou, Andreas Behnke, and Hilbourne Watson placed the first chapter of the book through a rigorous testing ground, focusing especially on the challenge of talking about 'the' postcolonial subject. I am also grateful to the audience present at that panel, including Ann Tickner and Himadeep Muppidi, again both contributing points that I have taken on board. I am grateful too to Mustapha Pasha, Ritu Vij, and Charlotte Epstein for their friendship and for always asking the difficult questions. Parts of this project were also presented as contributions to the Leverhulme Network project 'Cosmopolitanism or Empire', coordinated by Costas Douzinas, and I am grateful to Costas for providing an intellectually invaluable forum for discussions of the global implications of a cosmopolitan late modernity. At King's, Claudia Aradau, Peter Busch, and Didier Bigo are, as ever, a constant source of support and intellectual engagement. I am also grateful to the editors of the Routledge series *Interventions*, Jenny Edkins and Nick Vaughan-Williams, for including this book in this wonderful, critical series in international relations scholarship. I am grateful to them for their patience, as I am to Nicola Parkin at Routledge and the reviewers of the original proposal.

I could not have written this book without the unconditional love and support provided by Mary Nankivell especially, and by Dorian Jabri and Chris Smith. All, as ever, are always there for me.

INTRODUCTION

The past in the present

> We have to discard the past.
>
> Pablo Neruda, 'Past'

Recent events in the Middle East place into sharp relief questions relating to change and political transformation in the postcolonial world. The primary call of the 'Arab Spring' is for a renewed notion of political community being made at a historical juncture that is of the postcolonial on the one hand and of late modern modes of colonisation on the other. That these events are taking place in a region that has witnessed its share of war in Western military intervention and practices deemed to service the so-called 'war against terrorism' reflects the intersection between globally articulated modes of power and local political contestations. It is as if the promise of independence, though long recognised as remaining largely unfulfilled, is being reclaimed afresh, political community reclaimed afresh, and the right to politics itself being reclaimed in the face of external and internal violence and dispossession. The prevalent tendency is to see these events as rebellions against tyrannical and dictatorial regimes. Indeed they are reflections of a seemingly widespread expression that fear itself is transcended, so that confrontations between civilians and the security apparatus of the state are the overwhelming feature. However, the reclaiming of the political must be conceived in terms of both local as well as global structures of domination and control and their complex and contingent intersections.

It is not too difficult to see interventions such as those in Iraq and Afghanistan, not to mention the continued incursions into Pakistan and yet other more subtle forms of interventions elsewhere, as reflective of continuities with the colonial past. These are, at the same time, distinctly late modern forms of intervention; from the high technology military machines unleashed upon populations, to their interpellation as 'peacebuilding' and 'statebuilding', to the seemingly paradoxical combination of technologies of control and regulation, from the direct use of warfare to the rebuilding of schools and hospitals, to the pedagogical aspects that come in the form of 'training', gender-awareness, human rights, all function at a limit point wherein distinctions seem to disappear – between war and security, violence and care, public and private, inside and outside, the military and civilian. The terrain that confers meaning to the postcolonial, namely the 'international' conceived as a distinct location of politics, seems itself challenged in the face of a global juridical-political trajectory that is transnationally defined, that seeks the trumping of the international by the cosmopolitan terrain of the human.

While Kwame Nkrumah (1965) foresaw the continued implications of what he referred to as 'neocolonialism', the workings of capital across, and despite of, the limits of the sovereign state continuing to dispossess the formerly colonised, late modern transformations, those that confer positive force to that other transnational terrain, humanity at large, are equally monumental in their implications for the postcolonial world. My interest in writing this book is exactly the trajectory of the postcolonial subject,[1] but as will be seen, this is by no means a linear trajectory, a historical narrative that has a beginning and an end. Rather, this is a trajectory that sees the intersection of past and present, a past lived in the present as well as a present that was always there in the past. This is a trajectory that sees movement, not just in time, but also in space, so that the spatial articulation of the postcolonial subject is not simply confined to the postcolonial state but shifts and moves on a landscape of streets and neighbourhoods, gallery spaces and film archives, on the pages of literary productions, and in the virtual space of mass communications. The reclaiming of the political that I want to identify here is bound up with this temporal and spatial trajectory, in complex ways that not only defy easy cause and effect relationships, but also elude easy capture. That the attempt is made exactly to capture the postcolonial subject as this subject negotiates and seeks to reclaim the terrain of the political should not be taken to mean a total capture in a theoretical and conceptual frame, for the postcolonial subject escapes, and it is a recognition of this excess to the subject that renders this work critical.

The theme of the book emerged from a number of sources and motivations. My last book, *War and the Transformation of Global Politics* (Jabri, 2007a) explores the implications of liberal cosmopolitanism, focusing on violence as its constitutive moment. Conceiving of war as a technology in the government of populations, the book focused on the implications of interventionist wars and security practices on relationships of power and emergent subjectivities. Inspired by Michel Foucault's analytics of war,[2] the book argued that the permeation of war into the social sphere is suggestive of what I refer to as a 'matrix of war', the practices of which have implications not only for the structure of the international, but for subjectivity – the liberal self conceived as possessing global reach on the one hand, and the other of the liberal self, located largely in the postcolonial world, target of practices that range from direct violence, to incarceration, to surveillance, and pedagogic practices aimed at the redesign of societies. Two inter-related issues that emerged from the book included on the one hand the question of the implications of racially defined hierarchical inscription of the subjects of liberal cosmopolitan projections of power, and on the other, the question of how resistance might be conceived in the face of such projections. This then is the intellectual background that informs the present book, a background that is brought into sharp relief by recent events in international politics, namely the invasion and occupation of Iraq, the war in Afghanistan, practices constitutive of the so-called 'war against terrorism', Gaza, Lebanon, Iran, to name but a few locations where the 'government' of populations,[3] variously using technologies from the violent to the pedagogic, comes face to face with the postcolonial subject.

Conventionally in International Relations, reference to the 'cosmopolitan' is suggestive of Kantian-inspired liberal discourses informing conceptions of transformation towards peace and justice. Seeing realist conceptions of the international system as a hindrance to such transformation, liberal cosmopolitans have long projected a self-image that proclaims a critical and an emancipatory agenda in social and political theory and in the realm of practice.[4] Theory and practice meet in advocacies around international law and its transnational reformulations, human rights, interventions in the name of rescue, global governance, and measures aimed at what is referred to as 'human security'.[5] The agents of such transformation are assumed to be the liberal democracies of the West, seen as holding the 'moral resources', to oversee its actualisation.[6]

When viewed from a Marxist, a poststructural, or a postcolonial perspective,[7] the cosmopolitan ceases to be a benign aspiration, but acquires a material and a discursive presence that is imbricated with relations of power globally rendered. Conceived in this way, liberal cosmopolitanism comes to be understood as the projection of power through practices of discipline and government aimed at other societies. The 'apparatus of security' that, according to Michel Foucault, identifies liberal government,[8] is what I argue constitutes the transformation of the international into cosmopolitan space. This apparatus is realised through practices that range from violence to pedagogic practices geared at 'training' target societies towards liberal modes of self-articulation. The structural transformation of the international is hence also accompanied by operations of power and knowledge that seek the transformation of subjectivity itself, so that the now postcolonial others come to have a self-understanding that somehow reflects the frame through which the liberal cosmopolitan might view them, just as, to borrow from Parama Roy (1998), the colonial subject reflected colonial inscriptions.

The cosmopolitan terrain I am highlighting here is also a terrain of contestation and resistance. The subject of late modern operations of power might be seen as traversing transnational spaces, somehow defiant of the re-formulated limits defined and inscribed by those in possession of legislative authority in this transformed space. Where the liberal self is constituted as being in possession of global reach, engaged in the government of others, the other of the liberal self, located largely but not exclusively in the postcolonial world, is somehow reinscribed in terms of the dichotomy of modernity and tradition, civilisation and barbarism, freedom and unfreedom; dichotomies that are reproduced through a powerful racialised, culturalist, as well as gendered discourse. My claim here is that the apparatus that seeks to constitute the global in security terms, that extends its machinery, indeed its technologies, both military and civilian, across the terrain of the global is also one that is enabled through discourses of legitimisation that draw upon a racialisation of populations, a hierarchical rendering of societies despite the universalising claims of the human as a category and target of action. The legacy that enables this projection of power and one that is drawn upon in contemporary practices is colonialism, but its present articulation is distinctly late modern in its construction.

What do I mean when I claim that the articulation of the colonial legacy is distinctly *late* modern in its construction? I mean that it is imbued with the features of our time; the intensification of the institutions of modernity, to borrow from Giddens, the modern state as a cluster of institutions that permeate all aspects of lived experience, and a capitalist international political economy that incorporates most exchange within its remit, that stands in tension with the regulative aspect of the territorial state, and that overwhelmingly determines life chances through inequalities of access to resources. Ultimately, the most significant feature of late modernity, what Bauman refers to as 'liquid modernity', is the fragmentation, indeterminacy, and uncertainty associated with these institutions of modernity, elements that are recursively related to the globalisation of the economic and the socio-political. In times of 'liquid modernity', to use Bauman,

> power has become truly exterritorial, no longer bound, not even slowed down, by the resistance of space ... It does not matter any more where the giver of the command is – the difference between 'close by' and 'far away', or for that matter between the wilderness and the civilized, orderly space, has been all but cancelled. This gives the power-holders a truly unprecedented opportunity: the awkward and irritating aspects of the panoptical technique of power may be disposed of. Whatever else the present stage of the history of modernity is, it is also, perhaps above all, post-panoptical.

> *(Bauman, 2000: 11)*

What does this shift from the panoptical to the post-panoptical mean for the postcolonial world? How is this global terrain of the late modern viewed when the lens is held by the postcolonial subject? There are, of course, no easy generalisations that can be made, though the broad-brush stroke approach that Bauman uses is all too tempting. Nevertheless, we might say that the 'postcolony', to use Achille Mbembe (1992), is increasingly incorporated, some would say co-opted, into the time and space of the post-panoptic articulation of power, so that the wielders of power locally are but easily bought off local managers of a globally instantiated de-regulative imperative authored elsewhere, in financial institutions that have always functioned transnationally, but always with the assistance of the military and security apparatus of the state. We might say that where the colony in modernity was subjected to conquest, the postcolony is subjected to the post-panoptic governmentalising manifestation of power, where populations, and not simply individuals, are shaped and regulated into governable, manageable entities. When viewed from the postcolony, the postpanoptic is not necessarily about the end of confinement; indeed it might mean the use of incarceration to an ever increasing extent, not just of errant individuals, but of populations through the control of their movements. The postpanoptic might also make use of a military machine no longer simply engaged at state boundaries, but a global military machine the function of which is the governing of errant populations and their movements.

Colonialism has always been viscerally felt, in modernity and in its late modern versions. This is not just about the racialised inscriptions of the colonised, the degradations, humiliations, and violence, both epistemic and physical, to which the colonised is subjected, but it is also profoundly about the traces that such inscriptions leave behind, only to re-emerge in the subject's consciousness, at times articulated in discourse, but more often remaining un-articulated, forming a backdrop of knowledge that is constitutive of the subject's past and present, even as this past is often inherited, learnt in narrations of a past told and retold. It is in this sense that we might think of Fanon's colonised subject *and* the 'insurgent' fighting American troops in Fallujah, both viscerally related to the condition of colonisation: 'At the level of individuals, violence is a cleansing force. It frees the native from his inferiority complex and from his despair and inaction; it makes him fearless and restores his self-respect' (Fanon, 1967: 74). The visceral is all too apparent in the confrontation that the coloniser seeks to subdue and, importantly, this visceral aspect of the colonial encounter is not confined to the individual: 'The settler-native relationship is a mass relationship. The settler pits brute force against the weight of numbers. He is an exhibitionist. His preoccupation with security makes him remind the native out loud that there he alone is master' (Fanon, 1967: 42). Over and above the immediacy of the encounter and its constitutive violence, the *post*colonial condition too is, for Fanon, also visceral in its manifestation: 'The well-being and the progress of Europe have been built up with the sweat and the dead bodies of Negroes, Arabs, Indians and the yellow races' (1967: 77). The structure of the colonial relationship is rightly conceived in terms of this constitutive inequality; however, this is an inequality that is carried in and upon the body of the colonised, past and present.[9]

There is then a materiality to the colonial relationship and this materiality might be conceived in a number of ways that can potentially reflect the nexus of power and resistance as this negotiates the time and space of modernity. This materiality might first be conceived as relating to bodies as these come to be inscribed in and through the colonial encounter. When bodies are placed at the nexus of power and resistance, they come to have a presence in all presence's sheer physicality of form, so that just as power seeks to variously obstruct, kill, harm, confine and incarcerate, so too resistance seeks to interject the body into the spaces of power, so that such interjection seeks to variously disrupt, and harm in Manichean return, as Fanon shows, or it might create alternative spaces for movement and circulation defiant of the carceral remit of power. As we know from Michel Foucault's analytics, power operates upon bodies and populations, disciplining the former and governing the latter, and we know too that such disciplining and government take place in an architecture of space that exactly serves to produce disciplined and governable individuals and populations. This architecture of space is then a material force that has effects, in the shaping of subjects and in their potential to resist. Reflecting continuities of past and present, this architecture of space might come in the form of so called 'green zones' – high security enclaves and walled compounds – and it might come in the form of road blocks, prison buildings, and other locations of confinement aimed at the control of movement, both temporally and spatially.

The postcolonial subject bears the imprints of the colonial legacy, not just in relation to a colonised past, but in the constitutive role of the past in shaping the present. This is an imprint that sits closely, if somewhat uncomfortably, with the imprint of the postcolonial state and what I will refer to as the promise of 'independence'. It is these imprints together and in all their complexity and diversity that then come to the fore in a late modern cosmopolitan terrain wherein the very idea of 'independence' as a political construct comes face to face with a governmentalising remit that can be authored elsewhere. The profound implications for the political cannot be overstressed. While the machinery of government is not confined to Western agencies and institutions, that much of the postcolonial world has witnessed and continues to witness a separation, or a disjuncture, between government and politics – between the machinery of provision and the institutions of state – raises fundamental questions relating to the meaning of political community and its relationship to the state. As we will see, where the postcolonial state relied for its legitimacy on the anti-colonial, nationalist struggle, the late modern postcolonial state comes up against the question of political community in a context wherein the limits and boundaries of such community can no longer be conceived in terms of the state. As will be seen as the argument of the book develops, the core concepts I use in rethinking postcolonial political community are the 'declaration of independence' and the 'moment of founding'. I borrow these terms from Hannah Arendt's engagement with the American Revolution, but find them of immense significance in thinking of the postcolonial subject and this subject's claiming the political, the right to politics. Of core interest here is how the declaration and the moment of founding are articulated, in modernity and now in late modernity. The conception of resistance I seek to develop in this book is constitutively related to the 'declaration' and the moment of 'founding' and the forms that both take, in relation to political community, to the 'international', and to the 'cosmopolitan'.

The book is structured around and through a number of interrelated themes aimed at uncovering the postcolonial subject's claiming the political. The idea of 'claiming the political' suggests the articulation of a 'right to politics' in the context of the postcolonial state, the postcolonial international, and the late modern cosmopolitan. To suggest a subject engaged in claiming, or an 'articulation' is at once to suggest the emergence of political agency. While much in the constructivist turn in International Relations seeks to resolve the agency-structure dynamic, the more challenging question, and one that is preferred intellectually in this context, relates to the subject and how we can conceptualise this subject's constitution as a subject of politics. The first chapter, therefore, explores the ontological and epistemological challenges in tracing the postcolonial subject. The second locates the postcolonial subject and articulations of resistance in the temporal and spatial contingencies of modernity, focusing in particular on what I refer to as 'policing access to the political' as a colonial rationality. The first two chapters must be read as servicing Chapter 3, which is devoted to providing a theorisation of the subject of politics in postcoloniality. The concepts I elaborate in this chapter run through the book, providing its conceptual schema, and driving its curiosities. These include 'the subject of politics', the 'right to politics', and the 'declaration of independence' as core concepts in understanding the constitution of the subject of politics in postcoloniality, drawing in particular on Hannah Arendt and Etienne Balibar, and then focusing on the 'negativity' of the subject of politics, focusing on Fanon's negativity. The aim throughout is to rethink resistance in terms of the subject's claim to politics, locating this claim in a constitutive relationship with political community, the international, and the cosmopolitan. The last three chapters of the book are therefore devoted to the postcolonial struggle over the political, starting with Chapter 4, which focuses on the claim to politics and what I refer to as the 'heteronomy of the international'. The chapter focuses in particular on the constitutive role of 'independence' in relation to the constitution of political community and the struggle of access to the 'international'. The aporetic relationship between the postcolonial and the international comes into sharp relief here, but is seen in all its resonance in Chapter 5 where the 'international' as such is challenged through what I have suggested are cosmopolitan operations of power, what I refer to as the cosmopolitanism of government. The ultimate aim of this chapter is to reveal how the subject of politics emerges in these spaces of cosmopolitan government. Chapter 6 retrieves the subject of politics in late modernity, culminating in what we have come to know as the 'Arab Spring', suggesting that this perhaps signs in a moment that we might come to know temporally as the 'beyond the postcolonial'. The regional reference point is primarily, though not exclusively, the Middle East.

1

TRACING THE
POSTCOLONIAL SUBJECT

> It wasn't easy getting out of the city. There were so many roadblocks and
> soldiers were all over the place ... At every one of the roadblocks the soldiers
> commented on the food I had at the back. Then they would ask if I thought that
> people were hungry. When I said no, the soldiers would take some of my food
> and wave me on.
>
> Ben Okri, *Worlds that Flourish*

The postcolonial world, having emerged from the violence of colonialism, finds
itself once again subject to colonial reason, as violent and dispossessive as it was in
its previous articulation.[1] The difference now in late modernity is that the
technologies of power used in the control of populations are not manifest in direct
rule, but rather through complex forms of government the agents of which might
be states, international institutions, or non-governmental organisations, all engaged
in practices that have the global as the purview of their operations. The architectonics
of this military/socio-political/institutional framework are never fixed and can be
mobilised at relatively short notice. This absence of fixity is somehow suggestive of
a rapid response mechanism whereby emergencies and conflicts are resolved
through practical problem solving.[2] The technologies drawn upon can range from
the use of force to the provision of welfare, to pedagogical exercises the aim of
which is the transformation of societies into governable entities. The conditions of
possibility that enable this late modern articulation of colonial reason are at once
discursive and material, both implicated in a hierarchical constitution of the global
order and those who inhabit it. However these are also the conditions within
which modes of resistance take place and just as the colonial legacy continues to
have its imprint on the present, so too this legacy is present in postcolonial
articulations of resistance, defined in this book, as claiming the right to politics.

The postcolonial literature in the social sciences generally and in international
relations in particular tends to focus on the implications of discourses and their
underlying philosophies, pointing to the politics of representation that deny
equality to the postcolonial world, that denigrate postcolonial self-determination,
and that universalise at the expense of postcolonial difference.[3] The scripting of
global politics in terms that exclude or that subsume the postcolonial world confers
agency, and hence authorship and legitimacy, to the 'West', thereby generating a
conceptual schema that is not only inadequate to the task of understanding the

international, but one that is framed in both analytical *and* normative terms. The politics of anamnesis is all too apparent here, in that Europe's colonial encounters, their genocidal, extractive, and exploitative practices, remain unaccounted in narratives relating to the global political order and its constitution.[4] More profoundly, the postcolonial world has not been considered as agent involved in the shaping of the international, but, rather, as the recipient of its rules and normative structures. This scripting out of the postcolonial is not confined to realist or liberal perspectives in international theory, but has also been apparent in much critical and poststructural work.[5]

The achievement of the postcolonial critique in international social and political thought is at once both deconstructive and generative of a research programme that seeks to script the postcolonial into the analytics of international and global politics. This scripting is not based on modernisation theory and its 'developmental' discourse, one that provides the edifice upon which concepts such as 'failed states' are built.[6] Rather, the lens shifts towards questions relating to postcolonial agency, not in a generalising, simplifying, idealising mode, but in revealing its complex intersection with matrices of power and domination and their contingencies. Considered in this way, postcolonial articulations of agency come to be understood in constitutive terms, so that the international and its discursive and institutional transformation can be as much a product of the agentic assertions of the postcolonial as the attempts of the powerful to constrain or limit transformation along lines that serve structures of domination. The constitutive is revealed when the postcolonial is understood as always already constituted in the discursive and institutional framing of the international, but one that has the capacity to reconstitute and hence transform.[7] At the same time, this shift of the lens towards postcolonial agency has invited engagements with what is referred to as 'non-Western' international relations. In revealing these voices, we gain insight into an alternative framing of the international, its discourses and power structures.[8]

With this shift of the lens towards postcolonial agency in the spatial and temporal location of the international, attention focuses on the substantial expression of such agency, its negotiations with global matrices of power and regulation, and its articulations of resistance. From Al-Qaida's violence, perpetrated cellularly in the 'West' and the 'East', to India and Pakistan's nuclear tests against the rules of the nuclear non-proliferation treaty, to the United Nations General Assembly recognition of the Palestine Liberation Organisation, to the more recent UNESCO recognition of Palestinian statehood, to the plurality of spaces across the world where the 'international' emerges in local spaces and where resistance based on inequalities of class and gender is manifest in such spaces, all these and more represent articulations of agency in the contingencies of power that define the international.[9] However, these are also diverse forms of negotiation and resistance, diverse in their articulation, in their mobilising potential, their meanings in different socio-political settings, and their constitutive and transformative capacities. Such diversity might at first hand suggest that postcolonial scholarship might be able to critique the exclusion of such forms of agency, and to provide empirical content to its articulation, but that it fails to provide a political theory of postcoloniality as such, including reflection on what it means to be a subject of politics in the 'aftermath of sovereignty'.[10]

The aim in this book is to take up this challenge – to provide an international political theory of the subject of politics in postcoloniality. Locating the subject in relation to the political immediately suggests a conceptualisation that is relational and hence inter-subjective. To talk of the subject of politics is indicative of a subject formed and constituted in relation to community, but also the subject who constitutes community in relations with others. Conventionally in international relations, the question of 'community' has been rendered in normative discourse as suggestive of either the 'communitarian' or the 'cosmopolitan'.[11] However, this particular debate has tended to eschew the question of politics as a distinctive domain of human interaction, and how politically, the question of 'limits', as Rob Walker (2010) highlights, comes into form and places the lens on 'sovereignty'. In this latter frame, and in an age of interventionist practices in the name of the 'human', the debate has primarily recently been constructed in terms of the location of political authority, the choice being either with Kelsen, and the transcendence of sovereignty, or with Schmitt, and its celebration.[12] However, an alternative framing of the question would be to place the lens on politics, the subject of politics, how this subject is specifically constituted as 'political', and how such constitution relates to the constitution of political community.[13]

With the focus of this book being on the subject of politics in postcoloniality, the question of interest relates to how the subject of politics emerges, how such emergence relates constitutively to political community and its limits. To suggest the subject claiming the political is hence to acknowledge the contingent matrices within and through which this constitutive and constituting relationship takes place and becomes actualised. One way of capturing the emergence of the subject of politics, in anticipation of Chapter 3, is in terms of the Arendtian notion of 'founding' or 'beginnings',[14] both concepts that direct attention to declarations of independence, declarations that I argue are core to understanding the postcolonial subject. This should not be taken to mean that the postcolonial subject is entirely 'captured' so to speak, by the 'national' moment, but acknowledged the constitutive power of the struggle for 'independence'.[15] The subject in this sense does not stand outside of the political relation but can be denied its articulation and expression. Such denial is directed at the reconstitution of the subject and their extraction from the domain of the political. At the same time such denial and extraction are in themselves acknowledgements of the subject of politics and of the salience of political community. Unravelling the subject in relation to the political is hence to account for the constituted self and the self's constituting relation to the political and the situatedness of these relations in contingent matrices of power and knowledge.

Locating the postcolonial subject of politics hails forth a temporal and spatial specificity that stems from the colonial legacy. At the same time this is also a legacy that is firmly situated in modernity and modern institutions, the modern state, the modern international, and an international political economy of exchange relations.

This legacy is profound in its implications for the postcolonial subject, for this is a subject whose articulation of the political is constitutively dependent on the modern international as a distinct location of politics that historically confers legitimacy to the limits of the national state as political community. To understand the postcolonial subject of politics is hence to unravel the temporal and spatial constitution of the subject and this subject's struggle for access to the political and the international. The aim in this chapter is exactly to trace the postcolonial subject, focusing in particular on the epistemological and ontological challenges involved in understanding the temporal and spatial constitution of the subject.

The postcolonial critique of international relations as a discipline, as highlighted above, focuses on its essentially Eurocentric conceptual schema and methodologies, arguing that while these are taken to be universally applicable, they nevertheless exclude the non-Western world at worse, and at best merely represent this world from the vantage point of the European. For the postcolonial critic, this vantage point represents the source of continued domination in a postcolonial era still defined by a powerful colonial legacy where even to possess access to the domain of the international is to acquire the tropes – sovereignty, the territorial nation-state, the government of a territorially defined population – that have their genesis in Europe (Grovogui, 1996). Viewing the international from the vantage point of the non-West is hence to, first of all, gain access to the international and on terms equal to that of the European, and second, having gained access, to draw upon the political-juridical structure of the international as guarantor of freedom from resurgent colonial domination and subjugation. So powerful is the legacy of colonial rule that the subject of the postcolonial condition is always already somehow predetermined, somehow stamped, indeed inscribed by the colonial experience. Viewing the international from the vantage point of the non-West is hence to do so through a lens that is already prescribed and shaped by coloniality and the continued desire to resist its continued economic, social, political, and epistemological domination.

At the same time there is a reluctance to reiterate dualisms and oppositions – the 'West' and 'non-West' being one such – that inform essentialist discourses that inadvertently confer primacy to a logocentric European subject through what we might understand as the culturalisation of the 'other', where this other is only identifiable through tropes of cultural difference, exoticised, nativised, and forever determined by the signifying effects of culture. The culturalisation of the 'other' is hence as complicit in the reproduction of a hierarchical conception of subjectivity as are discourses that simply assume Europe as the universal terrain of the international. As Homi Bhabha (1994: 25) points out:

> The Language of critique is effective not because it keeps forever separate the terms of the master and the slave, the mercantilist and the Marxist, but to the extent to which it overcomes the given grounds of opposition and opens up a space of translation: a place of hybridity, figuratively speaking, where the construction of a political object that is new, *neither the one nor the other*, properly

alienates our political expectations, and changes, as it must, the very forms of our recognition of the moment of politics. The challenge lies in conceiving of the time of political action and understanding as opening up a space that can accept and regulate the differential structure of the moment of intervention without rushing to produce a unity of the social antagonism or contradiction. This is a sign that history is *happening* – within the pages of theory, within the systems and structures we construct to figure the passage of the historical.

There is then the intersubjective terrain of a back and forth and the spaces created in-between. To understand the claim to the political by the postcolonial subject is hence to reveal the ways in which articulations of struggle and antagonism at once draw from structural continuities in the form that they take and the substantive content that they express while understanding at the same time that such articulation and expression might constitute 'instances that open up hybrid sites and objectives of struggle' (Babha, 1994: 25). We might therefore state, in anticipation of what is to come, that the postcolonial subject's relationship to the international is one that is not determined by the colonial legacy, but generates a new political relationship that is not confined to the relationship between the West and the postcolonial, but includes relationships within, through the constitution of forms of political community suggestive of a space of hybridity, negotiation, and articulation.

The language of critique is at the same time concerned with revealing the location of the subject of postcoloniality in relation to power and resistance. How does power operate in the present and what form does resistance take in a context wherein the international and its structure have and continue to undergo profound transformation, politically and juridically, as well as sociologically and economically? Power reveals its operations through the discourses and institutions of the state, of the international and of a transnational terrain of movement and circulation that is not just of the market and its interactions, but also of human beings on the move, of ideas and affiliations, and communicative practices the implications of which are comparable in their global effects to the rise of the industrial revolution (Findlay and O'Rourke, 2007). Articulations of resistance in the postcolonial world are as much of this terrain as are operations of power, and underline the monumental task that is the former in relation to the latter.

This chapter provides the epistemological and ontological backdrop to the question that frames this investigation; namely, how is the claim to the political articulated and how do these articulations relate to postcolonial resistance? As I highlight in the Introduction to the book, the aim is to trace the postcolonial subject as this subject traverses three distinct and at the same time inter-related temporal and spatial locations: colonial modernity, the postcolonial international, and the late modern cosmopolitan. The form that the claim to the political takes is intimately related to these locations and has at its core 'independence' and the founding of political community, moments that run through and connect the anti-colonial struggles of the past with contemporary articulations of the political in the context of the late modern cosmopolitan.

An epistemological quest for the postcolonial subject

It is all too easy for the hegemonic discourses of European social science generally, and the science of politics in particular to simply assume the universality of concepts and theoretical frameworks, a universality that derives from the conferred ontological primary of the European self. 'Knowing' the postcolonial subject hence becomes a matter of the incorporation of the 'other' into established and un-problematised discursive formations authored in the West. As I state above and as argued by other postcolonial scholars, the assumed primacy of such discursive formations is as much of orthodoxy as it is of certain modes of critique. Where the former takes its universality for granted, the latter, while acknowledging difference and providing powerful critiques of logocentricism, nevertheless include the 'other' through forms of exoticism or even nativism, tropes that reify cultural difference so that culture is seen as a mark of essential difference rather than a matter that is of the political (Said, 1993; Spivak, 1999).

Both forms of epistemic framing are present in Michel Foucault's writings, even though Foucault's analytics have had an undeniable influence on much postcolonial writing including this one. The first form, that of negation, can be seen in Foucault's lecture, 'What is Enlightenment' (1984a). He states: 'We must try to proceed with the analysis of ourselves as beings who are historically determined, to a certain extent, by the Enlightenment. Such an analysis implies a series of historical inquiries that are as precise as possible', where the Enlightenment,

> is an event, or a set of events and complex historical processes, that is located to a certain point in the development of European societies. As such, it includes elements of social transformation, types of political institution, forms of knowledge, projects of rationalisation of knowledge and practices, technological mutations that are very difficult to sum up in a word, even if many of these phenomena remain important today. The one I have pointed out and that seems to me to have been at the basis of an entire form of philosophical reflection concerns only the mode of reflective relation to the present.[16]

The 'ontology of the present' and the 'critical ontology of self' that this present allows is inaugurated in the European context, and specifically in the French Revolution, which becomes, as Homi Bhabha (1994: 243) highlights, 'his sign of modernity'. For Bhabha, the 'Eurocentricity of Foucault's theory of cultural difference is revealed in his insistent spatializing of the time of modernity'. The Eurocentricism of Foucault's reading of modernity is revealed through a postcolonial reading, one that interrogates this signification of modernity from the point of view of those other, colonial spaces where the 'reflective relation to the present' would not be located in Europe. The point I want to make here is that while Foucault, in this particular text, provides the tropes through which we might think critically, and indeed, provide a conception of what it means to be 'critical', at the same time this is a spatialised ethos that most definitely does not consider non-European moments of critique and self-reflection.

The second form of epistemic framing is not one of negation but of an essentialised, culturalised nativism wherein culture remains unproblematised and is instead reified as the marker of difference. This emerges in Foucault's engagement with the Iranian Revolution, a rare venture beyond the European and the American. Just as the French Revolution is considered a signifying event hailing forth modernity and the Enlightenment, so the Iranian Revolution is seen as the historic sign for the emergence of the non-Western subject capable of resistance against the modernising imperatives of the liberal West. According to Foucault, the antagonism that defines Western rationality directs its focus on the 'Orient':

> We could write of the history of limits – of those obscure gestures necessarily forgotten as soon as they are accomplished, through which a culture rejects something which for it will be the Exterior … In the universality of the Western ratio, there is this division which is the Orient: the Orient thought of as the origin, dreamt of as the vertiginous point from which nostalgia and return are born, the Orient offered to the colonising reason of the Occident, but indefinitely inaccessible for it always remains the limit.
>
> *(Foucault, 2006: xxx)*

For Foucault, the Iranian Revolution represented a rejection of the hegemony of Western rationality and its drive for domination: He states: 'Recent events did not signify a shrinking back in the face of modernisation by extremely retrograde elements, but the rejection, by a whole culture and a whole people, of a modernisation that is itself an archaism'. The Revolution represented a resistance to the attempt to 'modernise the Islamic countries in a European fashion'.[17] What emerges here is a theory of cultural difference that does not negate, but that essentialises cultural difference. To quote Ian Almond (2004: 21), 'Foucault's conviction of the Orient's immobility, untameable nature and essential homogeneity are all gestures which come straight out of the nineteenth century, out of a hegemonic European tradition of comment on the Orient'.

Tracing the trajectory of the postcolonial subject requires first and foremost a move beyond negation and essentialisation. Such a move might be suggestive of a cartographic project that somehow identifies the territorial locations wherein the postcolonial subject resides, animating the object world of global maps with narratives of existence.[18] However, such a tracing is not simply confined to spatial articulations or representations, but is at the same time crucially temporal, so that the postcolonial subject is somehow imagined as inhabiting history and the present where the latter continues to be marked with the discourses and practices of the former, powerfully present in contemporary articulations of self and of community. This tracing is hence at once both spatial and temporal, but these are in themselves not confined to a linear understanding of space and of time, nor are these somehow divorced from the articulations and representations that confer them form and content. Rather, there is complexity and fragmentation, just as there is uncertainty as to how, methodologically, we can trace such complexity while avoiding the epistemological violence that can be done when seeking to somehow situate the subject of politics, and here specifically the subject of postcoloniality. Any such situatedness, while acknowledging the significance of the socio-cultural, political, and economic context, nevertheless has a capacity to assume unproblematic embeddedness or sedimentation, denying the subject that capacity for movement and for negotiation of the discursive and institutional continuities that give form to present and past.

It is commonplace to start with modernity and to reveal the constitutive place that colonialism played in shaping the modern West and its relationship to the rest of the world, specifically the world that the West came to colonise. We might also start with how modernity and the colonial experience shaped in turn the colonised subject and the forms of resistance to colonial rule that emerged and that continue to inform the shape of things in the so-called global South. Tracing the postcolonial subject is hence dependent upon what might be referred to as a 'periodisation' of global history, a periodisation that reveals the construction of 'non-European alterity', which, according to Siba Grovogui (1996) can be identified with three very specific genres of discourse: the fifteenth century and the ecclesiastical context that legitimised the 'discovery of the New World'; the Enlightenment and the hierarchical construction of peoples and civilisations; and the colonial discourse that accompanied nineteenth-century natural history. The periodisation I offer here has its focus on the colonial legacy, framed as it is by the so-called 'modern' period, a period that generated colonial rule on the one hand and anti-colonial resistance on the other. The 'historical imagination' clearly informs the ways in which the periodisation of global history is conceptualised, but is itself subject to not just the limits of imagination, but also the paucity of linguistic constructs that have capacity to capture the complexities of the interconnections and movements of communities and populations, their cultures and modes of governance, the material conditions defining the limits of the possible, and the matrices of discursive and institutional power recursively related to subjectivities.

The historical imagination expressed here is not of the Kantian variety that sees the forces of nature and of reason being complicit in the linear progression that takes us from here to an elsewhere, that makes possible a future defined by 'perpetual peace' and one that, moreover, comes to be defined in terms of the limits that the cosmopolitan can place upon sovereign authority.[19] Nor is the historical imagination one that envisages, following Hegel, the emergence of 'World Spirit', the assumed apotheosis of reason, the limit against which all else can be judged.[20] The historical imagination that informs and permeates this study is best expressed by Walter Benjamin when he states: 'History is the subject of a structure whose site is not homogeneous, empty time, but time filled by the presence of the now' (1999a: 252–253). It is, in other words, in the complexity of the now, in all its fragmentations and uncertainties, that the traces of history emerge, even as the historical itself permeates the present. In a critique of what is essentially a Kantian conception of historical progress, Benjamin states:

Social Democratic theory, and even more its practice, have been formed by a conception of progress which did not adhere to reality but made dogmatic claims. Progress as pictured in the minds of Social Democrats was, first of all, the progress of mankind itself (and not just advances in men's ability and knowledge). Secondly, it was something boundless, in keeping with the infinite perfectibility of mankind. Thirdly, progress was regarded as irresistible, something that automatically pursued a straight or spiral course. Each of these predicates is controversial and open to criticism. However, when the chips are down, criticism must penetrate beyond these predicates and focus on something that they have in common. The concept of the historical progress of mankind cannot be sundered from the concept of its progression through a homogeneous, empty time. A critique of the concept of such a progression must be the basis of any criticism of the concept of progress itself.

(Benjamin 1999a: 253)

Representations of the non-Western world, from the Enlightenment to the present, have relied, as Dipesh Chakrabarty argues (2000: 23), on this conception of 'progress', so that it is indeed conceived in terms of 'homogeneous empty time', a time, in other words, devoid of history and subjectivity, a time understood only and solely in terms of the West, in relation to the West. The implication is that to understand other peoples, other regions, other histories, is always to do so in terms, in concepts, and in theoretical frameworks provided by the West, so that the other is always somehow lagging behind, perpetually identified in terms of a lack or an incompleteness. This structural inequality is built on a distinctly modern assumption whereby the concepts of European Enlightenment are always universal in application, being based on 'Man', as universal being, whereas the frameworks of the rest are particular to locality and culture.[21] This hierarchical rendering of the universal and the particular suggests that the understanding of the latter must always be in terms of the former, the universal categories provided by reason and nature. There are, therefore, both ontological and epistemological limits to any endeavour that seeks to view the international from the vantage point of the 'other', the non-Western, the regional. Even the term 'non-Western' seems to imply a negation, or even a 'not-yet' aspect, so that all those beyond the boundaries of the West and its constructs might, one day, be of the West. The question that immediately turns up is how those who refuse such co-optation might then be understood or even 'explained', when the concepts' inability to capture the subject suggests not simply exclusion, but a refusal to admit, a construction of a forever outside of the seemingly universal.

Despite these epistemological limits, the achievement of the historical imagination is that, far from reifying the past, the subject is seen as being formatively constituted in the continuities and discontinuities of social and political life, continuities and discontinuities that at once both shape the subject and inform the subject's capacity to form and transform these (dis)continuities. We might then refer to the subject of history and of the present; the subject of late modernity traversing the terrain of the global, interpellated by the discourses and institutions that surround them, while at the same time carrying the traces of history and memory that not only define difference but enable its articulation. There is no linear narrative here that constitutes the subject, but rather a subject whose location in the present carries fragments of history that emerge, often unexpectedly, as traces of memory that then situate the subject in a formative past. There is here a profound intimacy to the subject, an intimacy that can only be revealed in narratives of self. The evocation of the traces of memory and their place in the formation of the subject can be illustrated through Julia Kristeva's narrative of the exiled, hybrid self:

> I have not lost my mother tongue; it comes back to me with greater and greater difficulty, I confess, in dreams, or when I hear my mother talking, and after twenty-four hours of immersion in that water that had been so distant since that time, I surprise myself by swimming quite comfortably … And yet, Bulgarian is already an almost dead language for me. That is to say, a part of me was slowly extinguished as I learned French with the Dominicans … and finally, exile cadaverized this old body and substituted another for it – at first fragile and artificial, then more and more indispensable, and now the only one that is alive, the French one … And yet, when the plot thickens, that is, every time Being comes back to me like a story … a surge that is not made up of words but has a music all its own imposes an awkward syntax on me, and these unfathomable metaphors that have nothing to do with French politeness and obviousness infiltrate my calmness with a Byzantine unease.
>
> *(Kristeva, 2000: 165–166)*

Every utterance of the 'and yet' reveals the subject in all their intimate and complex locations. At the same time these are locations that express a profound sense of loss as well as new beginnings, the past interjecting into the present, consciously invited at times, and at other times uninvited. The 'and yet' also reveals the hybridity of self that is so formative of the subject of exile and, as has been suggested, of the postcolonial subject. To borrow from Kristeva (2000: 167) again to iterate the point I am making:

> for almost fifty years now my French taste has not always been able to resist the jolts of an early music coiled around a memory that is still vigilant. From these connected vessels there emerges a strange language, a stranger to itself, neither from here nor from there, a monstrous intimacy. Like the characters in Proust's refound time, whose long years of voluntary and involuntary memories are embodied in immense spaces, I am a monster of the crossroads.

The presence of the past can hence be of the public and the private, revealed in articulation, in moments of intersubjective communication and even mobilisation. However, it also inhabits a profoundly intimate location that then emerges, sometimes in jolts of memory, jolts that awaken a long forgotten past. At the same time, these are jolts that are in themselves awakened by the present, as the subject traverses the time and space of the present. Kristeva is not herself of the postcolonial, yet her evocation of the condition of exile provides a profound sense of the temporal and spatial hybridity that is of the postcolonial self.

Kirin Desai's *The Inheritance of Loss* (2006) provides us with a picture of the postcolonial subject as this subject traverses the terrain of the global, inhabiting spaces across cultures and national boundaries, urban spaces that present their own forms, paradoxically, of cosmopolitan exclusions, and rural terrains that, again, paradoxically, present the sanctuary of 'home' as well as its dangers. Desai's subject is not only presented, and indeed made possible as a construct, through the historical imagination, but this is indeed an imagination that is at the same time a dialectical one. The cosmopolitan terrain of the global city that is New York provides our migrant protagonist with the spaces of potential that define the migrant's struggle for survival, but these are spaces that microcosmically contain the dynamics and parameters of a global neoliberal order that permeates every aspect of lived experience and in doing so renders vulnerable the fragile terrain that our subject travels. Just as the subject returns to the sanctuary of home only to find new dangers, so the cosmopolitan terrain of the global city travelled faces its own vulnerabilities in the face of transnational violence.

Hence the historical and dialectical imagination informing our attempts to trace the postcolonial subject: historical, for history is always present, and constitutively so in the subject traced and the subject lost, and dialectical, in that theory is understood to be to be always implicated in practice, and always emergent from contestation and contradiction. However, beyond the historical and the dialectical, such a tracing is also informed by a distinctly postcolonial imagination, one that reads modernity through the colonial legacy and specifically the colonial experience and the frameworks of domination and dispossession formative of the postcolonial subject, of agency, and of positionality upon the terrain of the global. Writing of the postcolonial suggests both a temporal and a spatial trajectory where the former highlights the 'shaping power of a colonial past' upon a contemporary present, as Ania Loomba (1993: 209) highlights, a present that is constituted by the economic, cultural, political, and epistemic dominance of the West.

In unravelling the temporal trajectory of the postcolonial subject, the temptation is to frame the subject in terms of a colonial past and a postcolonial present, acknowledging at the same time the constitutive presence of the colonial past in the discourses, institutions, and subjectivities of the present. However, despite this persistent and continuing presence of the past in the present, there is at the same time, and constituted by the prefix 'post' in the postcolonial, the assumption of a break, a limit, a borderline in time that hails forth a moment of emergence, of presence – an interjection into time of a significant and signifying moment that inaugurates a rejection of the past; a culminating moment registering the place of resistance in the colonial experience and a claim to a future free of colonial subjection. There is, in this moment what we can refer to, looking back historically, as a 'declaration of independence', a declaration that clearly asserts rejection of foreign rule and hence a symbolic claim to the cultural and material resources of a political community constituted through anti-colonial struggle. This declaration of independence is the defining moment that places a break, that defines the limit dividing the colonial and postcolonial despite the persistence of the colonial legacy in the present. This moment is as constitutive of the postcolonial subject as is the colonial past and its ongoing power in shaping the present.

There is a powerful argument in the postcolonial literature that places emphasis on questioning the 'post' in the postcolonial, preferring instead the construct 'modernity/coloniality', especially in a context where the case for relegating the moment of national independence to the margins seems appealing to any critical thinker all too aware of the matrices of power, inequalities, and complicities with global neoliberal power within the postcolonial sovereign national state (Mignolo, 2000). There is, in addition, an awareness of the limitations of the postcolonial experience of sovereignty when we view the economic, social, and political conditions that prevail in regions in south Asia, Latin America, Africa, and the Middle East; that the moment of national liberation did not and has not hailed liberation from poverty and continued subjection to Western domination and local national elites at once both complicit with and complacent about the continued dispossession and domination of the global 'South', its human and material resources (Hall, 1996). When government itself, the government of postcolonial populations, is often so clearly subject to an ever-increasing penetration by Western power, both state and non-state, then the moment of independence is so clearly of the symbolic than the real.

A recognition of the persistent inequalities and domination that continue to impact upon societies of the global South does not, however, negate the historical moment that comes to constitute these societies as 'post' colonial, as having experienced modernity exactly through coloniality, and indeed as having experienced resistance to the colonial configuration of global power and its political economy. The formulation – modernity/coloniality – must hence remain at the heart of any attempt at tracing the postcolonial subject and its trajectory of resistance in modernity and late modernity. At the same time, the imaginary of a future to come suggests a constituting capacity that looks towards both the reshaping of the international and the reconstitution, indeed re-founding, of political community. As I stress at the outset, the subject of postcoloniality is at once both constituted and constituting, and it is this double moment, so to speak, that lies at the heart of this investigation.

On temporal trajectories

Time is not separable from space and any construction of either somehow implicates both. There is no easy correlation of the two elements, however, so that time may be distanced from space just as the materiality of space can somehow defy temporal projections. The subject shifts and moves with time and across space, as we have seen in the previous section. For the postcolonial subject, the encounter with the

European constitutively relocates the past into the present so that articulations of political subjectivity in the present are never far removed from the past. As will be argued in this section and the next, and in anticipation of the chapter to follow, situating the postcolonial subject in relation to time and space is core to understanding articulations of resistance and their claim to the political.

Crucial to both liberal and Marxist renditions of the global is the idea of 'Europe' as the birthplace of 'Man' and of 'capital', both universal categories against which the rest are defined. In philosophical terms, it is the category of the 'human' as universal subject that is the defining moment of modernity, a moment constructed as being of Europe and authored by Europeans. Writing the postcolonial subject into history is, as shown by Dipesh Chakrabarty among others, always a matter of locating this subject in relation to historical narratives that have constructed Europe as the reference point, so that the 'subalternity of non-Western, third world histories' is always measured in terms of 'lack' or 'incompleteness'. Europe becomes the 'subject of all histories', a condition enabled by the discourses of the social sciences where 'theory' is assumed to cover the 'whole of humanity'. As Chakrabarty (1992: 3) points out,

> Only 'Europe', the argument would appear to be, is *theoretically* (i.e., at the level of the fundamental categories that shape historical thinking) knowable; all other histories are matters of empirical research that fleshes out a theoretical skeleton which is substantially 'Europe'.

When Europe is the universal referent, the histories of non-Europeans, the non-West, is always written in terms of historical transitions so that the measure of the non-West is constituted by terms such as development and modernisation, measured in terms of the rationalised modern state and engagement in the modern (i.e. capitalist) mode of production and exchange. The 'Third World', or what we now prefer to call the 'South', is hence perpetually interpreted in terms of negativity – a lack, an incompleteness, and in contemporary discourses, a failure.[22] I will argue later in this book, that it is precisely this 'lack' that we might read as the basis of resistance; as providing the ever uncapturable excess that is mobilised into resistance. These discourses of historical transition reflect a mode of interpretation that was already in place during colonial times and are the defining feature of nineteenth- to twentieth-century nationalist discourse, framing the subject of Indian progress in the spaces between what Chakrabarty (1992: 6) calls 'homologous sets of oppositions', namely 'despotic/constitutional, medieval/modern, feudal/capitalist', so that 'Within this narrative shared between imperialist and nationalist imaginations, the "Indian" was always a figure of lack'.

Europe, through its universal categories, brings the 'global' into being, and through its colonising discourses and practices, comes to constitute the reference point against which all others are judged. Epistemologically, the 'other' comes to be known only through categories that are forever European – the modern state, the modern citizen, and the idea of 'citizens' rights', which, as Chakrabarty highlights, quoting Marx, 'splits the figure of the modern individual into "public" and "private" parts of the self'.[23] However, this 'private' part of the self comes, in colonial discourses, to represent the 'backwardness' of the colonised subject, especially in discourses that highlight the 'condition of women'. In developing the discursive strategies that shaped the nationalist struggle, the aim was to 'construct cultural boundaries that supposedly separated the "European" from the "Indian"', but that nevertheless sought to reshape the 'private' realm in terms that would reflect the modernity of the Indian self, measured in terms of 'discipline' and 'order' in domestic as well as public life. The 'colonial subject' is in this sense the 'split subject':

> As such a split subject … it speaks from within a metanarrative that celebrates the nation-state; and of this metanarrative the theoretical subject can only be a hyperreal 'Europe', a 'Europe' constructed by the tales that both imperialism and nationalism have told the colonised. The mode of self-representation that the 'Indian' can adopt here is what Homi Bhabha has justly called 'mimetic'. Indian history, even in the most dedicated socialist or nationalist hands, remains a mimicry of a certain 'modern' subject of 'European' history and is bound to represent a sad figure of lack and failure. The transition narrative will always remain 'grieviously incomplete'… On the other hand, maneuvers are made within the space of the mimetic – and therefore within the project called 'Indian' history – to represent the 'difference' and 'originality' of the 'Indian,' and it is in this cause that the anti-historical devices of memory and the anti-historical 'histories' of the subaltern classes are appropriated … Much like Spivak's 'subaltern' … this subject can only be spoken for and spoken of by the transition narrative that will always ultimately privilege the modern (i.e., 'Europe').
>
> *(Chakarabarty, 1992: 18–19)*

Writing of the postcolonial subject is hence always bound up with this paradoxical situation, one that seeks a move away from the European, but is always reflective of the signifier of theoretical knowledge and hence of universal knowledge, namely the modern European condition and its sovereign subject. The subaltern, even when allowed to speak, is always in subordinate position, according to this line of argumentation.

In seeking to trace the postcolonial subject and the subject of resistance, there is always the danger of what Spivak refers to as 'representational realism', making reference to 'concrete experience' or the reality of lived experience, but one that is actually 'disclosed through the concrete experience of the intellectual, the one who diagnoses the episteme' (Spivak, 1988: 69). The diagnosis is clearly not equivalent to the experience, and the latter cannot fully be captured in the conceptual schema produced by she who writes. If only Europe is theoretically known, and the rest of the world is theory's empirical domain, the hierarchical relationship generated, that between European theory and the world as its object of knowledge, suggests that the latter is always catching up with the former.

For Chakrabarty, one way of dislocating Europe from its pivotal position is to 'provincialise' it, so that it becomes one discourse amongst many, and in doing so enabling a radical critique that unravels the taken for granted categories that forever place the 'other' in subordinate position to the European. This is not a cultural relativism, but rather an engagement with how certain categories of thought come to constitute taken for granted discursive formations which then become the markers of truth and progress, enabling, for example, Europe's 'acquisition for itself' of the term modern.

While Chakrabarty's move is to 'provincialise Europe', the move I want to make here is to suggest that the postcolonial subject is not only constituted by a modernity claimed by Europe, but in the moment of emergence is also constituting and reconstituting. As we will see later in the book, the moment of emergence of the postcolonial onto the 'international' had profound impact on this terrain of the political. To trace the postcolonial subject is to focus on the constitution of the postcolonial subject as well as the ways in which this subject reconstitutes the international and the global. As many a postcolonial author has shown, the subject of knowledge has, in modernity, always been the European, the author of what is regarded as legitimate knowledge, holder of universal categories of selfhood, the state, and the international. To prioritise the Other of the European does not mean the negation of the encounter with the European and its formative influences in colonial modernity, but to shift focus onto the gaze of the non-European, a gaze that is not entirely formed from the historical legacy of coloniality, significant though this is. Nevertheless, we remain confined within knowledge systems that assume the European as the originary position from which all else is defined, or against which all else is compared, so that the other of Europe is forever defined by the lack. Yet it is this lack that potentially can inform our investigations into resistance and the forms it takes. However, it would be a mistake to assume that resistance is always in opposition to.

Such is the constitutive moment that comes with the temporal framing of the epistemic subject we can refer to as the postcolonial; at once both the Other of Europe and of Europe. The temporal cannot, however, be assumed in ontologically separate terms from the spatial, even though, in Kantian terms, the two are distinct categories of the a priori, the presocial, the pre-contextual, and hence the universal. Yet, it is the temporal that is the more powerful element in the framing of the postcolonial self even as this self shifts and moves spatially across the global terrain, for it is the traces of the past that somehow shape the present and its understandings. The expressions and articulations of the present, in other words, always reflect memories of the past, a form of practical consciousness that is always already in the background, and comes to be foregrounded as the subject encounters the world epistemologically.

This subject is also of the modern, but this is a modernity that is differently experienced and differently articulated. There is something here of what Fredric Jameson (2003: 699) refers to as 'existential uneven development', so that, as he states, 'modernism is to be grasped as a culture of incomplete modernisation'.

Socioeconomic temporalities, to use Jameson, are not uniform in experiential terms, and variations therein suggest multiple positionalities of the self and how the self experiences the modern, its association with industrialisation, expanding technologies, their penetration into lived experience, and the rationalisation and bureaucratisation of life. Bringing populations into the modern is hence about the changing claims that populations can make in relation to modernity and its various structuring elements. For Fredric Jameson, 'imperialism masks and conceals the nature of its system'. And yet, such concealment has never been more apparent and more blatant and all pervasive than its present articulations in liberal cosmopolitan discourse and its enabling institutions. In words that have clear resonance in contemporary modes of intervention into other societies, Jameson (2003: 701) states:

> As far as modernism is concerned ... the epistemological separation of colony from metropolis, the systematic occultation of the colony from metropolis, the systematic occultation of the colonial labor on which imperial prosperity is based, results in a situation in which ... the truth of metropolitan experience is not visible in the daily life of the metropolis itself; it lies outside the immediate space of Europe, in the colonies. The existential reality of the metropolis are thus severed from the cognitive map that would alone lend them coherence and reestablish relationships of meaning and of its production.

In the era of globalisation, however, the distance that enabled the separation of colony from metropolis is suppressed. Nevertheless, this temporal distanciation, one that holds history apart from contemporary articulations of cosmopolitan interventionism remains a powerful influence in the anamnesis that informs contemporary practices. The tensions and contradictions of the past, the public and the private, the particular and the universal, the subject and object, for example, re-emerge as contradictions in the dialectic between the local and the global. However, the macro systems, their enabling militaries and bureaucracies, have not suddenly transformed themselves into entirely new forms, for these are apparent both in the everyday and in the various 'liberal' interventions of the 1990 and to the present, practices enabled by and sustaining of these very 'macrosystems'. The point that underpins this book, therefore, is that the colony and metropolis are and can be re-emergent, channelled in different form, but still reliant on armies and bureaucracies servicing a liberal cosmopolitan project, now engaged in the re-shaping of postcolonial societies deemed locations for governmentalising intervention.

This re-emergence of the colonial past, rendered in twenty-first-century form, is not entirely reflective of the operational modalities of the past, nor does it produce subjectivities that might be reflective of the colonial and colonised subject. While decolonisation hailed the postcolonial subject into being, contemporary forms of colonisation and the macro systems that enable their operations face a subject steeped in the historical trajectory of the colonial past, but one that is at once also of the globalised present, so that any articulation of resistance is not simply territorial, if indeed it ever was, but is also a claim to history and hence to temporality in the shrunken spaces of the globalised present. In relation to art, and in the context of postmodern structures of finance capital, Jameson (2003: 703) suggests the following distinctions:

> the formal abstractions of the modernist period – which corresponded to the dialectic of value of an older monopoly stage of capitalism – are to be radically distinguished from the less palpable abstractions of the image or the logo, which operate with something of the autonomy of the values of present-day finance capital. It is a distinction between an object and its expression and an object whose expression has in fact virtually become another object in its own right.

Jameson's evocation of the aesthetic in the West, I want to argue, has its parallel in the West's relationship with its Other, the Other deemed variously as source of identifiable threat and future scenarios of risk. It is the Other whose expression, in representational form, that has become the 'object' in its own right, the object that comes to be the target of an apparatus of security that sees its articulation in global terms, a global matrix of war that involves militaries and bureaucracies, the armed and the civilian, taking place not simply at the level of the territorial state, but permeating lived experience, in dispersed locations from neighbourhoods, to households, in urban centres as well as rural sites. The expression, or the discourse of representation, comes to be materialised in this late modern global apparatus that seeks to incorporate the Other within its purview of surveillance, discipline, and control.

We know from Edward Said that the discursive representation of the Middle East and of Islam is one steeped in what he calls an Orientalist discourse that contains tropes of exoticisation, objectification, and feminisation, not to mention demonisation. Such is the power of Orientalism in contemporary representations of this region and its dominant religion that it permeates political and geo-strategic practices and informs regional alliances and decisions relating to intervention. Just as philosophy proclaims the sovereignty of the modern self, it at the same time reinforces subject positions that relegate the Other to a subordinate position, a place devoid of autonomy and subject to technologies of control that render entire populations in culturalist and racialised terms. There is no intersubjectivity here, at least not one where the subjects are equal in any sense, nor one that can assume a Habermasian inter-cultural dialogue without already defined rules of engagement, the authorship of which lies with the West. So deep rooted are these rules of engagement that they do not simply inform the form and content of intersubjective interaction between the West and its postcolonial other, but also the discourses of the theorist and their epistemological categories.

In this exposition of the temporality of postcolonial life, or of postcolonial subjectivity, we might say that there are distinct periods – the colonial, then the postcolonial, then the late modern, thereby associating the modern with the colonial, as in coloniality/modernity, and the postcolonial with the late modernity of globalised existence. The 'post' as such suggests a temporality beyond time, somehow the 'end of temporality' as Jameson would have it. Just as each 'mode of production has its own unique and specific temporality' as Jameson phrases the Althusserian position, so too we might say that the colonial and the postcolonial have theirs, but these remain enframed within the temoralities of modernity and late modernity. In some way, we might say that, for the non-West, for the formerly colonised and more blatantly for the colonised of the twenty-first century, this shrinkage of time is radically felt when the routine of daily life is so dramatically disturbed by the sudden and unexpected violence of the drone silently unloading its deadly cargo unto populations below. We might say there is a certain politics of time at play in late modern wars that target the populations of the Other of Europe. Such is the firepower unleashed that the temporal positionality of the target population is no longer in its own hands, no longer of its own efforts of creativity and commitment, no longer a matter of choice, but subject to a formula decided elsewhere. It is as if the West, despite of, and indeed because of, the uncertainties of a radically globalised era, wishes to retain control of temporality as time shrinks, as temporality itself is reclaimed by the postcolonial subject, so that this subject claims a vision of destiny.[24]

Decolonisation had inaugurated what Jameson refers to as 'an explosion of otherness unparalleled in human history' (Jameson, 2003: 709) such that the comforting racial categories of the colonial mind are somehow swept away in the face of an 'immense multitude of others' claiming, indeed forcing, recognition as equals. It is this recognition of a multitude of others that somehow disturbs the 'bourgeois self', for no longer can this self claim a universal presence, a pre-ordained destiny to rule the world, and to forever reduce the Other to a status of inferiority. Perhaps it is exactly this disturbance of self that reorients the bourgeois self to an existential moment where the colonial past could be reinvented into the present.

However, this is a present that, despite its registers of the colonial past, nevertheless denies any acknowledgement of the past; its primary achievement, it might be said, is in its concealment of the past from the present, so that liberal interventionism might indeed be understood in terms of saving lives as opposed to killing them into discipline and control. Such are the practices of the present order of things that force is not force, war is peace, and killing is care. This making the present self-sufficient, independent of the past and future, is clearly most radically enacted in the high technology warfare currently played out in the theatres of intervention that are forever those of the postcolonial world. Nowhere is this 'presentism' more radically expressed than in the concept of 'suddenness', where we can, in agreement with Jameson, see the 'association of violence and an aesthetic reduction to the present'.[25] To step 'out of history', however, has its conditions of possibility, which are historical. In other words, what enables the presentism of liberal warfare are conditions that are borne of history, and specifically that of coloniality/modernity.

The expropriation of time as a technology of domination comes face to face with modes of resistance that seek to re-appropriate time so that the presentism of liberal governmentality is confronted by articulations of subjectivity steeped in the trajectories of the colonial *and* postcolonial past. Bodies and societies configured as devoid of history come to reclaim subjectivities steeped in history, and in doing so reframe the liberal interventionist in their midst in terms of the colonial past so that despite liberal cosmopolitan presentism, the past comes to have materiality in the present. As we will see in the second half of the book, the reclaiming of time comes to be expressed in a number of diverse ways, from the battlefield context to the art gallery. However, this reclaiming of time should not be read in simplistic terms, and certainly not in terms that confine the past to the colonial order. For this past is also of the postcolonial, contained in the postcolonial state and its place in relation to postcolonial political community. These are the complex locations of the postcolonial subject, at the nexus of modernity and late modernity, and whose struggles are as much of the temporal as they are of the spatial.

The spatial and the postcolonial

What I have argued in the first section of this chapter is that the temporal constitution of the postcolonial, the specific historic rendering of the subject of coloniality/modernity, is an aspect of the postcolonial self that must be understood in juxtaposition to the late modern, cosmopolitan tendency to seek an escape from temporality, a blurring of the boundary between past and present. Such is the constitutive power of history and its imprint on the postcolonial self that any attempt to dissociate contemporary practices from that history is at the same time an act that seeks to dispossess the postcolonial self of subjectivity. To seek the end of temporality is hence not simply a denial of the historical imagination, but is a technology of power that seeks to deny the subject the frameworks of knowledge and contingencies that confer meaning to the subject's sense of being in the world. How the postcolonial subject sees the international is as much determined by the temporal as it is by the spatial, and it is the latter aspect that I will elaborate in this section, even as it is fully understood that the relationship between the two is one of mutuality rather than a dualism.

One way of conceptualising the spatial constitution of the postcolonial is in terms of the accession of the decolonised to the space of the international, a space constituted in modernity's ordering of the global into territorially defined states. Another is to emphasise the idea of the postcolonial as the 'recovery of geographical territory', to use Edward Said (1993: 252), as a moment in the constitution of political community. Where the first places emphasis on the European genesis of the 'international' and its constitutive elements, the latter places emphasis on repossession and reinscription as prerequisites in the process of founding a bounded, hence recognisable political community. Both are clearly constitutive of the postcolonial condition and hence of postcolonial subjectivity.

The spatial constitution of the postcolonial denotes the elsewhere of the West – those colonised spaces expropriated of resources, of history, and often, of people. This geopolitical configuration of the postcolonial becomes especially pertinent when we consider Said's reflection on the postcolonial as being somehow of the 'past'.[26] I want to argue later that even when we consider the postcolonial to be of the past, it nevertheless not only has moments of recurrence, but is a condition, a state of being, a continuity defined by the colonial experience and recurrent not simply in neocolonialism, but in late modern, indeed cosmopolitan, forms of intervention.

The spatial connotation or constitution of the postcolonial often refers to the regional; the three continents – Asia, Africa, and the Americas – are seen as representing the colonial/postcolonial, though there is debate about the appropriateness of a term that suggests a temporal break between the colonial and the postcolonial when there is so much of continuity as opposed to discontinuity.[27] Nevertheless, as I state earlier in this chapter, the 'break' inscribed by the term 'post' is historically of such significance, epistemologically and ontologically, that to relegate it to insignificance is to depoliticise the distinctiveness of the postcolonial experience and to deny recognition to the distinctly *political* subjectivity of the colonised, the decolonised, and the postcolonial encounter with the rest of the world. More significant still is how the 'break' from the past relates to the spatial, and especially the spatial constitution of the 'international', for the 'break' is inscribed as such by the spatial domain that is the international and the forms of recognition that the international enables, institutes, brings into form. The 'post', in other words, would be meaningless without this spatial inscription, the international as hailing forth the distinctly *post*colonial subject.

The spatiality of the international is hence a significant moment in the constitution of the postcolonial subject. However, this is not to argue, as did Sartre when writing of colonialism and the anti-colonial struggles, that the latter's success hailed the colonised's entry into 'humanity' – that what was considered by the coloniser as the 'subhuman' could now enter the realm of the human.[28] Rather, the argument made here is distinctly political, in that it underlines the crucial constitutive role played by the international as such, in its conferment of *'political'* recognition to the populations of the formerly colonised. There is then a difference I want to highlight, a difference that is as much ontological as it is epistemological as it is political: recognition of the postcolonial as a distinctly political being is ontologically of a different register than recognition as a 'human' being in that where the former confers recognition of political struggle, the latter diminishes the opponent. Fanon (1967) uses Hegel's master-slave dialectic to make the point. As highlighted by Edward Said (1993: 253), Fanon re-reads the Hegelian dialectic, suggesting that the 'master in imperialism "differs basically from the master described by Hegel. For Hegel there is reciprocity; here the master laughs at the consciousness of the slave. What he wants from the slave is not recognition but work."' While the Hegelian dialectic does not connote a spatial relationship, significant in Fanon's emphasis on 'recognition' is his (and Said's) spatial imaginary; that the colonised comes to 'self-consciously' occupy and 'reinscribe' places the colonial culture signified as subordinate. As will be shown in Chapter 4, the post in the postcolonial suggests access to the space of the international, and through such access reconstitutes a terrain of juridical and political contestation over the charting of sovereign rights beyond the merely territorial, though in agreement with Said, the retrieval of the territorial is a core element in the constitution of the postcolonial subject of politics.

The transition from the human to the political is of profound importance in the history of those who experience government by others, the formerly colonised and their contemporary counterparts. As is evident from the first section of this chapter, liberal cosmopolitanism is an apparatus of security that works through a deterritorialisation of its target populations. Such deterritorialisation is enabled by discourses of rescue and development in equal measure and by practices that transform states into zones of military and civilian operations. Concepts that emerge from liberal cosmopolitanism, from global governance to global democracy, to global civil society, and to the most 'homely' rendition of this discourse, Martha Nussbaum's 'global village' of 'human' loyalties (Nussbaum, 2006), are all implicated in this deterritorialising endeavour, one that feeds into and is itself enabled by a political economy the workings of which, in production processes and in the mobility of finance capital, rely upon a deterritorialised domain of global interaction. What should be emphasised, however, is the authorship of such deterritorialisation, for this was and is not of the target populations, but of the discourses and practices of liberal cosmopolitanism, held firmly in the hands of the liberal self of global reach, the self of a capitalist global order sustained and reinforced by a global surveillance and military machine itself dependent on this political economy. To deterritorialise is hence to depoliticise. However this is a differential depoliticisation, one built on hierarchies of worth and reason, so that the agency for a deterritorialised terrain of humanity at large lies with he or she who has global reach.

This Deleuzian deterritorialisation is a direct product of what Foucault refers to as 'heterotopia' in reference to the plurality and multiplicity of locations wherein subjects engage. However, heterotopias in Foucault are always 'disturbing' because 'they secretly undermine language, because they shatter and tangle common names, because they make it impossible to name this *and* that ...' (Foucault, 1970: xvii–xviii) There are hence heterotopic spaces, from urban locations to prisons and schools, whereby alternative modes of doing things emerge, suggesting perhaps alternative modes of politics. However, even though Foucault recognises that space is 'fundamental to any exercise of power',[29] and is critical of discourses that 'devalue' space, those that treat space 'as the dead, the fixed, the undialectical, the immobile', his is a project concerned with spatialisation as a technology of power. Such spatialisation may hence in itself be thought of in terms of deterritorialisation, for this is indeed a practice of displacement and extraction, the removal of the subject to deterritorialised locations. To reterritorialise might hence be seen as an articulation of postcolonial resistance, of situated subjectivity, and a distinctly political expression of a specifically defined consciousness that has a sense of time *and* space.

The spatial constitution of the postcolonial subject is intricately bound up with the temporality of modernity/coloniality. The 'international' as such emerges as a juridical-political construct the articulations of which differ both historically and spatially, so that what the 'international' means in relation to the European state system differs substantially from what the international means in relation to the European/non-European context. There is, in other words, no essential, historically transcendent meaning we can confer upon the space of the international, so that the meaning of the international, and the all too important question that occupies this study, what the international means when seen from the decolonised spaces of the South, will be imbued with the discursive and institutional continuities of contingent social, economic, and political relations. The international must hence be understood culturally, in constructivist terms. However, this should not suggest that the materiality of the international is insignificant. Rather, there is a mutually constitutive relationship between the cultural, the realm of meaning, and the material, and both are implicated in the colonial past and the postcolonial present, as will be indicated in the following chapters, which deal respectively with how discourse came to constitute the subjects involved in colonial modernity, and how the subjects of colonial rule came to negotiate and navigate their colonised spaces, discourses, and epistemes.

The following chapter will seek to unravel the conditions that rendered possible the emergence not just of a hierarchical international juridical-political order, but of hierarchically constituted subjectivities that bear their imprint in present-day articulations of the international. Colonial practices of racialisation had a two-fold purpose – dispossession on the one hand and the policing of the boundary of modernity on the other. The Other of European subjectivity, despite the imbalance of power that variously exoticised, demeaned, and dispossessed, nevertheless remains a powerful figure, at once desired and feared, a combination of factors that inform Europe's interaction with the rest of the world to the present. The encounter with the non-European subject, by the seventeenth and eighteenth centuries, had developed into one that actively sought to relegate the 'other' to subordinate status juridically and politically so that the colonial project that sustained the unhindered spread of capitalist accumulation could be set in motion. Policing access to the modern came to be the primary technology of control, for in the modern lay the aporetic condition whereby colonialism would generate, enable, and produce the subject of resistance.

Policing access to the modern was a trope of colonial rule and could be articulated at a number of different sites, from access to education and defining/ determining those included and excluded, to access to the bureaucratic machinery of the colonial state, to access to the rule of law and the judiciary, and access to social sites of interaction such as clubs and societies. However, one of the most significant such sites, at least as far as the present context is concerned, was that of the 'international' as a distinct juridical/political space. Just as access to the bureaucratic and juridical machinery of the state was limited to the white settlers and the few selected to service them, so too access to the international, for the leaders and populations of the non-European came to be determined by the political economy of the juridical inscription of the international and who had the right to police it and be protected by it. To understand the contemporary articulation of power through the government of populations, and to understand the modes of resistance that have emerged in relation to this power is to focus on not simply the continuities of the past in the present, but to reveal practices that somehow define the conditions of possibility for the emergence of the postcolonial subject as subject of (international) politics.

2

POLICING ACCESS TO THE MODERN

Power, fear, resistance

> We are accused of terrorism:
> if we write of a ruined homeland and the ruins of a homeland
> torn, weak ...
> A homeland without an address
> and a nation with no name ...
>
> Nizar Qabbani[1]

The postcolonial subject carries a legacy of resistance against foreign domination. Narratives of resistance range from those inherited from generations past to those learned through a postcolonial educational system where the teaching of history in much of the postcolonial world is dominated by recollections of acts of resistance against colonial occupiers. There is a temporality and a spatiality to these all too constitutive narratives – from moments of resistance that emerge as instantaneous reactions to domination in routine encounters to enduring political mobilisations that sought a sustained, multi-layered, and multi-targeted campaign again aimed at the colonial other. These are not separable narratives, but are in fact mutually constitutive, so that the apparent intimacy of the first is but a constitutive moment in the all too public terrain, variously of the strike, the published pamphlet, or the violent uprising.

As argued earlier, the definition of resistance I am developing here focuses on the claim to the political, suggesting therefore a transition from subjectivity to political agency; a self-conscious articulation of claims to the sites of struggle and contestation. The use of the term 'transition' suggests a temporal lag – from subjectivity to political agency – that is all too evocative of instrumental rationality. While the instrumental must be taken into account in any discussion of action as such, my use of the term 'transition' does not imply a time-lag, for to do so would suggest that the articulation of agency is separable from subjectivity. As will be shown in Chapter 3, my aim is to provide a conceptualisation of 'resistance' that relies on a mutually constitutive relationship between subjectivity and political agency where each is in turn in a mutually constitutive relationship with structures of power, both discursive and non-discursive. The conceptualisation I provide is also premised on the idea of 'negativity'; that articulations of agency and the all too constitutive structures of power never fully capture the subject of resistance, and this uncapturability must somehow also have a presence in this conceptualisation of the subject of resistance. These then are the themes that emerge throughout the book, forming as they do so the conceptual/theoretical frame of these reflections on resistance and the postcolonial subject.

In anticipation of the chapter to follow, my aim here is to situate postcolonial resistance, or the postcolonial claim to the political, in the continuities that link colonial modernity and postcolonial late modernity. This wider historical context places the lens on 'modernity', the temporal-spatial limits of the modern and its constitutive features. This discourse on modernity is important in that how we understand modernity has implications for our understanding of postcolonial claims to the political and the forms in which such claims come to find expression. Much postcolonial writing directs its critique against 'modernity' as such, a modernity that is inconceivable without coloniality. The formula 'modernity/coloniality' that can be found in the writings of Walter Mignolo and Enrique Dussel among others, is all too powerful a discourse, providing as it does a vision of a violent modernity that is far from liberal renditions that celebrate its emancipatory potential.[2] For Mignolo (2005: xi), rejecting the prefix 'post' in the postcolonial, the epistemological frame must move to the 'coloniality' side of the formula, 'the untold and unrecognised historical counterpart of modernity'. As we saw in the last chapter, however, the 'post' in the postcolonial is highly significant for the perspective I take here, for I take it to be constitutive of the subject of politics in postcoloniality being elaborated here.

My aim in this chapter is to develop the theme of modernity/coloniality, but to do so in a different direction. My starting assumption relates to what I and many others refer to as the 'paradoxes' of modernity; its emancipatory potential on the one hand, and its violent dispossessive potential on the other.[3] These are not exclusive potentials, nor are they necessarily related causally, though they indeed could be. Much discussion in the postcolonial literature focuses on its critique of 'modernity' as such, so that the different articulations of modernity or the emergence of alternative modernities and negotiations therein often disappear from view. More seriously, the attribution of certain concepts to specifically European modernity, concepts such as juridical sovereignty, loses sight of how the tropes of modernity come to find expression in non-European contexts; tropes such as 'self-determination', 'free expression', 'progress' and 'scientific' knowledge, the primacy of mathematical thinking, contractual obligation, satire, and critique. The point is not to argue over the temporal genesis of these,[4] but to rethink them historically and dialectically. To do so means a rejection of dichotomous thinking that makes use of formulations – seen in contemporary times – such as modernity/tradition, modernity/counter-modernity, and their other, hierarchically ordained terms such as reason/religion, the universal and the particular. To think historically and dialectically is to acknowledge the paradoxes of modernity, its complexities of articulation in lived experience, and the negotiations and contestations that take place over its discourses and institutions.

Given the historical and dialectical imaginary I have defined, this book is hence not written in opposition to modernity. Rather, it seeks to reveal how resistance emerges in and through the modern, its discourses and institutions. In this chapter, I focus in particular on the notion that I refer to as 'policing access to the modern'. I argue that a fundamental strategy of resistance to colonial domination stemmed from a desire to retrieve access to the 'modern', to reclaim territory and political community, to gain and regain access to the international as a juridical-political space and as political economy. The colonial violence directed at anti-colonial resistance might hence be conceptualised in terms of policing access to the modern, wherein the technologies of policing included warfare, 'counter-insurgency' violence, internment and incarceration, partitioning and collective punishment, as well as regulated access for a selected 'native' few. Such practices of policing, as will be shown, derived from a fear of specific instances of resistance. However, as will be argued below, they also stemmed from a more generalised anxiety, thereby directing policing and regulation to the wider populations of the colonised.

Ultimately, as will be argued throughout the book, policing access to the modern has its postcolonial articulations, the difference being that in the postcolonial condition, the subject of resistance, as will be shown in Chapter 4, is or can be the postcolonial state, and where the stakes relate to claiming access to the modern international and the founding of political community. The continuities into late modernity are stark, and as will be shown in Chapters 5 and 6 respectively, policing access now finds a global remit; articulated now in terms of humanity at large, transnational in its discourses and modes of operation, and aimed at a fear of the particular other and a more generalised anxiety about the other's claim to the political.

The paradox that characterises modernity for the colonised is that it at once instantiated in their midst the emergence of empire and its consequent structures of power and dispossession *and* modes of resistance that sought to capture the space of the modern, its discourses and institutions. The assumption of the colonisers was that they possessed access to the modern, indeed were its authors. However, theirs was a particular rendition of the modern, an all too powerful rendition that sprang from the legacy of the European Enlightenment and specifically the rejection of the absolutist state for Europe while seeking to practise the absolutism of the colonial state upon the populations of the colonised. The aim in this chapter is not to replay colonial history, but to highlight aspects of the past that live into the present – the racialisation of the cultural other, the disciplining and pacification of populations through violence, and exclusionary practices premised on the imperative to police access to the modern and its potentials in the production of the subject of resistance.

The notion of policing access to the modern does not imply the wholesale exclusion of the other from the discourses and institutions of modernity. Rather, the idea suggests control and regulation, so that practices of 'modernisation' – those that led to dispossession – went hand in hand with those that sought to subjugate the self-definition and indeed self-determination of the other. The imperative of the colonial subject is constitutively based on domination and dispossession, and being so relies upon the subjugation of the colonised, a subjugation built on the premise that the colonised will resist, ultimately. Policing the modern is hence built on a combination of the fears specifically related to particular acts and agents of insurrection/sedition/rebellion, and a much more generalised and indeterminate anxiety that stems from the knowledge that irrespective of the forces of imperialism, the forces of domination, the colonised remained essentially unknown, escaping imported categories, and having the ever present potential for rebellion and resistance. My intention is to reveal both the continuities of past and present and to highlight that in both instances of foreign domination/intervention we see the driving imperative is the disciplining and pacification of populations understood to be the sources of an ever-present danger. As will be shown below, the violence of colonial occupation is structured, as Ranajit Guha (1997) argues, by the imperative to discipline and pacify a population perceived as constitutively seditious and hence always a source at once of both a directed fear and an indirected, indeterminate, generalised anxiety that the seditious will erupt.

The hermeneutics of danger that inform 'the prose of counter-insurgency' (Guha, 1994) in colonial modernity and in postcolonial late modernity dominate the epistemological grounds through which resistance is understood. The discourses and practices of counter-insurgency provide an 'enframing' of the subject of resistance, so that alternative narratives on resistance, those that do not emerge from what I am referring to as the hermeneutics of danger, are not only constitutive of a counter-hegemonic move in the 'episteme' on resistance, but also provide, as I hope to do here, a critical ontology of resistance, and hence of subjectivity. I will return to the hermeneutics of danger later in the chapter. However, I begin with an engagement of narratives of resistance in the context of colonial modernity, distinguishing between 'fragments' and 'trajectories'. I use the term 'fragment' to suggest a temporality of the idiographic; a picture extracted from a landscape, not for its representation of a generality necessarily, nor for its revelation of causes and effects, but for the hesitant insights it can provide on subjectivity. I use the term 'trajectory' to suggest a related but a different temporality, one that does not imply a linear narrative, one moment leading to the next, but that enables distinctions to be drawn based on the contingencies of resistance. The fragments are mine and the trajectories are those I borrow from Edward Said. The fragments and trajectories of resistance to coloniality that I highlight function to immediately 'show up', so to speak, the poverty and the all-too-present epistemic violence of the discourses of 'counter-insurgency' that purport to provide understandings of resistance. The significance of these latter discourses is twofold. First, they provide a picture of the discursive formations that inform discussion of resistance. Second, and more importantly for my purposes, they provide an indication of the continuities in discourses and practices between colonial modernity and postcolonial late modernity, continuities informed by cultural and racial signification.

Narratives of resistance

There are fragments of resistance and there are trajectories. There are also those instances that remain unrecorded, missed out of the archive of anti-colonial struggle. These might be traces of memory that emerge as asides to wider stories about family or friendship. The trace seemingly vanishes, if not for its enduring impact on the listener, the postcolonial subject who inherits and retells the tale. This inheritance includes not just traces, but the historical narratives of resistance that shaped and continue to shape the subjectivities of the postcolonial self. There is necessarily a process of selection involved in the writing, and the aim here is to reveal practices of colonial domination that I am referring to as 'policing access to the modern' through the modes of resistance that the colonisers sought to confront and to eradicate.

Fragments

The students in occupied Egypt

The authorities had decided to embark on a policy that aimed at once to both discipline and punish, but also to use violence as a means to terrorise and intimidate the population into submission. Pacification was the ultimate strategy, and the tactics used sought conformity with the edicts of rule. Sovereign authority instantiated its imperative through a performance that spanned military power and institutionalised exclusion so that the costs incurred through rebellion were so high that participation would be unthinkable. Then when killing the rebellious was found to be futile, the authorities hit where it would hurt most, at the very heart of aspiration and hope for the future. The authorities in this case were the British in 1919 occupied Egypt, and their strategy was to subdue the Egyptian national liberation movement. Having killed and exiled its leaders, the aim of the British was now to hit at the heart of its popular support, and the education system of the schools and colleges seemed a target where technologies of discipline and punishment could be designed to greatest effect. However, in so designing these technologies, they at the same time enabled and constituted the discourses of resistance.

The Ministry of Education under British rule had introduced the 'conduct and application' act in the autumn of 1919, which determined that students could be expelled on failure of these two subjects. The timetabling of examination was also used as a means through which striking students missing their first schedule would be prevented from re-sitting in the second, thereby ensuring failure. School administrations also sought a submission of a formal apology from students who had taken part in previous strike activities. The aim was not only to punish these activities, but to prevent the recurrence of future strikes and demonstrations. Students from schools and colleges went on strike, as reported in *Al-Ahram*, 'in order to eliminate a hurdle that has been cast in our path for no crime we have committed, unless the love of one's nation and selfless dedication to the service of one's nation can be considered a crime'. While there were immediate grievances against the tactics of the educational authorities, the broader narrative of the striking students was framed by the discourse of national liberation. One major grievance expressed by the students was that the Arabic language itself was being undermined by policies that favoured English over Egyptian teachers and lecturers. These practices of exclusion and intimidation are made all the more evident on reflecting upon the decision of the British to close the women's Al-Saniya Teachers College, one of the first to be subjected to the punitive measures imposed against the dissenters. Writing to *Al-Ahram*, the women's leaders proclaimed: 'We, the students of Al-Saniya School, take this opportunity to inform our fellow Egyptians of our plight. We are vulnerable to expulsion for the slightest cause ...' Their strike aimed to prevent the school's closure and to have Arabic as the medium of instruction, calling on the nation 'to rise to the call of justice and rescue the innocent and oppressed young women who seek to advance the cause of their nation while fettered in the chains of despotism'.[5]

The British response to the student resistance highlighted above must be placed in the wider context of British education policy since the occupation of Egypt in 1882. Overturning over fifty years of government-sponsored education under the Ottoman Khedives, the aim of its principal architect, Lord Cromer, was to limit access to a modern educational provision. As indicated by Mona Russell (2001: 51), 'Cromer had seen first hand in India that it is indeed better to "trade with civilised men" than to "govern savages", but, at the same time, that too much education makes for an unwieldy, critical populace'. Cromer sought to achieve this variously by raising school fees, restricting access, and controlling the curriculum, this last even including encouragement for the religious schools, seeing these as a way of combating nationalism. However, of far more significance historically is the British attempt to restrict instruction in Arabic, thereby limiting the teaching of history. As seen above, far from obliterating nationalist allegiance, such measures saw some of the most significant confrontations against British rule in Egypt's socio-political history. At the same time, it would be a mistake to interpret these events in simple oppositional terms, the British colonials on the one hand and the Egyptian nationalists on the other, for significant class divisions within Egyptian society meant that the 'order' constructed by the colonists often served the purposes of the Egyptian upper and middle classes who shared an interest in 'order' and 'discipline'. Timothy Mitchell (1991: 119) stresses this shared interest in the following statement:

> Nationalism was not a singular truth, but a different thing among these social groups. My concern here is with those who secured new wealth and political power under the British, and maintained it as the British withdrew. Their political writings were concerned with the threatening presence of the mass of working and unemployed Egyptians. This threatening presence took most often the form of the crowd. Somehow this crowd was to be ordered and made obedient and industrious. Its individuals were to be formed into an organised and disciplined whole. It was this obedient and regulated whole that was to be imagined under the name of the 'nation', that was to be constructed as Egyptian 'society'. And the word for this political process of discipline and formation was education.

While Mitchell's aim here is to emphasise, perhaps too strongly, the fear of the 'crowd' as the driving imperative behind commonalities of interest between coloniser and a certain class of the colonised, what is significant is that education policy, irrespective of such commonality, was certainly one of the major battlegrounds upon which policing access to the modern took shape. Schools and universities were at the same time understood to be primary sites of mobilisation and resistance for a nationalist cause, the discourses of which were in the public arena prior to Cromer's arrival. This particular fragment illustrates the nexus between resistance and power and the productive force therein.

The artist in colonial India

Visiting the National Museum of Modern Art in Delhi in 2010, this particular postcolonial subject is struck by a contrast apparent in two of the museum's gallery spaces. In the first were oil paintings that seemed to represent in full garish form the British colonial's perception of Indian society, an exaggerated orientalism depicting exoticised, sexualised subjects constructed entirely for the gaze of the colonial occupier. It quickly became apparent that these were indeed works commissioned by the British as decorative items for their colonial homes. Moving on to the next gallery space, the sense of discovery was overwhelming. For here was a completely different art form, at once both modern in its chosen medium and in its substantial thematic, while being of India. This, I discovered, was the Bengal School of Abanindranath Tagore. The subject matter in these paintings seemed somehow of an everyday India, its landscape and its people. The invitation here was not to the gaze of the colonial, but that of a nation. The modernity of the works seemed to derive from their minimalism, their use of tempera and not oil, and their quiet reflexivity. This, however, appeared very much a local rendition of modernity, one that derived from a local as well as an international space. At the same time, the 'fusion of horizons', to use Gadamer, was all too apparent for the viewer looking on, for here was difference articulated and in doing so somehow hailed the viewer into the interpretative space of the artwork.

There is a long history of Western writing about the non-West, Africa, the Middle East, Asia, that assumes these lands to be simply accumulations of population, without history or art, blank slates upon which Western knowledge could make its imprint. The history or art that is recognised is read variously through archeological or anthropological lenses, orientalised, and certainly never related to innovation or an imaginary that relates art to social and political production. Edward Said, reading Gide, finds in the latter that 'The people of Africa, and especially those Arabs, are just there; they have no accumulating art or history that is sedimented into works.' There is here what Said refers to as the 'European authorial subject' entitled to 'hold on to an overseas territory, derive benefits from it, but ultimately refuse it autonomy or independence.' (Said, 1993: 232)

What emerges in a discursive formation that always places the European authorial subject in a hierarchical relationship to the non-European other is a political economy of representation that comes to be structured in time and across space, so that it emerges not just in the colonial era, but has its reiteration in the contemporary context. The power of interpretation, of art or history, but also of events and practices, remains primarily with the European subject. In relation to our subject matter in this chapter, policing access to the modern is at once also policing access to the interpretative, and this can best be illustrated by engaging briefly with how Indian artists, at the turn of the twentieth century and under British colonial rule, negotiated their terrain in the face of technologies of control used in art education. Of significance here is not only that any resistance had to steer its course between 'tradition' and 'modernity', but rather how the latter, modernity as such, could be open to the interpretation, and rendition, of the non-European, colonised subject. Limiting this capacity, or indeed governing its directionality, came to be a matter for the art education establishment in the colonial state. Where the artist, in substance and in method, sought to locate his art in a modernist rendition of a pan-Asian aesthetic, the discourses and practices of 'art education', though sympathetic in places, sought to confine Indian art to orientalist interpretations, thereby negating the nexus between art and the political.

Abanindranath Tagore (1871–1951) was the founder of what later came to be known as the Bengal School, which, at least for the Delhi Museum of Modern Art, represented a 'philosophy of pan-Indian art' that sought to develop 'an indigenous yet modern style in art as a response to the call for "swadeshi", to express Indian themes in pictorial language that deliberately turned away from Western styles' constituting a 'pan Asian aesthetic' in rejection of the 'colonial aesthetic' of the time. Inspired by Japanese artists such as Okakura Kakuzo and Indian miniature art, Tagore and his followers used the wash technique to portray historic figures as well as scenes from daily life. The clear curatorial juxtaposition in the museum aimed to show this art in contradistinction to the 'orientalist' art that was commissioned by British colonials during the Raj; the 'pan-Asiatic aesthetic' of the former and the 'colonial aesthetic' of the latter.[6]

The problem with the above representation of Tagore's art is that it places him in a binary construct – nationalist versus orientalist – that not only overlooks the agency and complex hybrid subjectivity of the artist, but does not allow the revelation of how this subjectivity and agency could emerge from a matrix of governmentality that sought to shape (and hence to police) aesthetic production in India. The agency to resist cannot hence be reduced to a re-found tradition, or indeed Indian 'spirituality', as the Orientalists would have it, but rather, a resistance that sought to make a claim to the political landscape exactly through an alternative, locally articulated modernity that was in dialogue with past and present, with the local inheritance of a complex, textualised art, and techniques deriving from elsewhere, including Persian Islamic art, Japanese art, European art, and the British arts and crafts movement. This is then a complex trajectory that makes the identification of a distinct moment of resistance difficult to identify, politically tempting though such an identification might be to any interpretation of the anti-colonial struggles of the past. There is hence a case to be made for interpreting Abanindrabath's art as occupying, as Banerji (2009: xxxi) suggests, a 'liminal hybrid zone' suggestive of a cultural politics 'made up of dialogic negotiation and the constitution of hybrid identities in-between the modern and the communitarian'. This 'liminal engagement with modernity', as Banerji puts it borrowing from Chakrabarty, suggests not a uniform subject of nationalism nor indeed of colonial orientalism, but a fragmented self whose frames of reference are of the local and the transnational, but never reducible to either locale, for each of these is defined by complexity. While the political agency of the artist might be said to have derived exactly from this complexity, the trajectory of colonial art education was to render such complexity uniform and manageable, conforming to the orientalist aesthetic of colonial hegemony.[7] Read in this light, the nationalist rendition of the artist constructed in curatorial decisions comes to be problematised, for even the liminal engagement with modernity can be seen as agency constituted not simply by the artist's consciousness and sense of self, but also as a product of the shaping imperative of pedagogic practices.

The Iraqi poet

The point of these fragments is to suggest that the colonised, in being confronted with European modernity and its colonising imperative, come to reconstitute and indeed reinterpret modernity, reinscribing self into its complex landscape, thereby performing an insurrectionary politics that comes to be a moment in the visioning and potential founding of political community. The Egyptian and Indian examples highlighted above are suggestive of the complex terrain that constitutes these negotiations with modernity; negotiations that seek to reclaim not just territory, but political agency, and hence the imaginary formative of a future to come, a future not simply based on decolonisation but of the constitution of political community. What is especially pertinent in the last of my three fragments on resistance in the midst of the policing imperative of the colonial state is that here we see a creative agency rendered in the poet's own language, Arabic, reinventing poetic form, and in so doing claiming a language of modernity and freedom that can be said to derive from the poetic as such and not from externally prescribed sources, though here too there is a spatial and temporal liminality of expression. At the same time it is this negotiation of a liminal spatiality and temporality that confers agency to the subject, in this instance one that traverses the colonial and the postcolonial.

Reading the Libyan author Hisham Al-Mattar's latest novel, *Anatomy of a Disappearance* (2011), devoted to the subject of the disappearance of his father at the hands of the Gaddafi regime, I am surprised to find reference to the Iraqi poet Badr Shakir Al-Sayyab and his famous poem *Rain Song*, as the book from which the narrator child's father 'hardly departed'. The recollection is of a conversation where the child seeks to know the father's past, a curiosity born of a life lived in exile:

And if I came to him with questions, he would smoothly deflect them:
'It was all so long ago.'
I rarely persisted because I knew that he was being true to Mother's wishes.
'Don't transfer the weight of the past on to your son,' she once told him.
'You can't live outside history,' he argued. 'We have nothing to be ashamed of. On the contrary.'
After a long pause she responded, 'Who said anything about shame? It's longing that I want to spare him. Longing and the burden of your hopes.'

(Al-Mattar, 2011: 26)

We carry history with us, we feel its visceral proximity as we traverse the present and its spaces.

The poet Badr Shakir Al-Sayyab (1926–1964) is widely seen in the Arab world as the founder of the 'free verse movement', combining the metrical rules of classical Arabic poetry with the flow of the vernacular.[8] To locate Al-Sayyab temporally is to place him in colonial and postcolonial Iraq, a temporality that is at once also spatial; the southern Iraqi city of Basra and the city's nearby villages, and specifically Jaykur, the village of his birth. However, al-Sayyab is at the same time of the Arab world, recognised throughout as a major figure in the much reified world of Arabic poetry. Al-Sayyab's political milieu was first and foremost nationalist, finding expression after the execution by the British of the leaders of the anti-colonial Rashid Ali Al-Kilani Movement of April-May, though the household of his youth included portraits of nationalist leaders such as that of the Egyptian Saad Zaghlul, and the Turkish nationalist and moderniser Mustapha Kemal Ataturk. Al-Sayyab's political formation must hence be seen as being not just of the colonial period, but of the post-independence Arab world that saw the loss of Palestine in 1948 and the political disappointment associated with repressive Arab regimes; in Al-Sayyab's case, experiences of incarceration, exile, and a life-time of politically instigated impoverishment under a nominally independent Iraq still under British control until 1958.

There had been previous attempts to 'liberate' Arabic poetry from the strictures of metric rules, but al-Sayyab's poetry must be seen as providing the moment of creative agency responsive to the call of social and political challenges of the time. As Issa Boullata suggests, the free verse movement was 'initially a reaction against a technique', and hence concerned primarily with form, it came to move away from the romanticism of its early days towards a concern with content:

It stopped being concerned with putting an end to neo-classicism, and began to pursue its own raison d'être. The new form of free verse began to be seen rightly as part of the content itself … the major poets recognised in the new free verse form not only a vehicle of new themes altogether at variance with old ones but an expression of some of the very themes treated, such as liberty or new life for the Arab nation. No modern poet could sincerely write on liberty, they thought, if in his writing he used the shackles of traditional ways of expression. Nor could a modern poet really express the hopes of a new life for Arab society if he used old and out-moded methods of versification and rhyme schemes. To be modern meant to be a rebel.

(Boullata, 1970: 251)

For Boullata, free verse 'expressed a psychological necessity in the Arab world; otherwise it would never have been accepted … By the time al-Sayyab and Nazik al-Mala'ika began their first experiments in free verse, the Arab countries of the Middle East had been independent for some time, but their intellectuals had begun to doubt whether they were really free' (Boullata, 1970: 251).[9] The revolutionary process needed to 'modernise' the Arab world had to be reflected in a revolutionary expression of an emerging 'realist' poetry. For al-Sayyab:

> Every mature revolution has to start with the content before the form, because the form is an attendant that serves the content. It is the new substance that looks for a new form for itself, and breaks the old frame as a growing seed breaks its shell. I am sorry to say that the stupendous innovation that has affected the form is not commensurate with the slight innovation that has affected the content. This leads us to confess that the 'revolution' of the young poets against form – against rhyme and metre – is a superficial revolution, and that if it remains so, it will cause the gravest harm to Arabic poetry.
>
> *(Quoted in Boullata, 1970: 253)*

The content that mattered for al-Sayyab related to freedom from imperial domination, repression, and poverty. In *Rain Song*, written in 1953 while in exile in Kuwait and pursued by the British-backed regime of Nuri-al-Sa'id, the subject is projected onto the landscape of his country, at once reclaiming and expressing a sense of hopelessness carried in a cyclical repetition of words:

> I can almost hear Iraq abound with thunder,
> Storing up lightening in valleys and mountains
> Until, when men broke its seal,
> The wind left of Thamud
> Not a trace in the valley.
> I can hear the palm trees drinking the rain
> And I can hear the villages groan, the refugees
> Wrestling with oars and with sails
> Against the storms of the Gulf and the thunder, singing:
> Rain
> Rain
> Rain …[10]

For Terri DeYoung (1998: 16), the 'specific imagery of the passage relies heavily on apocalyptic discourse as it appears in the Koran. This is signalled most explicitly by the mention of "Thamud", which was a pre-Islamic tribe destroyed by God for refusing to listen to a prophet who was sent to them'. The vision does not suggest an 'end of history', but a historical moment preceding the emergence of Islam. However, this should not be read as a religiosity in this distinctly secular poet whose allegiances were first with the assertively named 'Non-religious Party' in 1940s Iraq and then with communism. A preferred reading derives from Issa Boullata's (1970: 255) interpretation of the poet:

> If al-Sayyab insisted on themes of tragedy, sacrifice, martyrdom and death, it is because life did not treat him mercifully on the personal level. On the other hand, the tensions which the Arab world was undergoing politically, socially, and existentially, and the psychological crisis in which the Arab people found themselves as they were torn between conflicting ideologies and contradictory methodologies, had a great bearing on his poetic vision. He refused to be on the margin of things and hurled himself vehemently in the whirlpool as the Arab nation, during his lifetime, was undergoing perhaps the most acute tests of identity, and passing through the most severe ordeals of anxiety and self-determination.

In the 'projection of self' onto the realm of the political, al-Sayyab's poetics are at once reflective of a creative agency that seeks to transcend the limits of discourse, finding expression in a location of excess beyond the formality of rules, and yet articulated in the 'real' of lived experience. Yet this is a troubled, fragmented subjectivity, one that portrays at once the despair, longing, and hope of the exile as he seeks to reclaim lost territory and redraw a political future. In Issa Boulatta's (1970: 255) words, 'To write poetry was to take a position, to commit oneself to an attitude in relation to the world ...' The modernist in al-Sayyab, reflective of the free verse movement that describes modern Arabic poetry and its location in Arab society, is well expressed by him:

> I am one of those who believe that the artist has a debt which he must render to this unhappy society in which he lives. But I do not accept that the artist – and especially the poet – be made a slave to this theory ... If a poet is sincere in his expression of life in every respect, he will necessarily give expression to society's woes and hopes without being forced to do so by anyone. Likewise, he will give expression to his own woes and private feelings which, in their deepest, are the feelings of the majority in his society.[11]

There is a certain intimacy in the self projected onto the world, and we see this in the liminal postcolonial negotiations with modernity highlighted here. These liminal spaces reveal a time and place of contestation, of efforts to reclaim lost territories in the face of colonial dispossession and postcolonial discontent. In traversing the terrain of the colonial and the postcolonial, in these fragments, from Egypt, through India, and back again in the Arab world, and specifically Iraq, and from the expression of political agency on the streets of colonial Cairo, to the art world of the much contested Bengal School, and then the poetics of the free verse movement in Arabic Poetry, what is revealed is the complex terrain that connects subjectivity to political agency. This complexity brings into view both the 'intimacy of revolt', to use Julia Kristeva,[12] and the subject's constitution in regulative practices and discourses that seek to police and shape the colonised and postcolonial subject. At the same time, we see revealed forms of agency that are in themselves constituting of postcolonial modernity, providing an opening into not just the anti-colonial struggle, but the moment of emergence, the founding of political community. We see at the same time, that this is perhaps a deferred moment, emerging now in the twenty-first century, as the populations of the Arab world seek to reclaim their moment of self-determination afresh, a point I will return to later in the book.

Trajectories

For Edward Said (1993: 256), 'The post-imperial writers of the Third World bear their past with them as scars of humiliating wounds, as instigations for different practices, as revised visions of the past tending towards a post-colonial future.' The spatial and temporal constitution of the postcolonial subject that I have been stressing throughout finds expression here, so that the writers drawn upon have the imprint of imperialism upon their bodies, an imprint of a domination that is manifest in its immediate territoriality. The temporal contains the past in the present of the writing, and in an imagined future to come, a temporality that contains within it the anti-colonial struggle, the moment of self-determination, and contestations relating to the political community of the post-colonial future. Primarily, and like the fragments highlighted above, these are part of the 'global history of modernism', excluded and marginalised though they have been from the writings of this history, moving the 'contest of decolonisation from the peripheries to the centre', and constituting a 'voyage in' of 'hybrid cultural work' (Said, 1993: 294–295).

Said selects four texts that he locates in two distinct historical moments. The first contains C.L.R. James's *The Black Jacobins* (1938) and George Antonius's *The Arab Awakening*, where the former deals with an eighteenth-century Black Caribbean insurrection, while the latter writes of a twentieth-century Arab one. Both are seen as possessing a prescience at the time of writing; for the continued 'agonized' life of the Caribbean and the continuing impact of Palestine in the life of the Arabs; though in the immediate context of the ongoing 'Arab spring', the latter work seems remarkably prescient and salient. James and Antonius were writing from the perspective of national independence movements, according to Said. The second two works are distinctly *post*-colonial and include Ranajit Guha's *A Rule of Property for Bengal: An Essay on the Idea of Permanent Settlement* (1963) and S.H. Alatas's *The Myth of the Lazy Native: A Study of the Image of the Malays, Filipinos and Javanese from the Sixteenth to the Twentieth Century and its Function in the Ideology of Colonial Capitalism* (1977). These latter works are, according to Said, 'archeological and deconstructive', seeking to reveal the workings of colonial exploitation through the microcosm of discourses and practices; in Guha's case dealing with the 1826 Act of Permanent Settlement for Bengal and the extraction of rents and revenues in Bengal, and in Alatas's case, revealing the practices that produced the construct of the 'lazy native', for purposes of exploitation and subordination.

The trajectory assumed in Said's differentiation is significant for present purposes in the contrasts it draws out between these anti-colonial and postcolonial writings. The first contrast that might be highlighted here relates to the authors' standpoint in relation to the European Enlightenment. Where James and Antonius view the 'enemy' as the colonial West, both find their political inspiration in the Enlightenment project, seeing here the ideas of critique and liberation constitutive of national liberation struggles in Africa, the Caribbean, Asia, and the Middle East. For James, according to Said, the French Revolution produces both Toussaint and Napoleon. Antonius, on the other hand, provides a reading of the Arab Revolt that reveals the voice of Arab leaders and Arab thinkers in formulating the case for independence. Both James and Antonius, though respectively Marxist and liberal, write from the 'standpoint of an ongoing mass political struggle', Negro Revolution in James's case and Arab Nationalism in Antonius's. Both, in this sense, were writer/activists; their 'voyage in' was, and indeed continues to be, an intervention, not just into the politics of representation, but the claim to politics.

Guha and Alatas, for Said, write from the point of view of a postcolonial subject, making a 'gesture of decolonisation' targeting the writing of history. The audience here is a limited academic one; what Said refers to as a 'community of method', informed respectively by Foucault and Marx, and critical of historiographies that limit their analytics to the European context. There is no linear narrative here committed to a moment of 'emancipation' conceived along European lines, but a standpoint of 'irony', challenging the claims of imperialism to 'civilise' and to 'enlighten', revealing its practices of expropriation and dispossession as being located precisely in the philosophies and knowledge systems of European modernity, revealing this in all its calculative, administrative, and instrumental rationality, one placed in the service of empire.

What is significant about Said's construction of this unlikely comparative base is its implied trajectory. First, there is the subject of the anti-colonial struggle at home with the Enlightenment project and indeed whose narrative relies on Enlightenment notions of critique and emancipation in formulating political choices; a hybrid engaged subject position where primacy is conferred to national self-determination. Second, there is the postcolonial author seeking to deconstruct the European Enlightenment, revealing the deeply imbricated systems of power that link the philosophies of rationalisation within Europe to the administration of its colonies. Significantly, the latter two are also suggestive of both a 'voyage in' first, with respect to the politics of representation, and second, what we might see as the 'occlusions' of critical thinking and the 'community of method' to which these authors belong. Where the first has as its object representations of European modernity and its far from emancipatory practices, the second has as its target critical social and political theory and the absence of reflection on the nexus between the metropole and the colony. For Said, all four authors provide instances of 'cultures of resistance'.[13]

Culture and the politics of control

The insurrectionary emerges despite the odds, despite the technologies drawn upon in the control and regulation of the colonial and postcolonial subject. The insurrectionary politics I have highlighted above and will continue to do so throughout the book cannot be reduced to the constitutive potential of the discursive and institutional structures of domination that form the context for rebellion. As we have seen in the fragments of resistance highlighted above, there is a complex localised, indeed alternative modernity that articulates a temporality and a spatiality that is not simply a product of the colonial encounter. However, within the deeply sedimented archive of the imperial project, the authorial voice remains with the West, thereby denying or indeed negating the autonomy of voice that can be articulated by the colonised and the postcolonial subject. Such negation is a product of an epistemic, bureaucratised, and a direct violence that has its roots in the colonial period, but persists into the present. The use of direct violence as a technology of control and continuities therein between the colonial and the postcolonial will be covered in the next section to this chapter. This section focuses on 'culture' as a technology of control.

One defining trope that lies at the heart of these practices of control is 'culture', for here we have not just a convenient concept that can be used for hierarchical differentiation and identification, but one that, in the political economy of representation, comes to 'determine' the subjectivity of the other, so that the determination is in fact an interpellation, to use Althusser. Within this epistemological frame, 'recognition' is actually a mode of exoticisation, so that the subject can never be anything other than the attributed inscriptions determined elsewhere, in the cultural productions of the West. These productions become material when cultural difference and articulations thereof are seen as interjections into the political, and nowhere is this more clearly the case than in the context of the Middle East and the Islamic world.[14]

There is much in contemporary discourse that focuses on the question of culture as the organising principle around which and through which individuals and populations express their identity, political affiliation, and relationship to others. The assumed homogenisation of a globalised world of commerce and consumerism is seen as being dialectically related to the rise of localism and the reification of tradition. Cultural difference hence becomes the 'cause' that produces conflictual effects, the explanation, in other words, of conflictual dynamics that then generate transnational violence and threats to security and well-being.[15] In this form of explanation, the global progress seen to emanate from globalisation is hampered by the insularity of cultural affiliation interpreted as constitutive of tradition. In this hegemonic discourse of a rampant neoliberal political economy, societies joining in are then labelled 'emerging'[16] as compared with the perceived stagnancy of those steeped in conflict, violence, poverty, and state breakdown. Where the former somehow emerge into a homogenised 'world spirit', so to speak, the latter are yet to be subjects of a universal historical trajectory that culminates in one universal, homogenised space.

It follows then that when culture becomes a problem, the liberal response is not to obliterate it in the cause of homogenisation, but rather, to govern it, to render it amenable to the workings of global capital and the power relations that determine its political economy.[17] The liberal response to culture is hence composed of two inter-related elements: the first is to interpret culture as somehow differentiating the other of Europe and hence as being constitutive of problems associated with conflict and violence, and the second is to govern, contain, the effects of cultural difference when these are interpreted as problematic. The point here is that where liberal political theorists interpret liberalism's dealings with cultural diversity in terms of toleration and accommodation, the suggestion here is that liberalism's dealings with cultural diversity are framed by the imperative to govern populations, to shape communities and their relations, so that difference is not manifest as conflict.[18] To interpret liberalism's relationship to cultural diversity through toleration is to suggest a fundamental inequality between s/he who tolerates, the liberal subject, and s/he tolerated, the other of liberalism. If toleration ends or is somehow challenged, this is not due to the s/he who confers toleration, but the actions of the subject tolerated.[19] To interpret the relationship in terms of government has the merit of not taking for granted the accrual of benevolent motives to majority communities. Rather, liberal power operates through the abstracted, microcosmic management of biopolitically defined spheres – health, education, the economy – the maintenance of which serves the overall running of a liberal, juridically contained, political economy. Culture is hence a trope in the government of populations, a technology that is drawn upon not to repress but to control. At the same time, culture can also be the trope through which the other is racialised, inscribed hierarchically in relation to the European self, so that such inscription comes to inform the 'eventness' of events, the worth of bodies subjected to violence, and a political economy of impunity and its attendant righteousness.[20]

This hierarchical interpellation of subjects is hence also evident in the construction of 'events' and their interpretations. The constitution of an 'event' as such emerges in the interpretative world of the author, the design of the text, and its ontological and epistemological commitments. We might, for instance, highlight the staging of a play, or the inclusion of a particular artwork, as significant events that can contribute to our hermeneutic engagements with the present. Such is the case with a staging of Aeschylus' *The Persians*.[21] That the play is an 'event' in the artistic calendar is perhaps not too surprising given the rare number of times that this particular play is staged. The particularity of a production can also contribute to its 'eventness', so to speak. That the recent production was staged at an army training site on the Brecon Beacons was in itself bound to add to the play's contemporary salience, given the subject matter. My reasons for highlighting this play are more pertinent to the subject matter of this book, for Aeschylus' *The Persians* is seen by some of its interpreters as being the first 'orientalist' play and certainly as having informed later representations of the East. The play was first produced in 472BC and is about how the unexpected defeat of the Persians is received at the Persian court. For Charlotte Higgins, reviewing the play for *The Guardian*:

> The Persian wars – in which a tiny, fragmented, and often argumentative coalition of between 30 and 40 Greek city-states, or poleis, fought off invasion by a mighty empire stretching from Turkey to Iran and from Egypt to the Aral Sea – remains one of the most sensational events in world history. This is partly because it was so unlikely, but chiefly because it prepared the ground for the Athenian enlightenment and its great flowering of philosophy and history, of rhetoric and drama, and poetry – ways of organising intellectual and public life that are at the core of so much later Western thought.[22]

Higgins places the play in a context of what I refer to as the nexus between war and politics, so that we see here the staging of a play, eight years after the actual battle, so that the play itself would have constituted an 'event' for members of that audience, just as its performance in the present, in a time of war in Afghanistan and continued troop presence in Iraq, is an event that carries much resonance for a contemporary audience. However, what Higgins does in the above statement is place the play in what might be referred to as a civilisational context, so that the war itself, and specifically, the defeat of the Persians at the hands of the then much smaller Greek side is a 'sensational event' for it represents the event that later made possible the dawning of the age of Western Enlightenment and Western rationality. As Higgins correctly points out, two conflicting interpretations stand out: the play might be interpreted as one that expresses empathy with the defeated on the one hand, while it might also be seen as a triumphalist statement that seeks to reignite the patriotic fervour of its audience and to demean the enemy. Edith Hall identifies the play as the first in line for orientalist interpretations of the East:

> the first unmistakable file in the archive of Orientalism, the discourse by which the European imagination has dominated Asia ever since by conceptualising its inhabitants as defeated, luxurious, emotional, cruel, and always as dangerous.[23]

Edith Hall is, of course, referring here to Edward Said's *Orientalism*, a work that reveals the extent to which the Western imagining of the East is framed by a discourse of superiority and prejudice, and how these in turn feed into and inform contemporary Western political responses to the Middle East in particular. For Said,

> Orientalism is premised upon exteriority, that is, on the fact that the Orientalist, poet or scholar, makes the Orient speak, describes the Orient, renders its mysteries plain for and to the West. He is never concerned with the Orient except as the first cause of what he says. What he says and writes,

by virtue of the fact that it is said or written, is meant to indicate that the Orientalist is outside the Orient, both as an existential and as a moral fact. The principal product of this exteriority is of course representation: as early as Aeschylus's play *The Persians* the Orient is transformed from a very far distant and often threatening Otherness into figures that are relatively familiar (in Aeschylus's case, grieving Asiatic women). The dramatic immediacy of representation in *The Persians* obscures the fact that the audience is watching a highly artificial enactment of what a non-Oriental has made into a symbol for the whole Orient.

(Said, 1978: 21)

As Said emphasises, what is circulated since Aeschylus are 'representations' that are rendered in terms of 'truth'. Such representations, found in literature as well as contemporary 'expert' tracts on the East, suggest that what informs Orientalism is, according to Said (1978: 201),

a fairly constant sense of confrontation felt by Westerners dealing with the East. The boundary notion of East and West, the varying degrees of projected inferiority and strength, the range of work done, the kinds of characteristic features ascribed to the Orient: all these testify to a willed imaginative and geographic division made between East and West, and lived through during many centuries.

This sense of confrontation between East and West is nowhere more apparent, indeed more present in its representation of the East as in contemporary texts relating to the Middle East, the Arabs, and to Islam as a whole. The sense of confrontation and the construction of a boundary emerge in representational practices that constitute the East as source of danger and this in turn as a product, variously, of unpredictability, passion, unbridled emotion, fanaticism, and an inability to fully conform to Western, hence enlightened modes of being. For Said, the Arab in particular is represented variously as 'the abject' and as a source of danger, and subject to so demeaning and discriminating a language that were this to be directed at any other community and in so wide a range of locations, from Hollywood productions to news channels, that it would invoke anti-discriminatory legislation.

The 'archive of orientalism' is deep rooted and permeates contemporary engagements with the Middle East. While Said places particular emphasis on structures of representation present in academic, journalistic, as well as literature and film, the proper context that enables these discursive productions is a wider and deeper 'imperial epistemology' that elevates these productions to the status of truth which then informs policy. For Walter Mignolo and Madina Tlostanova (2006: 205–206)

The modern foundation of knowledge is territorial and imperial. By modern we mean the socio-historical organization and classification of the world founded on a macronarrative and on a specific concept and principles of knowledge. The point of reference of modernity is the European Renaissance founded, as an idea and interpretation of a historical present, on two complementary moves: the colonization of time and the invention of the Middle Ages, and the colonization of space and the invention of America that became integrated into a Christian tripartite geopolitical order: Asia, Africa and Europe ... Both epistemic differences, colonial and imperial, were based on a racial classification of the population of the planet, a classificatory order in which those who made the classification put themselves at the top of humanity. The Renaissance idea of Man was conceptualised based on the paradigmatic examples of Western Christianity, Europe, and white and male subjectivity. Thus from the Renaissance all the way down, the rhetoric of modernity could not have been sustained without its darker, and constitutive side: the logic of coloniality.

Hence, the capture of space and time, the classification of populations along racial lines, the supremacist discourse that places the European subject 'at the top of humanity' while others are in turn either denied a history or relegated to the margins of humanity so that they are barely human, constitute the epistemological ground that locates coloniality at the heart of modernity. This then is the epistemological frame that enables, not just the orientalism of the eighteenth and nineteenth centuries, but the discursive and institutional practices of the twentieth and well into the present whereby the figure of the colonised is reincarnated, re-configured, in late modern modes of colonisation where the white European, and white American, holds the epistemological reigns, so that other subjectivities are constituted in imperial epistemology either as 'resistant' (to modernity, enlightenment, progress) or as 'emergent' (into the social, economic, political, and epistemological world of the white European/white American).

Counter-insurgency: violence, fear, anxiety

On the day, 19 August 2010, when the American troop withdrawal from Iraq started, one US marine was recorded shouting, 'we won, we won, we brought democracy to Iraq, I love you America'.[24] Tony Blair, giving evidence to the Chilcot Inquiry, expressed the same sentiment, in effect that the invasion and occupation of Iraq had rescued the Iraqi population from a tyrannical regime. When Iraqi generals and prime ministers in post-invasion Iraq are thankful, then talk of dispossession seems somehow out of place, if not churlish, somehow extreme in its anti-Americanism, appearing to exonerate the excesses of a prior local regime bent on the destruction of its own society. Far from being a story of dispossession, this was one of liberation and empowerment, mistakes notwithstanding. Indeed, so prevalent is this discourse of impunity that much of the Chilcot Inquiry, set up to investigate the circumstances surrounding the decision to invade Iraq, has, in fact, been designed in such a way that its focus is not on the illegality of the war, but on the 'mistakes' made in the military planning, and issues relating to reconstruction.[25]

The line between benevolence and dispossession is not always clearly defined. The racialisation of bodies is, however, evident in both forms of discourse. Colonial domination and dispossession emerge from a paradoxical combination of fear and desire; violence is always perpetrated by the other, and any response to such violence is framed in terms of policing and the maintenance of order. The construction of the violence of the colonised and that of the coloniser/ occupier in terms respectively of barbarism and civilisation can be traced from the colonial period to present-day late modern articulations of colonisation, from Kenya to Iraq in the former time frame to Iraq and Afghanistan in the present. As Fanon (1967: 29) states:

> The colonial world is a world cut in two. The dividing line, the frontiers are shown by barracks and police stations. In the colonies it is the policeman and the soldier who are the official, instituted go-betweens, the spokesmen of the settler and his rule of oppression ... In the capitalist countries a multitude of moral teachers, counsellors, and 'bewilderers' separate the exploited from those in power. In the colonial countries ... the policeman and the soldier, by their immediate presence and their frequent and direct action maintain contact with the native and advise him by means of rifle butts and napalm not to budge. It is obvious here that the agents of government speak the language of pure force. The intermediary does not lighten the oppression, nor seek to hide the domination; he shows them up and puts them into practice with the clear conscience of the upholder of the peace; yet he is the bringer of violence into the home and into the mind of the native.

The coloniser and colonised inhabit, therefore, separate worlds – the protected, garrisoned, zone of the occupier, re-articulated in late modernity as the 'Green Zone',[26] and the thoroughly unprotected target that is the zone of the colonised. In Fanon's (1967: 30–31) all-too-prescient words:

> The town belonging to the colonized people, or at least the native town, the Negro village, the medina, the reservation, is a place of ill fame, peopled by men of evil repute. They are born there, it matters little where or how; they die there, it matters not where, nor how ... The native town is a crouching village, a town on its knees, a town wallowing in the mire. It is a town of niggers and dirty arabs ...

This zonality affirms the spatial distribution of the two, and materialises, renders factual and on the ground, the racial divide between the dominant and the dominated, and crucially, that which keeps them apart is pure force in all its materiality, directed at the all too material corporeality of the colonised population.

The zoning of populations can be enacted through confinement and latterly through the issuing of biometric identifiers to those under occupation. There are continuities with the colonial past, but there are also differences that are specifically late modern, a matter I will return to later, and specifically in Chapter 5. What distinguishes the modern colonial order was its sense of permanence, so that its legacies remain in present-day cities, from Rabat and Cairo to Delhi and Mumbai. The landscape of the colonial order demanded the separation of the European from the 'native', 'oriental' other; where the latter is admitted, then it would be along terms defined and legislated by the former. In the logic of a colonial order, there has to be separation, for it is this that is central to its technologies of control. Separation is also that which enables definition, indeed identification of self and other – a discursive machinery wherein there is the epistemic subject conferred the capacity to map the terrain of separation between self and other and, moreover, to describe the world of the other, to bring it forth into representation. Thus is the 'European city' divided from its 'Oriental' counterpart. However, as argued by Timothy Mitchell (1991: 163) in relation to French planning in colonial Cairo, the separation is materialised in the city itself, the limits and boundaries are always within: 'although the new order seemed at first to exclude the Arab town, in a larger sense it included it. Colonialism did not ignore any part of the city, but divided it in two, one part becoming exhibition and the other, in the same spirit, a museum.' The curatorial power remains with the European in the exhibition that is the colonial order; the world of the 'cosmopolitan' and the 'modern' and that of the 'traditional', the 'native', the 'static'.

Separation and the zoning of populations did not simply serve the representational practices of the colonial order, but through these enabled the servicing of i) a political economy that confined the 'native' areas to poverty, servitude, and (in the rural areas) productivity, and ii) a security apparatus geared for surveillance, disciplinarity, and the punishment of resistance. Indeed Bentham's panopticon was conceived as a method of control in the colonies (Mitchell, 1991). That the ordering of colonial terrain served an apparatus of security is evident in practices of colonial 'counter-insurgency'. There are clearly differences in application between measures used in former colonial times and the present context where there is some awareness of the constraints of international law. However, there are also parallels that derive from a hierarchical construction of worth between interveners and target populations. That discipline and punishment were/are the linchpins of the violence that constitutes any situation of coloniality, that such violence is often conducted with impunity, and that it comes to define the routine and the everyday to such an extend that it is considered to constitute the norm, that it comes to penetrate the consciousness and subjectivity of the colonised are features that are as evident today as they were in former colonial times.

During the Palestinian revolt of 1936–1939, British policy was predominantly defined by its military response to the resistance. The first response was to ban the Arab leadership, detaining and sending into exile those it accused as perpetrators. Having decimated the urban leadership, the revolt shifted to the countryside. New emergency measures were put in place, permitting such practices as the demolition of houses and detention without trial, practices that are prevalent in Palestine to the present day. As highlighted by Jacob Norris (2008: 28), apart from the establishment of martial courts, and the imposition of collective punishment which allowed for the 'forfeiture and destruction of any property (whether owned in common or privately) which has been used as a base for hostile action or outrage', the British, under the leadership of Sir Charles Tegart as chief adviser on terrorism and policing, also constructed 'seventy concrete fortresses at every main vantage point in Palestine and a wire fence erected along the 80-kilometre frontier with Lebanon and Syria designed to stem the flow of foreign weapons and insurgents' and 'classified rural villages as either "good" or "bad"'.[27]

What is significant about the practices conducted by the British and endorsed or formulated by the UK's Colonial Office was that these practices were premised on the constructs of 'security' and counter 'terrorism'. The geopolitical decision-making with regard to Britain's response to the Revolt must clearly be placed within the context of Britain's conflicting designs in the region concerning promises made about Palestine, and with regard to the immediate and impending European crisis and the onset of World War II. However, more significantly in the context of the present study is the focus on practices on the ground and in opposition to the local population. Norris (2008), through interviews with former servicemen, provides an account of how Palestinian bodies were used to crush the rebellion variously through the destruction of around 2,000 homes, the targeting of the domestic base of women, through the destruction of household food stocks and sewing machines, 'placing villagers in open-air pens for several hours while the living quarters were searched', and dehumanising the population by placing Arab prisoners at the front of trains and trucks to meet potential land mines or bombs, and the widespread stripping of Arab peasants during village searches.[28] Collective punishment became the norm in the British military's response to a local rural population and its resistance against colonial rule, a resistance deemed to be deserving of collective punishment due to what the colonials defined as 'corporate guilt'.[29]

This notion of 'corporate guilt' runs through the history of colonial responses to anti-colonial resistance and informs what is now referred to as 'counter-insurgency'.[30] While there are aberrant instances of atrocities committed by troops on the ground, the idea of collective or corporate guilt clearly informs such practices as the subjection of entire cities and towns in Iraq to searches, to the playing of loud rock music, and to the compulsory carrying of biometric ID cards as a condition of movement. The history of colonial rule and contemporary situations of occupation and invasion suggest that the use of violence against populations is not merely a matter of atrocity, but is constitutive of a strategy that seeks to collectively punish and discipline populations, the objective being the pacification of populations in the name, variously, of order, peace, and security. We might cite many examples from colonial history – the 1945 bombing of Algeria, the use of mustard gas in the 1920s bombings of Iraq, the 1948 massacre at Batang Kali in Malaya, mass detentions in response to the Mau Mau uprising in Kenya, the use of napalm in Vietnam – and reflect upon these either as singular instances of atrocity that might be subject to inquiry or situate these as being constitutively part of a strategy of pacification, a strategy directed at collectives of populations and not simply at individuals,[31] conducted and sanctioned by institutions and not simply by individuals, and realised through the use of pure force directed at bodies, the corporeal being of the racialised other. We might interpret these practices as reflective of a 'culture of impunity';[32] but a more informative interpretation is to see such practices, or to locate them in the context of the pacification (and hence the government) of populations.

The phenomenological aspect of colonial domination, in its historical context and in its more recent articulation, can only be understood in terms of how the forms of violence used against, or directed at the corporeal being of the other, is at the same time a mode of violence directed at the colonised population at large. The humiliation of the one is at the same time the humiliation of the many; the torture of one is the torture of an entire society and its future generations. The experience of sheer horror accompanying incessant bombardment is one lived not simply by those directly at the receiving end, but by these and others that follow at some future time and emergent in the most unlikely contexts as traces and fragments of memory, traces and fragments that shape subjectivities, that can never quite be contained or tamed by therapeutic anamnesis. The target of such practices is always the collective, in the form of the other's nation, its population, meanings shared, lives lived, accounts and narratives passed on, rendered in oral histories, diaries, documentaries, films, literature, and the visual arts.

That violence penetrates the temporal and spatial domains of the subject is well evoked in the work of Iraqi artist Halim Al-Karim, whose 'Hidden' series presents images/photographic portraits as triptychs depicting distorted faces abstracted from the specificities of time and place. The portraits are mainly genderless, though some are clearly women, some shown in high resolution, but the majority are blurred and distorted black and white photographs. The viewer is taken through the series of his work, from 'Hidden War', completed in 1985, and hence made during the Iran-Iraq war, to 'Hidden Face' and 'Hidden Theme' (1995) where the portraits are so distorted and darkened that we can only be aware of the effacing of subjectivity in contexts of extreme fear and violence, to 'Hidden Witnesses', constructed in 2007, and using lambda print, depicting, in the view of this author, the collective experience of violence, torture, and humiliation, all contained in the triptych of faces.[33] The portraits might be read to depict Iraqi individuals and the Iraqi population subjected to war and torture, and yet, the faces appear timeless and transcend any specific populations subjected to war. Halim Al-Karim's portraits capture what I seek to convey here; namely, that the individual whose body is targeted and subjected to violence is at once a carrier of populations deemed the 'enemy' other.

There is a certain banalisation of violence in contexts of invasion and occupation, those elements of late modern, twenty-first-century modes of colonisation. Such banalisation stems from the dehumanisation of a population and its construction as inferior to the occupying force, an inferiority associated with their defeat, abject surrender, way of life, mode of dress, and above all else, that an occupied population is by definition civilian subject to the rule of armed soldiers conferred the mandate to determine who will live and who will die with little prospect of accountability. Violence in these circumstances becomes routine and everyday, a task fulfilled, when, in contrast, its targets live in a continual state of fear, variously from violence, intimidation, and humiliation. The banality of violence in late modern modes of colonisation is perhaps most apparent when witnessed at checkpoints, which, by definition, are aimed at the population at large and the control of their movement. That foreign troops can establish checkpoints and subject a population to random searches, humiliations, and violence, captures the phenomenological side of colonisation, the grotesque imbalance of power contained in that context. This represents the fact, argued above, that such practices are aimed at the pacification of a population as a population, as a collectivity, and as subjectivity. Such banalisation comes across when the violence perpetrated against a subject population is depicted in emails and Facebook pages, photographs taken as one would holiday snapshots, all suggesting a continuity of form in the conditions that render such acts possible; conditions defined by the materiality of pure force.[34] Hidden wars, hidden victims, hidden witnesses, abstracted faces of a population and its victims who remain largely unnamed, uncounted. The point is not to suggest that such violence is 'hidden'; if anything it has most blatantly exhibited to a global public. Rather, it is the subjectivity of those targeted that is 'hidden' through their depiction as mass. The use of head sacks to cover Iraqis captured was not aimed at the protection of the anonymity of the prisoners, but at the production of a spectacle of victory and the vanquished enemy.

The banalisation of violence against the colonised other, in the past and in the present, can be seen as a by-product of a security apparatus writ large, one that uses violence as a technology in the disciplining, pacification, and re-shaping of those targeted. Of significance in this process of banalisation is that its constitutive practices are not necessarily directed by a leader of a government or the commander of a militarised unit, though such direction is all too apparent. Also of significance is that those in the service of the imperial project, past and present, are also complicit in rendering violence routine and everyday. Nowhere is this latter aspect in what I am referring to as the banalisation of violence better evoked than in Ranajit Guha's portrayal of the colonial encounter, where the lens of colonial history is firmly placed on military and civilian personnel serving in the distant locations of empire, and in this case India.

Within the structure of domination that is the colonial encounter, Guha reveals a phenomenological context that is replete with fear and anxiety of the colonised and this where the coloniser is the primary source of violence and intimidation perpetrated against the colonised. What we see in Guha's all too powerful piece, 'Not at home in Empire' (1997), is the coloniser as a subject who can never be 'at home' in the conquered territory for the 'limits' which confer ontological security, the limits of the known and the familiar, are never quite known in the space of empire, the space of otherness. Hence the clubs and the encampments, the separate European zones amidst the excluded terrain of the native. As Guha (1997, 484-5) highlights:

The isolation of rulers from the ruled was integral to the colonial experience in South Asia. It could hardly be otherwise considering that the raj was a dominance without hegemony – an autocracy that ruled without consent. Isolation was therefore a structural necessity. What made it worse and difficult to forget was the absurdity of Britain's claim to have fitted the roundness of colonial autocracy to the squareness of metropolitan liberalism.

This isolation of ruler from ruled was a product, according to Guha, not of a fear but of a generalised anxiety, and it is this distinction that I suggest is crucial in understanding contemporary practices of security that appear in discourse as 'counter-insurgency.' According to Guha (1997: 485), this differentiation remains concealed from orthodox accounts of the history of empire with their 'tendency to misconstrue the evidence of anxiety simply as fear'. The emphasis on fear stems primarily from a discourse of law and order, according to Guha, a discourse that relies on the specificities of the sources of fear rather than the 'indefiniteness so characteristic of anxiety'. Where 'fear' suggests specificity and causality, anxiety suggests indeterminacy. Where the former suggests that the enemy is knowable, and might hence be subject to an epistemological framing necessary for targeted precision, the latter is suggestive of the uncapturability of the other; the all pervasive character of a terrain that remains forever foreign, and hence 'uncanny'.

There is much effort in contemporary practices of security, including those taking place in contexts of intervention, to render the enemy 'knowable'. The technologies of 'counter-insurgency' utilised in locations such as Afghanistan and Iraq include directed military violence used in confrontations with armed insurgencies. However, they also include practices directed at the population which are rendered in counter-insurgency terms. NATO in Afghanistan has for long implemented operations directed at Afghan women, while the use of anthropologists is aimed at 'knowing' the enemy other through culturally sensitive communication or indeed the use of cultural tropes in the disciplining and government of populations.[35] The 'fear of sedition and rebellion' is the driving force behind such practices and assumes the potential of what we might understand as the epistemological capture of the enemy other.

However, the notion of 'anxiety' is suggestive of the indefiniteness of the unknowable and hence the un-capturable. In a statement that has profound resonance in relation to contemporary practices, Guha states:

Can we afford to leave anxiety out of the story of the empire? For nearly two hundred years the answer of colonialist historiography to this question has been one in favour of exclusion. It is not anxiety but enthusiasm that has been allowed to dominate its narratives. The latter is a mood which is consonant with all the triumphalist and progressivist moments of imperialism – its wars of conquest, annexation, and pacification in the subcontinent; its interventions in our environment and our economy by industrialization, monetization, and communication; its project of social engineering by administrative measures and its mission of civilizing by education. Its politics of expansion and improvement, its ethics of courage, discipline, and sacrifice, its aesthetics of orientalism have all been assimilated to this mood by a whole range of rhetorical, analytical, and narratological devices, so that enthusiasm has come to be regarded as the very mentality of imperialism itself. The result has been to promote an image of the empire as a sort of machine operated by a crew who know only how to decide but not to doubt, who know only action but no circumspection, and, in the event of a breakdown, only fear and no anxiety.

(Guha, 1997: 487–488)

I want to suggest that the banalisation of violence in the colonial past and its contemporary spaces of articulation can be understood in terms of this distinction between a fear that knows its sources/causes and a generalised anxiety that has an awareness of the unknowability of populations colonised/occupied. The shooting of civilians at road blocks, seen over and over again, and now available in imagery released by Wikileaks, is a reflection of the generalised anxieties produced by the otherness of the populations targeted, so that the violence perpetrated is always perpetrated with impunity, directed into the generality, the indeterminacy. Once inflicted, the targets of violence remain the indeterminate and the unknown, nameless in death as in life. At the same time, anxiety stems from a certain knowledge of the ever present potential of resistance, a potential that emerges in unpredictable temporalities and spatialities.

The colonial encounter is hence structured through domination – a material domination borne of dispossession and the force of arms, a juridical domination that subjected the colonised to the force of a law constitutive of the colonial state and its dispossessive practices, and an epistemological domination that relegated the colonised to the status of the over-determined, by nature and by culture, and hence to a racialised inferiority. Nevertheless, despite this pervasive structure of domination, the encounter is at the same time characterised by a fear of sedition and rebellion, a fear that directs the technologies of the colonial state against rebels, both actual and potential, and by a more generalised anxiety that stems from an awareness of the essential un-knowability of populations colonised. The colonised, in this scheme of things, always has the potential to resist.

3

RESISTANCE AS THE CLAIM
TO POLITICS

Even if the soldiers manage to erase all trace of the dungeon, they will never erase from our memories what we endured there. Ah, my memory, my friend, my treasure, my passion! We must hang on. We must not fail.

Tahar Ben Jelloun, *The Blinding Absence of Light*

Recent events in the Middle East might be seen as instances of new global imaginaries and of political creativity in the face of hostile forces, both local and external. Images of 'people power'; of bodies as mass; of a living, breathing public sphere, the symbolic expression of which was, and continues to be, Tahrir Square, gripped the viewing global public and inspired other manifestations of protest beyond the boundaries of the Middle East. The formative statements that seemed to capture these events and others – 'we have overcome the barrier of fear'; 'we can do what the Egyptians did'; 'Ben Ali, Mubarak, now it's your turn Cameron' – seem to hale a new era of rebellion, based not on ideology, but on a multiplicity of grievances the articulation of which differs from context to context, so that the overriding imperative does indeed appear to be the desire to resist the encroachment of the state and through it of the neoliberal order into the lived experience of peoples. Where Hardt and Negri's (2011) verdict on recent events is that they constitute the realisation of an emergent 'multitude' that is not so much external to 'empire' but imminent to it, what these events suggest is an overwhelming desire to re-capture the political, and in doing so, to re-capture the (postcolonial) state, not in the name of religion or some premodern form of authority, but in a very distinctly late modern articulation of the right to politics.

We saw in Chapter 2 that resistance is as constitutive of the postcolonial subject as are the technologies of power and domination that have sought, from coloniality and into postcoloniality, to suppress it. Placed in the context of postcolonial writings, the subject of politics moves from the anti-colonial struggle and into the postcolonial, where the first finds expression in the national struggle for self-determination while the second is suggestive of a disillusionment and a disenchantment with the enduring legacies of the colonial era and the complicities of the postcolonial state in the continued domination of postcolonial societies. However, this postcolonial disenchantment has opened up a fissure in intellectual engagements with the postcolonial condition. This fissure has been identified by authors such as Ahmad (1992) and Dirlik (1994) as an antagonism between the literary focus of iconic voices in postcolonial thought – Said and Spivak for example – and a Marxist-oriented critique of a global political economy that is the 'real' material cause of the continued subjugation of the postcolonial world. However, there is another stream of diverse postcolonial writing (see, for example, Mamdani, 1996; Ahluwalia, 2001; Chan, 2007; Mandaville, 2007; Amin, 2011) that rejects this antagonistic framing of the postcolonial intellectual effort, focusing instead, on the 'political' and specifically the substantial development of politics in the postcolonial condition, ideologically and institutionally, in a context of globalisation, in all its social, economic, and political ramifications. This stream of writing is not just interested in the politics of discursive representation, though it takes this very seriously, nor is it just interested in the implications of a capitalist global political economy, though this too is taken seriously; the discursive and material structures of domination, their differential distributions of enablements and constraints are recognised as formative and indeed constitutive of the postcolonial condition. However, significantly, this stream of writing focuses on what we might refer to as the substance of politics; for example, identity politics, state–civil society relations, the nexus between the local and the global in a globalised world, *and* the continued postcolonial struggle with structurated global inequalities. The substantive, empirical/historical content of this stream of postcolonial writing raises the question that engages this particular effort, what I am referring to as the subject of politics in postcoloniality. What does it mean conceptually and theoretically to talk of the subject of politics in postcoloniality?

We have witnessed much creativity in events taking place in the Middle East, starting from January 2011 to the present. However, there had been much by way of creativity preceding these immediate events, manifest not simply on the streets, but in galleries, and in film, not in simple renditions of suppression, but in moments of articulation that transcend easy categorisation or predictability. While the West's media, aided by politicians and academics alike, aimed its lenses at the Islamic 'threat', the populations of the Arab world had entered the worldly space of the late modern, had recognised as they had all along, that much had been compromised in their name, that the very ground on which they walked had been sold off, and not necessarily to the highest bidder, and that their right to politics, the most important right, had been denied them. Political conflicts and allegiances aside, to visit the region in the recent past meant to witness an unexpected revival, primarily of the intellectual and artistic kind, so that the locals were no longer solely reliant on an exiled community of poets, writers, and artists to be their voice of freedom, but on local expressions of what I am calling here the 'right to politics' (Balibar, 2002). This expression of the right to politics could not be interpreted in some Hegelian 'end of history' formula whereby the region could finally be admitted to a world spirit authored in the West, but rather, this claim to the political has happened in spite of the violence and the asymmetries of power that have characterised this particular world spirit and in whose name the region has been subjected over the years.

Global imaginaries and worldly subjectivities remain vulnerable to power and its instrumentalities of violence. However, the notion of creativity, as we will see below, is suggestive of a form of political subjectivity that is perhaps best captured in what I would suggest is a post-Arendtian politics, one that takes seriously Hannah Arendt's understanding of the political, but that takes this further to realise its potential in the practices and articulations of a worldly subjectivity, one that is at once of the discursive and the material. Two aspects of Arendt's writings are of particular significance in the present context. The first relates to her understanding of the subject of politics, as she puts it in *The Origins of Totalitarianism*, 'the right to have rights' (Arendt, 1968b: 296). The second, relatedly, and elaborated in her *On Revolution* (1977), highlights Arendt's understanding of the 'founding of political community' and with it her emphasis on 'presence' as core to political action. Arendt's understanding of 'founding' as the moment of revolution (Arendt, 1977), its formation in the 'declaration of independence' is especially valuable in rethinking the postcolonial moment, and its temporal and spatial articulation. These elements together provide very strong grounds from which to understand late modern manifestations of political subjectivity and agency. While Arendt's political thought in general and her conceptualisation of 'right to have rights' in particular, is not without controversy and has generated much discussion,[1] the aim here is not to engage with this controversy, for this would be beyond the remit of this book. The focus here is on how we might use Arendt's understanding of the specificity of politics as the context within which we might develop an understanding of the subject of politics and the postcolonial condition.

I use the term 'right to politics' not in a positivistic legal sense, suggestive of the institutional arrangements that enable citizens to express their views, variously through regular elections and a public sphere of deliberation. In place of this legal conceptualisation, I suggest that the 'right to politics' be defined as an enunciative move, one that makes a declaration, that claims a presence in the space of the political (Balibar, 2002: 6). Chantal Mouffe (2000) makes the distinction between 'politics', the realm of institutional arrangements, and the 'political', the realm of contested claims, of 'agonism' and 'antagonism', all terms suggestive of action and hence of political agency in situated contexts, so that we might indeed talk about 'political conflict', where there are declared stakes and presences associated with such declarations. The 'right to politics', I suggest, moves beyond Mouffe's distinction while agreeing with its underpinning assumptions. The move beyond is suggestive of the intersection between 'politics' and the 'political', an intersection that recognises action as being always constitutively related to what we might refer to as the 'spaces' of the political. Doreen Massey (2005) provides a useful conceptualisation of space as a product of interaction, that space is constructed and constituted. At the same time space is constitutive of subjectivity and of political agency, so that it is not possible to think about space as being external to the subject who acts, who enunciates.

So the claim to politics is the claim to the 'right to politics'. This is suggestive of a 'declaration' or an 'enunciation' and hence action. There is therefore a temporal and a spatial aspect to the claim. The temporal aspect is suggestive of a moment of intervention, a moment that, as I have suggested throughout, contains within it the complex intersections of past, present, and an imagined future. It is in this sense that the moment cannot be conceived in terms of instrumental rationality, nor in the formulaic terms of a Kantian ontology of self. Rather, this moment is only meaningful in relation to the subject whose articulations and expressions are constituted, formed, and re-formed, in the complex discursive and institutional matrix of the socio-political. However, these in turn find their expression through the subject's interpretative schema, the history that resides in the subject and emerges in traces and fragments. The temporal aspect of the claim to politics is in this sense the moment that encompasses past and present and the imaginary of a future to come.

There is also a spatial element to the claim or right to politics. The spatial comes into form, is constituted in the 'declaration', for this suggests interjection, a material presence that both constitutes and is constituted by existing spaces. The spatial constitution of the subject is suggestive of the imprint that material space makes upon the embodied self and the self's interaction with others. The public sphere is not confined to discourse, but is a landscape of architecture and planned locations that impact on circulation, enable or constrain collective gathering, and regulate the political economy of work and leisure.[2] Similarly the institutional arrangements that constitute 'politics', to use Chantal Mouffe's conceptualisation, are distinct spaces; in other words, are spatially defined in distinctive buildings that come historically to symbolise political authority, sovereign power, and the rationalised space of administrative government. The spatial distribution of functions is as significant in relation to the political as the spatial distribution of bodies, as we know from Foucault's analytics of power. Just as there is a temporal imprint upon the embodied self, so too there is a spatial imprint. This does not mean that we can easily separate the temporal and the spatial, for there is a complex imbrication of time and space. The spatiality of the body too must be part of this picture, not just in the sense that the body takes up space, claims a location, important though this is in relation to the political; but also in terms of the body as the landscape whereupon time and space make their imprint. However, the body is not simply 'object' dichotomously conceived in relation to subject, a tabula rasa awaiting subjective inscription, for the object in turn carries subjectivity, is imbued with subjectivity, as I will elaborate further later in invoking Theodor Adorno. It is in this sense that we cannot assume a separation of time and space, of subject and object, of discourse and materiality when thinking the right to politics.

This exposition of the theoretical framework to my understanding of resistance as the right to politics starts in the first section by highlighting core concepts that I rely on in a discussion of what it means to claim the political in the postcolonial condition. The main concept I rely on is the 'declaration of independence', though other concepts are of equal salience; as I suggest above, Arendt's conception of the distinctiveness of the political, her understanding of 'action', are all helpfully suggestive in conceptualising the subject of politics in the postcolonial condition.

The second section in this building block approach to political subjectivity and agency provides a theorisation of the space and time of politics. The third section of the chapter reveals the 'impossibility' of so capturing the postcolonial subject. The aim in this third section is to draw on postcolonial authors, specifically Frantz Fanon, to look to the constitution of the postcolonial subject and this subject's claim to the political. Of particular interest is what we might refer to as Fanon's negativity and its implications for the postcolonial subject of politics.[3] In anticipation of the next chapter, the final section of this chapter locates the postcolonial in the context of the international, arguing that the claim to politics, the right to politics, is at the same time a claim to the international. However, as we will see in this final section and as will be the subject matter of the next chapter, the aporetic moment for the postcolonial subject in all this subject's heterogeneity emerges in this subject's entry to the international, for while the modern international cannot be dissociated from the colonial legacy it is at the same time constitutive of the postcolonial subject. However, it is this very aporia that unsettles and through such unsettling generates a desire for the moment to come. Nowhere is this 'generativity' of 'negativity', to borrow from Diana Coole (2000), more aptly applicable perhaps than in relation to the postcolonial subject and this subject's continuing desire to constitute political community.

Claiming the right to politics

The subject of international political theory tends to be the bounded political community, represented by a territorially defined state as the institutional manifestation of its sovereign authority. Modern political community is hence only meaningful in this Westphalian understanding, so that even shifts beyond the state in juridical-political terms are meaningful in reference to the state. This conventional understanding of the international as a domain of inter-state politics is premised on the assumed distinctiveness of the international, a distinctiveness that historically derives from the juridical-political recognition of the sovereignty of the state and hence of the political community which the state is taken to represent. The transformation of political authority away from the state suggests a disjuncture between political authority and community, a disjuncture that in turn transforms the structure of the international and with it the relationship between political authority and political community. The subject of international political theory is hence not simply the state, nor simply political community, but the *limits* of political community and how these are drawn and redrawn in the temporal and spatial contingencies of social and political life (see, for example, Hardt and Negri, 2001; Kalyvas, 2005; Walker, 2010).

When the lens is placed on the limits of political community, the focus is not simply on how these limits are constructed historically, but also on their power to reconstitute the subject of politics. It is in this sense that the 'international' matters to the postcolonial subject, as we will see later in this book, for the international, while certainly of the modern colonial order, is at the same time (and aporetically) constitutive of the postcolonial subject. However, it is this very aporia that confers the potential of an authorial voice for the postcolonial subject, as we will see in the next chapter.

In rendering the limits of political community the subject of international political theory, the interesting question to ask is wherein lies agency in relation to the drawing and re-drawing of such limits. A juridical approach to this question focuses on sovereign authority, while a historical-sociological approach relocates the lens to practices of government and specifically the government of populations and their classification and distribution.[4] Both renditions of this Foucaultian-inspired distinction understand the capacity, or indeed agency, to draw and redraw the limits of political community on the side of power. As we will see below, another option we have in discerning or seeking out the agency to draw the limits of political community is to relocate the lens towards the subject of politics, the subject who claims the right to politics.

The question of limits is not only of significance in the history of the postcolonial world, but is of particular salience now in late modernity, when inside/outside distinctions can no longer be associated with the boundaries of the state, but are manifest in corporeal terms, both in relation to the individual self and in relation to populations. While the juridical rendition on the limits of political community is and continues to be a defining factor in the constitution of the postcolonial subject, it is the 'government' of the postcolonial subject and their capacity to draw and redraw the limits of political community that is core to any critical discourse on the postcolonial international. It is in the context of these practices of government that the claim to the right to politics must be understood.

The motivating force of events brings into sharp focus the seductions of the empirical domain, and especially when these concern resistance and mass protest. How do we capture this moment in a discipline whose historic remit is defined in terms of the state, international order, and material capabilities? This neo-realist rendition of the international has, of course, been long questioned and indeed discredited, variously by constructivists, feminists, postcolonial, critical, and poststructural theorists. These latter perspectives have rendered the international a political as well as a social domain, so that 'people', to borrow from Christine Sylvester (1994), are as much part of the picture as states and institutional arrangements. However, the problem has never simply been one of 'peopling' international relations, nor simply one of adding non-state actors to the so-called pluralist mix so that the relationships purportedly within the scientific purview of the discipline are not confined to one set of relations defining the inter-state system. The problem, rather, is one of interrogating the very limits of political community, how these limits are historically defined, pre-determined, naturalised, and ultimately complicit in the practices and discourses of inclusion and exclusion.

This problematisation of the limits of political community has taken many forms, not least of which stems from the recognition that globalisation, understood as the 'compression' of time and space relations (Giddens, 1991), and manifest in economic, social, and political relations, points to a domain of interactions that is transnational, suggestive of human communication and interaction, as well as institutional arrangements that seem to transcend the boundaries of the state, and in doing so, come to redefine the realm of the international as a juridical and political specificity. Any such re-definition brings into sharp relief the question of how the international, and its matrices of power, are manifest in the microcosm of practices and in lived experience. Nowhere is the 'weight' of the international, its political economy, and the structuring imperative of its matrices of power more closely felt than in the postcolonial world.

Many a postcolonial theorist has revealed the contingent character of the discipline's core concepts, underlining the legacy that continues to inform the hierarchical structure of the international.[5] However, the history of modernity is at the same time a history of the postcolonial condition, and hence incorporates the struggles for independence from colonial rule that hailed entry onto the terrain of the international. This moment of emergence for the postcolonial state forms as much a constitutive aspect of postcolonial subjectivity as the colonial past and must be taken into account in this investigation of postcolonial resistance. The discursive terrain that frames the postcolonial subject is all too powerful and deeply rooted in Europe's relations with its colonised others. The epistemic violence, to use Spivak, emerges in what Siba Grovogui (1996) identifies, as was shown in Chapter Two, as the three genres historically constitutive of what he refers to as 'non-European alterity', from the fifteenth century and the ecclesiastical context that shaped the 'discovery of the new world', to the Enlightenment and the production of hierarchies of civilisation, to the nineteenth century and the emergence of natural history as a discipline tightly related to colonising practices. The location of the authorial voice was hence established in Europe, as Talal Asad (2003) highlights, and came to be understood as the point of origin for defining the order of things, its discursive formations, and its limits. Edward Said, as highlighted in earlier chapters, reveals the power of such discursive formations, repeated as they are in the history of Western writing about the non-West, including Africa, Asia, and the Middle East. These lands appear simply as accumulations of population, always already inscribed in biopolitical terms, or exoticised and essentialised, and only emerging into history when called forth, or recognised, by the European subject.

Claiming the right to politics thus comes in the face of such power and its discursive and institutional continuities. To claim this right for the postcolonial subject is to come up face to face against what Said refers to as 'obligingly serviceable concepts' wherein the non-European other is forever trapped in 'tribalism' and 'primitivism', so that any attempt at claiming the terrain of the political on abstracted grounds, those that reject such racialised and culturally defined pre-determinations, is historically subjected to direct violence, as was shown in the last chapter, and to perhaps more subtle practices of government, including the use of violence as a technology in the government of populations, in the present late modern context, as will be shown in Chapter 5. Suffice it to say in the present context that to invoke a sense of 'a people' as such, to invoke the limits of political community defined in abstracted terms and not in familial or culturalist terms, is to exercise an autonomy of interpretation, to reinscribe the self onto the political landscape of the politically dispossessed. Some indication of such agency was illustrated in the fragments and trajectories of resistance I highlighted in the last chapter.

This act of re-inscription by the postcolonial subject does not imply extraction from modernity and its trajectories. Rather, and as Homi Bhabha points out in relation to Frantz Fanon, the postcolonial subject faces what he refers to as the 'problem of the ambivalent temporality of modernity', an ambivalence that calls for the 'inscription of alterity within the self' as an 'attitude of modernity' so that this hybrid form indeed comes to represent the 'condition of freedom'. Read in this sense, postcolonial agency 'opens up an interruptive time-lag in the progressivist myth of modernity and enables the diasporic and the postcolonial to be represented' (Bhabha, 1994: 240) Claiming the right to politics for the postcolonial subject thus means 'seizing the value-coding', to use Gayatry Spivak, constitutive of modernity's discursive formations, so that these formations are subjected to the performative, deformative, interruptive 'postcolonial translation'. This interruptive force of the postcolonial generates in turn not a repetition of a linear, progressivist philosophy of history, one wherein the postcolonial subject is always defined as somehow lagging behind, the 'not yet' construction that not only deferred the moment of decolonisation in the so-called Trusteeship system, but legitimised practices of violence and dispossession that continue into the present. Rather, the interruptive force might be interpreted as making possible the distinctly late modern concept of the 'altermodern', the idea of multiple, interconnected modernities wherein Europe is but one amongst a multiplicity of voices and hence trajectories.

Claiming the right to politics might hence be read as a claim to the modern and its reinscription and renegotiation. However, the problem with Bhabha's conceptualisation of postcolonial agency is that it often reads as an ethical assertion or indeed a derivation from a Foucaultian understanding of the ethical subject as having the capacity to reinvent, indeed to recreate the self. At the same time, the focus on the interruptive force of the performative in 'seizing the value-coding' involved in the signifying practices of the modern points to what we might understand as a revolutionary moment that can only be meaningful in relation to the postcolonial subject. I want to assert the revolutionary character of this moment in order to suggest specificity to the postcolonial subject, so that this subject's signifying practices are not merely read in terms that are already authored elsewhere.[6]

How do we methodologically (and hence ontologically) capture this revolutionary moment? Capturing this moment implies a methodological stance that is already of modernity, its discursive practices and ontological claims in relation to the subject of politics. When Hannah Arendt writes about what is seemingly the defining moment in the emergence of modern political subjectivity, namely the French Revolution, she argues, contra de Tocqueville, that instead of generating a 'science of politics', the French Revolution generated a new Philosophy of History where, as she puts it, the standpoint of the spectator is superior to that of the actors involved, and where 'historical necessity' is used as the explanation of events unfolding. This Hegelian reification of 'necessity' over the actuality of events unfolding meant that, as Arendt (1977: 43–44) puts it,

> Truth ... was supposed to relate and to correspond not to citizens, in whose midst there could exist only a multitude of opinions, and not to nationals, whose sense for truth was limited by their own history and national experience. Truth had to relate to man *qua* man, who as a worldly, tangible reality, of course, existed nowhere. History, therefore, if it was to become a medium of the revelation of truth, had to be world history, and the truth which revealed itself had to be a 'world spirit'.

For Arendt, the very idea of 'world history' is 'political in origin', for it was preceded by the events of the French and American Revolutions both invoking the idea of the 'rights of man', which even though subsumed by the nation-state, inaugurated the notion of 'world politics'. We can immediately see how these Hegelian categories are complicit in relegating the postcolonial subject to the 'not yet', the lag, and indeed the lack, even as this subject is being incorporated within a world authored/scripted in Europe.

More significant for Arendt, and for our purposes here, is the reading of revolution through these 'Hegelian categories' whereby 'historical motion is at once dialectical and driven by necessity'. This, to Arendt, is 'perhaps the most terrible and, humanly speaking, least bearable paradox in the whole body of modern thought'. This paradox suggests that the 'very moment of freedom' is always captured in the 'dialectical movement and counter-movement of history' wherein the necessity implied in astronomical motion is also present in the affairs of 'men'. However, Hegel derives his dialectic of freedom and necessity from the experience of the French Revolution, according to Arendt, and not the American Revolution. For Arendt (1977: 46–47), it is the experience of the American Revolution that provides her with an alternative conception of the revolutionary subject:

> For whenever in our century revolutions appeared on the scene of politics, they were seen in images drawn from the course of the French Revolution, comprehended in concepts coined by spectators, and understood in terms of historical necessity. Conspicuous by its absence in the minds of those who made the revolutions as well as of those who watched and tried to come to terms with them, was the deep concern with forms of government so characteristic of the American Revolution, but also very important in the initial stages of the French Revolution.

The defining feature of the American Revolution for Arendt was the 'founding' of an entirely new body politic. This foundational, constitutive moment is core to an Arendtian reading of politics and the political subject, a reading that places emphasis on the performativity of 'founding' and its 'declaration', both formative elements in the constitution of political community.

There is clearly a historic disjuncture between the 'founding' claims of the anti-colonial struggles that led to national independence and their capacities to create the entirely 'new' body politic. Far from creating the new, the leaderships of the emerging national states took hold of existing institutional frameworks, or even negotiated postcolonial arrangements with the former colonial rulers.[7] Clearly, there is much diversity in the postcolonial experience, in the anti-colonial struggles that preceded independence, in the negotiations held with colonial powers, in the ideological and institutional trajectories taken in the shaping of postcolonial societies as unitary polities. These diversities are as much intra-regional as they are inter-regional. However, a common feature of postcolonial writing relates to the disenchantments with postcolonial rulers, disenchantments voiced by figures such as Fanon (1967), Memi (1967 and 2006), Mbembe (2001), among others. Achille Mbembe, in particular, frames the problem of the 'postcolony' thus:

> In the postcolony ... I am concerned with the ways state power (1) creates, through administrative and bureaucratic practices, its own world of meaning – a master code that, while becoming the society's central code, ends by governing, perhaps paradoxically, the logics that underlie all other meanings within that society; (2) attempts to institutionalize this world of meanings as a 'socio-historical world' and to make that world real, turning it into a part of people's 'common sense' ...
>
> *(Mbembe, 2001: 103)*

For Mbembe, the category of '*commandement*' is the descriptor of the postcolony, and the 'signs, vocabulary, and narratives' produced by the *commandement* are not merely 'symbols', but are 'invested with a surplus of meaning' that is then made 'real' through its institutionalisation and occassional 'dramatisation' (Mbembe, 2001: 104).

At the same time, what is significant about the postcolonial experience, certainly in the context of Asia, sub-Saharan Africa, and the Middle East (the last is the subject of discussion in the next chapter), is that the colonial legacy looms large in the trajectory of the postcolonial polity and cannot be set aside in any investigation of the subject of politics in postcoloniality. As Mahmood Mamdani (1996) has argued in relation to sub-Saharan Africa, it is this legacy that has shaped what he calls the 'despotic' trajectory of the African state, a trajectory that witnessed the 'deracialisation' of civil society, but one that nevertheless failed to establish a new integrated polity over and above the colonial juridical construct of 'Native Authority', a device often used by the colonial state against the 'national' liberation struggle.

This disjuncture between the founding moment of postcoloniality and the creation of a 'new' polity has indeed led to despotic and oligarchical regimes in much of the postcolonial world, contexts wherein the security apparatus of the state is unleashed against individuals and categories of population seeking a voice politically. However, despite the all too powerful colonial legacy, and despite the subsequent overwhelming presence of the postcolonial state in the lived experience of the postcolonial subject, the moment of independence, the moment of retrieval of territories and hence the material spaces that held the potentiality of politics must be understood as constitutive moments in the formation of the subject of politics in postcoloniality. While Mbembe and Mamdani provide powerful insights into the workings of the postcolonial state in the African context, their analyses seem to negate the very possibility of politics as such, and specifically the potentiality of a subject making a claim to politics.[8]

I want to argue that the idea of 'founding' and the 'declaration of independence' is of core significance when considering the claims of the postcolonial subject and specifically claiming the right to politics. The 'declaration of independence' in the postcolonial context must be seen as the moment that enshrines 'liberation' from colonial rule, the moment wherein the challenge of founding a political community might begin. While much of the postcolonial literature, and specifically that deriving from 'subaltern studies', has been critical of any suggestion that 'national' liberation struggles equated with the voice of the subaltern, much of this critique can be encompassed in the political theory of postcoloniality that I am suggesting here. For it is the case that the postcolonial as such comes into form, is only meaningful, in relation to this founding moment and its declaration 'in words' as Arendt puts it. This 'constituting' moment of liberation then enables others that we might refer to as constitutive of postcolonial political community, others that might indeed involve further struggle, conflict and contestation. When Nehru proclaims India's independence, his emphasis is indeed on the declaration, the utterance of words that constitute:

> Long years ago we made a tryst with destiny, and now the time comes when we shall redeem our pledge, not wholly or in full measure, but very substantially. At the stroke of the midnight hour, when the world sleeps, India will awake to life and freedom. A moment comes, which comes but rarely in history, when we step out from the old to the new, when an age ends, and when the soul of a nation, long suppressed, finds utterance ...[9]

The issue here is not the promise unfulfilled, but the performative and its signifying, constituting power – in the affirmation of long years of struggle as well as entry into a future wherein the challenges and struggles of political community could be met. The defining moment is one that captures the stepping out and the stepping in, 'out' of the tyranny that denied the Indian population the right to politics, and when it claimed this right only to be met with violence, and 'in' to the condition wherein this particular and very specific right is redeemed, to use Nehru, in the formations of, and struggles over, political community. As Hannah Arendt highlights in relation to the American Revolution, the distinction between 'liberation' and 'freedom' must be kept in mind in any analysis of the revolutionary process:

> If ... one keeps in mind that the end of rebellion is liberation, while the end
> of revolution is the foundation of freedom, the political scientist at least will
> know how to avoid the pitfall of the historian who tends to place his emphasis
> upon the first and violent stage of rebellion and liberation, on the uprising
> against tyranny, to the detriment of the quieter second stage of revolution
> and constitution, because all the dramatic aspects of this story seem to be
> contained in the first stage and, perhaps, also because the turmoil of liberation
> has so frequently defeated the revolution.
>
> *(Arendt, 1977: 133)*

The act of 'constituting' has a different temporality to that which is constituted and
this difference is crucial in any understanding of the postcolonial international and
the ongoing struggle over the right to politics. The 'no-longer and the not-yet' is
suggestive of the hiatus that defines much of the postcolonial condition, a hiatus
wherein the inaugural moment of declaration, the founding of a 'new' body politic,
the constituting moment, comes face to face with the potentiality of constitution-
making. The founding moment is hence core to a political theory on postcoloniality
and to capture it is to recognise its significance in any discussion of postcolonial
subjectivity and the right to politics that is claimed and claimed afresh.

Locating the subject of politics

As is evident in the discussion so far, the temporality of the *post*colonial is core to
the understanding of postcolonial subjectivity I am presenting in this book. This is
an understanding premised on a recognition of the monumental significance of the
founding moment I take to be enshrined in the 'declaration of independence' from
colonial rule. Any political theory of postcoloniality must take this founding
moment seriously if it is to have anything to say about postcoloniality and political
subjectivity. Furthermore, any discussion of contemporary postcolonial politics, of
the continuing projects in the constitution of political community, have their
reference point in this founding moment.[10]

The moment of founding does not imply that the colonial experience or indeed
pre-colonial history are not influential in the formation of the postcolonial subject,
for history is, as I state in earlier chapters, carried in the subject, emerging in
fragments and traces and in the most unexpected locations. Even as the 'declaration
of independence' hails forth the 'new', constituting the *post*colonial subject, the
legacy of coloniality in all its structurating weight is never far removed. This does
not, however, negate the moment of emergence that Arendt ascribes uniquely to
the American Revolution and then to the 'new nations' of the twentieth century.

It is the latter that interest us here. If claiming the right to politics is the core
concept that then leads us to understand and indeed to appreciate the foundational
moment in postcoloniality, we find ourselves in the aporetic position whereby the
subject of politics is extracted from history in order to make a new history that is
only recognisable in terms of that against which she/he defines herself or himself.

However, Frantz Fanon, like Arendt, talks of new beginnings, but unlike Arendt, Fanon's political subject recognises that violence constitutes her/his moment of emergence. However, as we will see in the next section, while violence, in Fanon, can be understood as constitutive of the subject, his 'temporality of emergence', to borrow from Bhabha (1994: 236), is far more complex and indeed less determinate. Fanon's conception of 'beginning' is much closer to Arendt than she herself would accept or that is accounted for in comparisons between the two.[11] Suffice it to state at this stage, that just as the notion of 'beginning' for Arendt contains its own constitutive principle, so to speak, so too Fanon's 'temporality of emergence' is exactly suggestive of emergence containing its own constitutive principle.

The focus of this section, however, is the political subject and how this subject might be related to the idea, first, of the founding moment, the moment of emergence, the subject who declares independence, second, to the subsequent constitutive moments formative of political community, and third, where the latter is itself informed by the former. In the postcolonial context, we might refer to the moment of liberation and the potentialities of a moment to come, with the interregnum of constitution-making in between, the building of political community in between, with all the contingencies that enable and constrain the postcolonial subject.

In seeking to formulate a political theory of postcoloniality – one that answers to the question, what does it mean to talk about a distinctly postcolonial political subject? – I have drawn so far on the notion of claiming the right to politics, starting with a postcolonial reading of the aporias presented by modernity for the postcolonial subject, moving on to suggest an Arendtian rejection of the history as necessity thesis, and suggesting support for the idea of the founding moment of independence as constitutive of the postcolonial subject. The idea of the 'new' as we have discovered presents its own challenges, and these go to the heart of how we might think of political subjectivity in relation to the postcolonial.

Any formulation of the political subject comes up against the problematic dualism highlighted by Kant; the 'autonomy' suggestive of self-legislation and the 'heteronomy' suggestive of the causal influences of external forces.[12] In place of this dualism, one that, as we know, always already inscribes the European in the formalist/universalism of the autonomous, while relegating the non-European 'other' to the influences of the heteronomous, we might problematise the relationship between the 'autonomy of politics' and the 'heteronomy of politics' as Balibar suggests, pointing to a dialectical relation that has no synthesis. Taking such a problematisation into account, we might suggest that there is no sense in which we can talk about the revolutionary subject, the subject who strives independence and has the capacity to declare such independence without evoking the notion of 'liberation', *tahrir* in Arabic. For Balibar, the 'autonomy of politics' is suggestive of the figure of 'emancipation', itself based on the 'proposition of equaliberty'. In this understanding, the autonomy of politics points to the self-constitution of a 'people' as political community, wherein members recognise each other as political subjects, as having the 'right to politics.' To use Balibar (2002: 4):

> The autonomy of politics (in so far as it represents a process that has its origin and its end in itself alone, or in what will be termed citizenship) is not conceivable without the autonomy of its subject, and this in turn is nothing other than the fact, for the people, that it 'makes' itself, at the same time the individuals who constitute the people confer basic rights upon one another.

As is evident from the above, this statement resonates with Hannah Arendt's reading of politics and the self-constitution of a people. The controversies surrounding this distinctly Arendtian reading aside, what is significant for our present purposes is that, as will be seen in the next chapter, it points not to an essentialised reading of the subject of politics, but rather, the 'practices' constitutive of politics and their materialisation in 'the people' as these assert their presence in the context of coloniality. This assertion of presence and interjection, in the postcolonial context, raises the question of the postcolonial state and this state's presence onto the terrain of the 'international', a presence that in itself is intricately linked to postcoloniality and the constitution of political community.

The figure of emancipation that renders the 'autonomy of politics' possible is always and at the same time a subject constituted in the 'heteronomy of politics', again to use Balibar. This concept points to the conditions of possibility wherein the practices of politics might take place. These conditions and the structures of domination that define them do not, however, generate a uniform subjectivity, so that the relation between the two – subjectivity and its conditions of possibility – is what constitutes the practice of politics. There is in turn no uniform 'postcolonial subjectivity', but one that finds forms of articulation that are situated in the phenomenological experience of coloniality and constituted in the sheer weight of its history, but are at the same time creative constituting moments generative of the potentiality of a future to come. Read in this way, the latter would not be possible without the former even as there is no single formula that connects the latter to the former. While the tendency in postcolonial thought is to focus on the debate between those who stress the symbolic and cultural as opposed to the material conditions of production and exchange in the global political economy,[13] the point to stress here relates to the ontological understanding of the political subject, an understanding that recognises the mutually constitutive relationship between the *subject* of politics and the *conditions* of politics. At the same time, this subject should not be seen as being subsumed by these conditions, but rather, as creating its 'autonomy' exactly in relation to these conditions. Read in this sense, the practice of politics, the claim to politics, itself subjectivises just as and at the same time as it emerges into and transforms its conditions of possibility. It is in this sense that Michel Foucault can understand power as 'the conduct of conduct' or 'action upon actions', so that the analysis of the 'agonism' between 'power relations and the intransitivity of freedom is a permanent political task inherent in all social existence' (Foucault, 2001b: 343). For Balibar, the significance of this statement lies in the fact that Foucault 'reduces to a minimum' the distance between conditions and transformation, so that large-scale institutions (states, classes, parties, as he highlights) are 'divested of their monopoly' so that politics is brought 'at every moment within the reach of individuals or coalitions of individuals' (Balibar, 2002: 160).

However, even though Foucault divests large institutions of their monopoly, thereby pointing to the mutually constitutive relationship between the subject of politics and the conditions of politics, what of the possibility of conditions that seek to render the subject of politics impossible? We might say that the colonial condition seeks to render the subject of politics an impossibility, dispossessive as it is not just of territory and material resources, but of subjectivity as such, so that the colonised is configured exactly in terms of negation, a negation that persists to the present in discourses wherein the 'other' is always interpellated in discourse as the non-Western other, variously inscribed into a hierarchical structure of signification. Where Balibar talks of the 'heteronomy of the heteronomy of politics', pointing to the obliteration of the subject of politics through forms of 'banal cruelty', I see the colonial condition and its late modern articulation as being complicit in a form of negation that does not simply seek to depoliticise, but to obliterate the very potentiality of political subjectivity. However, as we will see in the next section, and through Fanon, this very negation provides the potentiality of the subject of politics and their capacity to claim a right to politics.

Fanon's negativity

How is it that the subject of politics emerges in the extremes of the colonial condition, where the colonised is subject not just to violence, physical and epistemic, but also to practices so disruptive and transforming of her or his country that the colonised is at the same time de-personalised and indeed de-individualised? What conception of self is possible when the familiar is rendered unfamiliar, when the very spaces that provided frameworks of identity were disappropriated or re-configured? What potentiality can be imagined by the subject whose very temporality, whose relation with history, is itself denied? It is all too easy to locate the subject of politics in a historicist schema wherein Europe remains the legislator of the time and space of the subject of politics, a time and space that can then be entered into by the postcolonial subject. Fanon, however, shows an alternative schema, one that conceives of the subject of politics in terms of presence and interjection, but one that, significantly, is about the founding of the 'new'. The claim to subjectivity, for Fanon, is a claim to politics, and this in turn is the constituent moment. The subject for Fanon exactly emerges in that self-created, self-generated space between the 'no-longer and the not yet', that space of negativity wherein the subject is never fully captured in and by the terms of autonomy and heteronomy, but is of an indeterminate space in between and beyond. Fanon's corpus of writing is exactly focused on the colonised as subject of politics, providing an understanding that defies uniformity and even identity. It is all too easy, without Fanon, to reduce the colonised as subject of politics into a one-dimensional subject of nationalist discourse. Fanon, however, and as Homi Bhabha puts it, 'suggests another time and another space', a time and a place of 'negativity', of the 'no-longer and the not yet'.

Fanon, I want to argue, provides us with a distinctly materialist understanding of the subject of politics. Apart from the constitutive role that violence plays in relation to the subjectivity of the colonised engaged in anti-colonial struggle, Fanon's subject has a material corporeal presence that somehow exceeds and defies linguistic representation. Fanon's intellectual points of reference, at home with and yet critical of a Hegelian and Marxist inspired dialectics, a writing reflective of a phenomenology that seeks to capture the self/other antagonism of the colonial experience, and the practice and theory of psychoanalysis, all point him towards a materialist epistemology that challenges the stability of concepts and significations. This epistemology serves him to conceive of the colonised and the racialised as subjects of politics in the midst of and despite the constitutive power of the heteronomy that is the colonial condition. Questioning in equal measure the universality of 'Man' and a general category of the 'Negro', Fanon at once disturbs the juxtaposition of Europe with Enlightenment, and with it the idea that Europe is the birthplace of 'Man', while also challenging Europe's construct of the 'other', and the 'automatic manner of classifying him, imprisoning him, primitivizing him, decivilizing him' (Fanon, 1986: 20). This imprisoning, fixing classification is not mere construction, however, nor is it mere inscription, though it is both, but is corporeal through and through. The weight of racism and the colonial order is already carried in the body, its comportment, and its movements. For Fanon (1986: 83), this is indeed the 'composition of … self as a body in the middle of a spatial and temporal world'.

The 'corporeal schema' is here imbricated with the 'historico-racial schema' for Fanon, so that the self is made into 'object' and somehow comes into recognition as object. If there is an epistemology that can capture the burden or weight that the latter bears upon the former then it is one that places primacy on she or he who is rendered object through the 'fact' of corporeal suffering. To use Theodor Adorno (1973: 17–18), 'The need to let suffering speak is a condition of all truth. For suffering is objectivity that weighs upon the subject'. To read Fanon in this way is to reveal the history that resides in the self who is 'object' and the object in turn whose identity exceeds the classifications imposed upon it. If the identity of the 'object' exceeds such determination, such fixity, then the object holds primacy. In Fanon, the object is indeed the colonised, the racialised self, the corporeal being never fully captured by the constellation of discourses that sustain the colonial, racist order of things. When Adorno insists on the primacy of the object, his targets of critique are idealist philosophies that place primacy with the subject, assuming identity between subject and object. However, what emerges in Fanon's negativity is exactly the 'non-identity', to use Adorno (1973: 183–197), of the object, the self made as object, that defines the potentiality of the subject of politics.

How does Fanon conceptualise this potentiality, this uncapturable excess? How is it possible to imagine a potentiality that refuses, as he puts it, 'the ontology of the white man' and hence the white man's historicity? The anti-colonial struggle, for Fanon (1967: 251), is not simply about 'a nauseating mimicry', which would instantiate a sublation of the colonised into a historicity authored in Europe, but is, or should be, about 'independence', but this is

> not a word which can be used as an exorcism, but an indispensable condition for the existence of men and women who are truly liberated, in other words who are truly masters of all the material means which make possible the radical transformation of society.
>
> *(Fanon, 1967: 250)*

However, national independence is not a finality, but rather a setting in motion, 'a temporality of emergence' that is always in process. This is the potentiality that, in the anti-colonial struggle and beyond, makes a claim to politics, interjects into the space and time of politics, so that the 'declaration of independence' is but one though necessary element in the constitution of the subject of politics. This potentiality is at the same time evocative of 'negativity', a negativity that enables Fanon to move beyond Hegelian dialectics, and beyond the phenomenology that is the colonial order.[14] If this order produces what Bhabha refers to as the 'overlooked' and the 'overdetermined' subject, one who is at once over-surveilled and always already defined, then this subject's agency derives exactly from that space of difference that escapes identification. There is at the same time a certain 'intimacy' to this space of difference, and hence an intimacy to Fanon's revolutionary subject so that even as this subject seeks to make his/her presence felt in the material spaces of his/her colonised, dispossessed, and reconfigured world, there is a psychic space wherein discourse is intra-subjective.

Fanon's subject is not simply a product of colonial discourse, European over-determination, and indeed a symbolic order that seeks to deny him or her presence. He or she is not merely a product of symbolic negation, but finds articulation in a space beyond such negation. Fanon's lens is directed exactly at this space of creative desire in the subject, a space that emerges from the 'temporal break' from 'the ontology of that white world' and its signifying moment in 'Man', as Fanon states in *Black Skin, White Masks* (1986). For the colonised to extract himself or herself from this moment is not to create another ontology in opposition to the white man, but rather to articulate a complexity the articulations of which cannot be reduced to singular, uniform representations, even as the subject variously shifts through, defies, or indeed negotiates the inscriptions and categorisations of the colonial order. At the same time, for the colonised to enact such extraction is to instantiate the moment of revolt, for it is this that constitutes the subject as political, that enables entry into the postcolonial international.

Claiming the international

The 'international' is the distinctive space that at once constitutes the emergent postcolonial world and is itself subject to transformation through the very presence of this world. It is perhaps too early to talk about late modern transformations of the recent past, and specifically the structural implications of the seeming shift of capital from 'the North' to the emerging economies codenamed BRIC (Brazil, Russia, India, China).[15] However, as shown in earlier chapters, the predominant discourse about the structure of the international and its political economy is that it is and continues to be structurally determined in favour of the West generally and the former colonial powers and against the postcolonial. Indeed, apart from the discourses in international relations calling for a 'decolonisation of the international',[16] Kwame Nkrumah famously coined the concept 'neocolonial' to capture the continuities of the colonial and postcolonial orders of the international, emphasising the point that political 'independence' had not translated to economic emancipation. The failure to achieve the latter, especially in postcolonial African states, dominates critiques of postcolonial leaderships, seen as being complicit in the continuing political subjugation and dispossession of their populations.[17] However, significantly, the critiques of the postcolonial states that authors such as Fanon and Mbembe provide are not confined to economic emancipation, but more clearly are concerned with the political emancipation of postcolonial populations. There is, in these discourses, an overwhelming sense of loss, and the loss refers not to evident resources lost, but to the constitutive moment that was 'independence' and the founding of political community. Fully understanding that the political economy of the international into which the postcolonial world was entering was unequal terrain, these authors nevertheless indict the failure of political leaders, depicted as using government for their own corrupt, self-aggrandizing ends. This is not a discourse of Western imperialists, but of individuals dedicated to the anti-colonial struggle, the lost promise of which they clearly mourn.

There is, however, another discourse that places primacy with the structurally unequal terrain of the international, even as, in this literature, political elites are seen as peripheral partners in globally exploitative structures of domination. What distinguishes this latter discourse is that the structure of the international, political and socio-economic, was always already scripted elsewhere, in the West. Independence was and, for some, continues to be a chimera, and never represented a founding moment. This latter literature is primarily the product of intellectual, social science discourse that seeks to identify causes to the continuing inequalities of the postcolonial world, causes that derive from the workings of a capitalist international political economy and from what we might understand as an epistemic and juridical order already determined and limited by concepts the origins of which lay elsewhere, outside the postcolonial world. Where the dependency school places the lens on structurally determined exchange relations between centre and periphery, postcolonial scholarship in international relations stresses the latter epistemic, juridical understanding of the international, arguing that sovereignty as a concept is a legacy of a European colonial order and has always constituted an epistemic imposition upon the formerly colonised. Independence for the latter especially, far from creating the new, was a moment complicit in the continuing destruction of local indigenous communities and their distinctive temporal and spatial ordering frameworks. Walter Mignolo, in this sense, talks of the continuing project of 'decolonisation'. The two perspectives might be represented in oppositional terms epistemologically and ontologically – the first structuralist and the second poststructuralist, the first focusing on the workings of international capital and the second focusing on discourse and the politics of representation.[18] These differences apart, of relevance to the present discussion is how each perspective might answer to the question of how the claim to the international is articulated. The answer to this question places the lens on the postcolonial state, the landscape of meaning into which and through which its identity is constituted, and the structures of domination within which and in relation to which this state authorises its capacity to negotiate the terrain of the international (see, for example, Muppidi, 2005; Krishna, 1999; Chan, 2007).

Claiming the right to politics must hence be seen in light of the constraints and enablements that derive from the realm of the international and that are complicit in the constitution of the postcolonial subject. If we understand the international variously in juridical-political terms as a realm of inter-state relations, in socio-economic terms as a realm of the workings of capital, and in epistemic-discursive terms as a terrain of hierarchically ordained signifying practices, then our understanding of the subject of politics might also be conceived in terms of the postcolonial state, postcolonial populations and classes therein, and the subject formed in discursive, representational practices. Where the accent is placed in defining the international informs the understanding of political subjectivity and the subject's articulations of agency. Much of the postcolonial literature, including especially Bhabha, Spivak, and other writers of the Subaltern Studies Group, would not see the anti-colonial struggle and independence as founding moments in the constitution of the subject of politics. Arguing against what they see as the totalising discourses of state and class, both seek to focus on heterogeneity and hybridity, so that just as the terrain of the spatial boundaries can shift so too the temporal ordering of the world, its cultures, and the lived experience of those on the ground so to speak. What Bhabha (1994) refers to as 'holistic social explanation' is rejected in favour of a hermeneutically oriented understanding of the 'split' or 'hybrid' subject of postcolonial politics, one whose articulations are not reflective of opposition to European modernity and power, but constituted within its modalities in all their hybridising potential.

However, even when the postcolonial subject is recognised as the 'split subject', the articulations of which are always reflective of the 'in-between' of cultures, this hybridity is in itself suggestive of the aporia of the postcolonial international – the moment of independence, and specifically its declaration and enunciation, is at once both self-constituting and constituted in the structural continuities that are and continue to be captured by the colonial legacy; the self-legislating and the already legislated. However, as already argued, there is a generativity and a potentiality in the aporia and it is in this sense that the subject of politics in postcoloniality makes a claim to the international, indeed has to make a claim in this distinctive socio-political terrain. The subject of postcoloniality is hence always subject to the codifications that stem from what I am referring to as the heteronomy of the international. While there might be disagreements about where the accent is placed in relation to the structural elements that constitute heteronomy, it is the all-too-powerful codifications, or inscriptions, that not only limit access to the political, and indeed the international, but provide its discursive potentialities of articulation.

Taking this understanding of the subject of politics in postcoloniality, an understanding that takes as its premise the materialisation of the subject, through declaration and presence, goes some way in reinforcing a strand of the postcolonial literature that is of the discipline of international relations as such. As has already been shown, this strand in the literature gives substantial content to the interjections of the postcolonial state and 'local' agents in the realm of the international and its discursive and institutional contestations (see, for example, Anghie, 2004; Muppidi, 2004; Grovogui, 2002; Chan, 2007; Krishna, 1999; and Shilliam, 2011). This literature constitutes 'voyages in', to use Edward Said's terms, revealing situated discourses and practices that have not formed part of the conventional literature in the discipline. There is, at the same time, a prior question to be asked, and this prior question relates to what it means to talk about the subject of politics in postcoloniality, a question that engages this particular text.

The question of subjectivity is all too present in postcolonial social and politics beyond international relations. However, there is an interesting (at least for this author) division in this literature when it comes to the subject of *politics* as such. In Edward Said, and some would say not surprisingly, given Said's regional focus, namely the Middle East, the subject of politics emerges very strongly in terms of the struggle for 'national independence', and the influences of Fanon are very clear. Both are formative and inspirational in the context of the theorisation of the subject of politics I am articulating here. Another postcolonial voice that will become significant here and specifically in relation to my conceptualisation of the subject of politics in late modernity, is Partha Chatterjee, a figure I will discuss further in Chapter 6. However, there is another strand of writing in postcolonial social and political thought where, I want to suggest, the subject of politics is either so over-codified as to lose presence, or is assumed to be in possession of a form of authenticity that is historically so subject to modernist epistemic violence that it can never speak its name. I want to suggest that while this third strand, represented by authors such as Ranajit Guha and Gayatry Spivak, is all too valuable in revealing the sheer weight of history in the epistemological framing of the postcolonial subject, it nevertheless reveals an internal tension when the stake is the losing sight of what constitutes the subject of politics. When it comes to politics, and specifically the subject of politics, these distinctions between these three strands I am highlighting are important.

Nowhere is this third strand and its tensions more clearly apparent than in Ranajit Guha. In his 'Prose of counter-insurgency' (1994), the peasant insurgent is already inscribed and constituted in the juridical, political, material, and social framework of the coloniser:

> When the peasant rose in revolt at any time or place under the Raj, he did
> so necessarily and explicitly in violation of a series of codes which defined his

very existence as a member of that colonial, and still largely semi-feudal society. For his subalternity was materialized by the structure of property, institutionalized by law, sanctified by religion and made tolerable – even desirable – by tradition.

(Guha, 1994: 336)

The subject of resistance is hence constituted through the 'codes' that structure domination, and these codes are themselves apparent not just in the performance of domination over the subordinate, but in the discourses that shape responses to resistance. These discourses are inevitably framed in terms that almost without exception negate or even deny the reasoning of the insurgent, highlighting instead factors such as natural inclination, cultural determination, or even an unreflective following of leaders, all of which are suggestive of causalities external to the consciousness of those who come to engage in insurgency or resistance. For Ranajit Guha, the historiographic is as complicit in this negation as are official discourses, and each of these is in turn heavily reliant upon the other, so that the narrating of events is always framed in pre-formed 'explanations'. In examining the colonial archives on imperial efforts at 'counterinsurgency', and in juxtaposing these with historiographic texts, the negation of the 'insurgent' is apparent:

> Yet this consciousness seems to have received little notice in the literature on the subject. Historiography has been content to deal with the peasant rebel merely as an empirical person or a member of a class, but not as an entity whose will and reason constituted the praxis called rebellion. The omission is indeed dyed into most narratives by metaphors assimilating peasant revolts to natural phenomena: they break out like thunderstorms, heave like earthquakes, spread like wildfires, infect like epidemics ... Even when this historiography is pushed to the point of producing an explanation in rather more human terms it will do so by assuming an identity of nature and culture, a hallmark, presumably, of a very low state of civilization ...
>
> *(Guha, 1994: 337)*

In her monumental essay, 'Can the subaltern speak?', Gayatry Spivak (1988) reveals the operation of power wherein the narratives of the European subject come to position themselves as those that have 'no geo-political determinations', thereby ensuring the relegation of all other narratives to spaces of particularity and determinacy. In this scheme of things, even where the 'consciousness' of the 'other' is retrieved, it is always in terms already set by the European subject, including the critical 'Western' intellectual. Asking the question, 'Can the subaltern speak?', Spivak articulates a philosophical, epistemological, ontological, and political question all-in-one, and indeed addresses the question not just to her immediate targets, namely Foucault and Deleuze as exemplars of critical thought, but postcolonial theorists and historians engaged in seeking the retrieval of the subaltern. In relation to Foucault, Spivak's critique is not just based on the fact that his analytics neglect imperialism, but that his conception of resistance privileges the West. She arrives at this conclusion by focussing on Foucault's notion of 'geographical discontinuity', using the term, according to Spivak (1988: 85),

> to distinguish between exploitation (extraction and appropriation of surplus value; read, the field of Marxist analysis) and domination ('power' studies) and to suggest the latter's greater potential for resistance based on alliance politics. He cannot acknowledge that such a monist and unified access to a conception of 'power' (methodologically presupposing a Subject-of-power) is made possible by a certain stage in exploitation, for his vision of geographical discontinuity is geopolitically specific to the First World.

For Spivak, Foucault's conceptualisation of resistance in relation to power and over and above 'exploitation' acknowledges what she refers to as 'localised resistance', but 'can lead to a dangerous utopianism', for it forecloses the topographical inscription of imperialism, an inscription that renders problematic the distinctions that Foucault assumes here, for the emergence of 'mechanisms of power ... more dependent upon bodies and what they do than the Earth and its products'[19] are in themselves reliant on European imperialist projections of (sovereign) power elsewhere. For Spivak, the (European) subject remains paramount in such occlusions of Europe's 'other', for even where, as in what she refers to as 'Third Worldism', the other of Europe is retrieved, the structure of the narrative is always hierarchically framed. As she states: 'Yet the assumption and construction of a consciousness or subject will ... in the long run, cohere with the work of imperialist subject-constitution, mingling epistemic violence with the advancement of learning and civilisation' (Spivak, 1988: 90).

Spivak herself provides the challenges in highlighting the 'epistemic violence' that is always at play in the retrieval of the subject, so that she, and perhaps we, must always acknowledge that, as she puts it, 'the subaltern cannot speak', for 'representation has not withered away'. However, at the same time there is a strategic/political imperative to seek out, or, in the terms of this book, to trace the postcolonial subject, albeit a subject that is always constituted by the contingencies of time and place and the power relations thereof. The positivity we find in Guha's attempts in seeking the 'consciousness' of the subaltern is, through Spivak's critique, confronted with a negativity that, as Rosalind O'Hanlon (1988: 191) puts it, suggests a 'tension between the desire to find a resistant presence, and the necessity of preserving difference and otherness in the figure of the subaltern'. This is indeed the aporia of the subject of politics in the postcolonial international.

Claiming the international in the late modern context, as will be argued later, can no longer be conceived in relation to the juridical-political constitution of the international as a realm of relations between states, but also and at the same time as a political economy of capital and of structures of signification. At the same time any transformation in the constitution of the international is itself complicit in transformations of claims to politics, so that the former somehow provides or indeed defines the conditions of possibility for the latter, just as the latter impacts upon such transformations. The transformations of the international emergent in late modernity are so monumental that we might indeed refer to a temporal stage that is 'beyond the postcolonial'. This does not imply the 'end of postcoloniality',[20] but rather, an appreciation of late modernity and its contingencies, where transformations in the juridical ordering of the international intersect with and are dependent on transformations in the political economy of the international and specifically the dominance of neoliberalism in the reframing of international institutions. To understand the international in terms of 'Empire', as Hardt and Negri (2001) do, suggests a conception of political subjectivity that is not external to Empire but imminent to its transnational spaces of articulation. The political subject is no longer nation or class bound, but is reflective of dispersed and unpredictable locations of resistance all constitutive of a 'multitude' of singularities. The sites, spaces, and temporalities wherein the claim to politics is made, wherein the subject of politics finds articulation, have now shifted, according to Hardt and Negri, from the terrain of the international defined territorially to a realm that is transnational and that comes into form through transnational practices.

As we will see later in the book, while for some, this shift means the end of a territorially articulated authority, for others, including this author, the claim to politics emerges in the complex intersection of the 'assemblages' that constitute the international in conditions of late modernity. Such assemblages, as defined by Saskia Sassen (2006), constitute the grid of 'territory', 'authority', and 'rights', so that the state and its transformations are never far removed from global transformations relating to the international political economy and the imperial projections of power. Such projections continue to bind the European and the non-European, not necessarily in an oppositional dualism, but in a mutually transformative and productive relationship, albeit one that is unequal in its constitution.

The claim to politics in late modernity and in the contingencies highlighted above might hence be given greater content and form than that which simply asserts hybridity and the ambivalence of identity. Understanding late modern assemblages of power and their differential implications for different populations does not point to the dislocation of politics, but rather the relocation and reinstantiation of the political subject so that the choices made and the mobilisations formed might well be transnational, but they at the same time can be directed at spaces that constitute the territorially defined polity, even as these spaces might be of the street, the urban neighbourhood, the virtual spaces of new media networks, and so on. Claiming the right to politics in a temporal context beyond the postcolonial and in the late modern suggests an imaginary that seeks another moment to come, the continued constitution of political community in a late modern context, the imperative of which has been to depoliticise in the name of a liberal cosmopolitan order the technologies of which remain uncannily familiar to a postcolonial subject still haunted by the colonial legacy and its imprint upon generations past and present.

Tracing the postcolonial subject into late modernity

This chapter provides a political theory of the postcolonial subject of politics. It argues for a conceptualisation of political subjectivity in terms of the constitution of this subject through the claim to politics, and specifically, the claim to the right to politics. The driving question focuses on what it means to be a subject of politics in postcoloniality, how this subject comes into form, is constituted through struggle against colonial domination and in the moment of 'independence'. The enunciative 'declaration of independence' is, in an Arendtian sense, taken to be a moment of constitution, a 'worldmaking' foundational moment wherein a people emerges as political community. Much of the postcolonial literature interprets this moment in terms of the nationalist movements' 'mimicry' of the European colonial powers, preferring to argue against an oppositional framework that sets coloniser against colonised while, somewhat paradoxically, suggesting such an opposition between the 'elite' nationalist discourse and the interests of the subaltern. However, this chapter suggests, through tracing the postcolonial subject of politics, that the anti-colonial struggle and the declaration of independence can be read as constitutive moments wherein political community emerges. In tracing the subject of politics in postcoloniality, it is also argued that the emergence of the subject must be conceived in relation to the 'heteronomy of politics', pointing to conditions of possibility wherein such constitution takes place. The temporal framing of the subject of politics, looking into Frantz Fanon's 'negativity', also pointed to what we might consider, through Fanon, as the ontology-defying move wherein the postcolonial subject of politics, now conceived as 'object', is not fully captured in concepts, suggesting an uncapturable excess wherein potentiality and the moment to come are also constitutive of the subject. There is hence no fixity in this conception of the postcolonial subject of politics, no totalising effort at sedimentation in 'homogeneous empty time' that takes the subject, in linear trajectory, towards a universally conceived 'Man'. Rather, there is heterogeneity and heteronomy, the subject formed in matrices of power and somehow in spite of them. At the same time, there is the promise of a moment to come, so that the constituting moment of emergence is never the final moment, but makes possible the struggles and contestations expressive of the continuing claim to politics. The constituting moment of emergence, as Fanon makes clear, is hence always in process.

The postcolonial subject of politics interjects, materialises presence onto the space of the political, and the space of the international, and in so doing is at once both constituted and reconstitutes this space. Tracing the postcolonial subject from the anti-colonial struggles of the past to the contestations of the present, what we see revealed is not a linear narrative, but rather the co-constitutive presence of past and present, so that the constitutive moment of emergence is at once also a moment of constitution-making, the struggle for political community and its design. Traces of the past re-emerge in the present as the postcolonial subject asserts presence in the temporal and spatial configurations of late modernity. There is here an overwhelming sense of the 'agonism' of power and freedom, as I indicated earlier in this chapter, an agonism that is never resolved as such, but goes to the heart of the possibility and potentiality of politics.

If, as Michel Foucault highlights, power is a mode of action upon the actions of others, then it is 'exercised only over free subjects, and only in so far as they are free' (2001b, 343). Foucault's idea of an 'agonism' between power relations and the 'intransivity' of freedom suggests a remainder or a potentiality that is always there in relationships of power, opening out the possibility of an imagined otherwise, an otherwise born of struggle and contestation. That potentiality is contained in this understanding of freedom is suggestive also of transience, of a moment wherein resistance is enacted, so that there is a constitutive temporal relationship, but one that once captured moves on to a future possibility, a future relationship. We might hence understand the colonial relationship as one that, despite the odds, never fully incorporated the colonised into its structures of domination, so that its matrices, while driven by totality, were always designed to contain and discipline, through violence and other means, in the full knowledge that their very design was informed by the potential of the dominated to resist. The anti-colonial struggles emerged from within this totality, their discourses and practices somehow steering the precarious space in between colonial structures of domination and an imagined future free of domination. In the very heart of the colonial order lived resistance, and in the very heart of every contemporary colonisation lives an ever continuing moment of resistance.

The notion of 'intransivity' suggests for Foucault a relational characterisation of freedom and not an essential understanding. The term 'intransitive' might also be approached linguistically to suggest a verb that does not require an object. This lack of an object is at once also suggestive of the potential of shifting limits, so that the end point of struggle is never quite reached, never quite completed, and hence the moment of freedom itself is somehow, not so much illusory, but of the moment to come. While Foucault himself is reluctant to engage with psychoanalytic concepts, nevertheless the understanding of freedom that he suggests somehow seems to require, in the understanding I have elaborated here, concepts such as desire, constitutively meaningful in relation to the 'lack'. The intransivity of freedom is hence, and in this sense, always a relationship of negativity. Where Fanon's subject, understood psychoanalytically, appears fully defined by the object of his/her oppression and hence targets his/her violence against this object, nevertheless we see here a subject that is somehow more fleeting, more of the intransitive in freedom, more reflective of the temporal relationship between the moment of coloniality and the moment of postcoloniality and the continuing quest towards defining the limits of political community.

4

RECLAIMING THE INTERNATIONAL

Resistance in cosmopolitan space

> Talk of national liberation excited great dreams in him. In that magical universe
> he could visualise a new world, a new nation, a new home, a new people.
>
> Naguib Mahfouz, *Palace Walk, The Cairo Trilogy*

Anticipating the megalith cities of Mumbai and Delhi, the expectation was of a
rampant neoliberalism having captured the postcolonial subject and with the
subject, the postcolonial space. This was emergence in all its late modern
manifestations, where deregulation and the opening out of spaces of production to
a global context of corporations is deemed a temporal moment of arrival, of new
powers emerging onto global space and thereby claiming the right to holding its
reigns of power – the veto power at the Security Council here, the chairmanship
of the International Monetary Fund there. The expectation was resoundingly met,
in all its complex and contradictory formations, and yet this was 'emergence' in
formation, directed and choreographed by a still powerful state, albeit one that, like
its counterparts in Europe, straddled the imperatives of the corporations and those
of a population the overwhelming number of which live under the poverty line by
any measure. Witnessing the contradictions is no easy matter, for the concepts and
theories that form the armature of the theorist are never adequate to the materiality
of suffering borne of the extremes of poverty. Here in the megalith of 'emergent'
postcolonial cities was a reminder that emergence is only for the few, and the
state's efforts at reconciling neoliberalism with welfare continues to be fragmentary,
and largely dependent on the creative survivability of the poor. Yet, in amongst the
contradictions, the state matters and could be seen displayed, not just in symbolic
representations, but in the practices that somehow mediated the nexus between
population and a global political economy that some, Hardt and Negri (2001) are
examples here, would suggest render the state a diminished if not irrelevant entity.

It was as if the postcolonial state, having first and foremost emerged onto the
terrain of the international, having indeed focused its efforts on the international
and its presence thereupon, having acquired its sovereign identity precisely from
this most distinctive of spaces, could, from henceforth, re-direct its efforts at its
own population. For here among the multiform images and narratives gained on

visiting the most significant of postcolonial states, India, were the un-anticipated elements; the introduction of biometric identifiers for the population of 1.2 billion; the conducting of a census of the population, the introduction of an education act that would ensure all children up to the age of fourteen attend school, the anti-famine legislation that would ensure all children and families had access to basic, nutritional foods; and projects aimed at the provision of basic sanitation to a population three-quarters of whom have no such access. Yet the baffling contradictions re-emerge once again in that the sovereign state that is India is at the same time an aid donor, so that travelling in yet another, altogether different postcolonial state, Cambodia, the theorist witnesses evidence of India's cultural largess in donations aimed not so much at Cambodia's poor, but at the preservation of a heritage that links this impoverished state to the icons of Hindu and Buddhist culture. Here is the sovereign postcolonial state, India, and its aid and security policy in Afghanistan, as it contributes, not in the Western way of war, but in the building of Afghanistan's infrastructure, so that a rival, Pakistan's, insurgent clients do not take hold in an already volatile region. A Foucaultian reading of the Indian state might suggest a trajectory not unlike that of the modern European state and the trajectories of power that took shape from the seventeenth century to the present. Power could no longer simply be conceptualised in terms of sovereign power, but in terms that took account of the Indian state's shift into a neoliberal order wherein the welfare of populations, indeed the lives of populations, could be seen as an element in statecraft; India's late modern attempts at the consolidation of a distinctly Indian political entity.

To invoke the postcolonial international suggests a commonality of experience, of a history almost over-determined by colonialism and a present that remains within what many a postcolonial theorist would argue is still in the grip of structures of domination suggestive of the colonial present. De-colonising the international is hence a call that might be said to describe the remit of postcolonial international theory (Jones, 2006). Many questions might be directed at this proposal; how do we recognise the decolonised moment when it is reached? What elements of the international require decolonising? Once decolonised, would the 'international' as such exist, or is it likely to be replaced by a transnational arena of interaction? What transformations of the spatial articulation of relations are envisaged in this decolonising project? What is the temporal articulation of the decolonised international? If the international is constituted by the modern state, and the international is always already of the colonial, does decolonising the international suggest the transformation of the state, perhaps its breakdown into localised forms of political expression? These are questions that somehow inevitably lead us back to the constitutive moment of the colonial legacy, the impossibility of thinking the decolonisation of the international without at the same time thinking the undoing of the colonial subject.

This chapter delves into the concept of the postcolonial international. I want to argue that the concept itself is immediately suggestive of transformation, so that the colonial past, while constitutively present, is at the same time subject to practices that seek to re-define, to re-constitute, to expose, and to transform. The postcolonial international hence suggests moments of founding, of declarations of presence, of struggle within continuing structures of domination the primary feature of which is dispossession. It also suggests the primacy of the distinctive place that is the 'international', a distinctiveness that stems from limits drawn territorially and in relation to political authority as well as political community. How these limits are drawn remains a matter of controversy to the present, in that even as limits are expressive of the very definition of founding and the declaration of the independence of political authority and community, they are, at the same time, remnants of a colonial past that can never be escaped, so sedimented is this past in the very constitution of the political subject and the structure of the postcolonial international. The aim in this chapter is to focus on the 'declaration of independence' as a moment of 'founding' that inaugurates the postcolonial subject and with this subject the specific spatial and temporal domain that is the modern international. The focus is always on resistance, and while aspects of such resistance relate to the decolonisation of the international, such decolonisation is not historically suggestive of the diminution of the international, nor its significance in the constitution of the postcolonial subject. The relationship between the postcolonial and the international is hence a dynamic one of mutual constitution, but that is unequally structured, materially and discursively. As will be seen in the chapter, the resistance of the postcolonial in relation to the international is not based on a relationship of opposition, but is rather, and continuing on a theme introduced in Chapter 2, defined in terms of access to the modern international, and through this, the assertion of presence onto the space of the international.

The chapter is divided into three sections. The first returns to the postcolonial subject and the claim to politics, or the right to politics. In the context of this chapter the claim made is exactly in relation to international politics. Historically, as will be shown, this claim is made through nationally defined struggle against colonial occupation, the form of struggle, as we saw in the last chapter, that comes to constitute political community. While there is a tendency with some postcolonial theorists to argue that the anti-colonial struggle, and specifically its representation in national liberation struggles, was confined to the elites and did not involve the subaltern, as I have argued so far, and in keeping with Said's understanding of the postcolonial subject, the struggle for independence was and continues to be a prerequisite for the founding of political community, heterogeneously defined though such community was ideologically, and in class terms. The first section is hence devoted to the postcolonial subject's claim to the modern international and the form of articulation suggestive of such a claim.

The postcolonial state is often represented in the literature as having failed the promise of independence. This is not surprising, if we look to the vast expanse of the postcolonial world where the complicity of states in the repression of their own populations, the levels of poverty and inequality as compared to the former colonial powers, the availability of vast resources alongside the extremes of violence and deprivation, the kleptomania of leaders sustained by external interests, of other states and global capital. The 'explanations', as we saw in the last chapter, tend to be divided between those whose emphasis is on discursive representation and the construction of a hierarchically ordained international sphere as opposed to the 'dependency' school of thought, where the emphasis is on the material structure of the capitalist global economy and the differential locations of 'centre' and 'periphery'. As indicated earlier, far from seeing these as mutually exclusive, the discursive and the material tend to be mutually constitutive and in being so suggest a dynamic relationship that can be subject to transformation. The second section of the chapter seeks to move the debate in an alternative direction, one that does not seek 'explanation' in the structure of modernity as such and its institutions – sovereignty or the capitalist political economy – but rather, problematises the relationship between political community, the postcolonial state, and the international. What I referred to in the last chapter as the 'heteronomy of the international' will be illustrated here in all its too powerful implications for the constitution of political community and its relationship to the postcolonial state. The lens in this section is steered towards inequalities relating to the right to politics.

The third and final section of the chapter looks to the postcolonial state as subject of resistance. The aim in this section is to reveal the ways in which the postcolonial state uses the discourses of the international to assert a voice in the transformation of its most formative constructs. What emerges from such an engagement is that while the structurated inequalities of the colonial past remain a powerful, if geographically unevenly spread, influence, the international as a distinctive 'space' of politics is drawn upon in the discursive practices of the postcolonial state and its populations in constituting agency, locally, internationally, and transnationally.

Declaring independence, claiming the right to (international) politics

There was always a reluctance on the part of the coloniser to simply leave. We might think of France in Algeria, and of Britain in Egypt, India, and Iraq, to name but a few colonies. The history of decolonisation is much documented and need not take up much space here. Of interest though is the constitution of the political subject engaged in resistance and the articulations of political subjectivity that emerged in this period. In particular, the point here is to explore the moment of 'founding' that I am seeking in this context. This is methodologically a difficult task, given the diversity of conditions and experience in the colonial and postcolonial world. Nevertheless, the conceptual categories I have highlighted so far locate the lens on the political subject and the conditions wherein articulations to the political were made. There are no case studies as such in this exploration, but rather locations of reference, primarily the Middle East, though other postcolonial spaces also come into the frame. The matter of interest here is not so much the diversity of histories of liberation across the postcolonial world, but rather, the ways in which claiming the right to politics is at the same time a constitutive moment of emergence, irrespective of the heterogeneity of expression, or indeed, non-expression, that might exist at the time.

Locating the constitutive moment I am describing as the 'declaration of independence' in conditions of persistent coloniality is challenging while also being revealing of the structural continuities that link the colonial to the postcolonial order. Egypt, to use an illustrative example, gained its independence formally in 1922.[1] However, the British remained in place in one form or another well beyond this date and up to 1952 and the young officers' revolt against the king. The Egyptian Revolution had taken place in 1919, under the leadership of Saad Zaghlul of the Wafd Party as a culmination of the previous five years that had witnessed the British take-over of Egypt as a 'protectorate' in December 1914, a small step from the actuality of control that Britain had exercised between 1883 and 1914, when the Consul General's sovereign powers far exceeded those of the Khedive. With marshal law being exercised by the British and the recruitment of other Commonwealth armies (Australians in particular) into Egypt, along with the indenturing of labour into the Labour Corps, the requisitioning of buildings, farms, and other resources, the liberation movement was transformed from an elite group to a mass movement. It is important to recognise, however, that the political milieu in Egyptian society at this stage was one that had seen the modernisation and internationalisation of the local economy, a consequent and increasingly powerful land-owning and technocratic class, and the increasing 'Egyptianisation' of government bureaucracies (Ayubi, 2006: 106). These factors, combined with a vibrant public sphere, meant that Egyptian aspirations were increasingly articulated in terms of the 'nation' as such, though differences of class were also apparent.

In the series of 'founding moments', the 1919 revolution perhaps best identifies the constitution of political community and the articulation of a political subjectivity that was 'national' in character. That this was the political consciousness expressed is especially apparent in Neguib Mahfouz's *Cairo Trilogy* (1991), where the character Fahmy is not satisfied simply to engage in the young Wafdist movement, but seeks martyrdom as the ultimate sacrifice in the name of the nation. However, the certainty of allegiance is at the same time disrupted by a vulnerability expressive of a conflict between responsibility to family and promises made to an anxious father in the face of British brutality and the desire for heroic expression in confronting the colonial occupier. The background is of a leadership, led by Saad Zaghlul, not just negotiating with an increasingly repressive colonial order under the High Commissioner, Reginald Wingate, but mobilising for mass support from the villages and towns across the country. It was indeed the emergence of just a mass movement that led to increasingly violent practices by the colonial power aimed at the Egyptian populace.[2] This included, apart from the killing of thousands of civilians, the burning of villages, the destruction of railways, as well as attacks on private property. When the demand for independence was transformed from an elite political party to a mass movement, the colonial authority used violence in spectacular form aimed at punishment, but also at the attempt to discipline the

Egyptian population. This strategy did not repress the movement, but like its Indian counterpart, sustained and reinvigorated it.

The mass movement came to involve men and women, Muslim and Christian, and ultimately succeeded in gaining independence in 1922. However, the British military continued its presence in Egypt, despite the constitution of Egypt into a parliamentary democracy with Zaghlul as its first Prime Minister.[3] Looking to Naguib Mahfouz once again, we witness colonial violence through the everyday experiential realm of the family, so that resistance in the public sphere and emergent divisions in this sphere – both reflective of the constitutive moments of the political subject – are juxtaposed with acts of resistance within the patriarchal structure of the family. The revolution manifesting on the streets of Cairo is so constitutive of the subjectivities portrayed that it has a presence in acts of resistance taking place within the private sphere and in the changing modes of articulation relating to identity. Any expression of the latter that strays beyond the distinctly nationalist affiliation associated with the young Wafdist martyr, Fahmy, is imbued with anxiety and a sense of betrayal.

The Revolution was, according to all accounts, a liberal/modern nationalist revolution. Its aim was independence and its methods evolved into a mass movement that succeeded in capturing a revolutionary moment. Some have argued that the anti-colonial struggle might be conceived in terms of three distinct phases – political, economic, and 'cultural-discursive', with this last being represented by the assumed rise of Islamist movements. However, the problem with this form of characterisation or indeed periodisation is that it assumes a discontinuity between the political, the economic, and the discursive/cultural, with clear-cut boundaries between these domains. However, conceived in terms of 'founding' moments, the 1919 revolution was indeed one where the limits of Egypt's political community were independently drawn, claiming sovereignty for the people, represented by a parliament that later saw itself consistently at odds with a king who was all too accommodating with the British. This was a distinctly modern revolution, inaugurating Egypt's liberal era (between 1919–1952), according to Bayat (1998), but more profoundly according to the argument I am making here, inaugurating, indeed founding, the political community as such with all the 'agonism' that such a community would suggest. Thus, even though the Wafd Party led the nationalist revolution, its connections with the landowning class and emergent industrial class led to increasing criticism, from factions within the party, other political parties, as well as increasingly powerful civil society groups. Engagement in agonistic politics, therefore, took place not just in parliament, but also within a public sphere wherein, according to Ayubi (2006: 107), Islamists, populists, and 'etatists' vied for position.

The moment of founding I am describing here is perhaps best articulated by the Arabic word Nahda, or awakening. George Antonius's seminal work, *The Arab Awakening: The Story of the Arab National Movement* (1946), is as relevant today as it was in its own day, for here is a powerful analytic of the elements that constitute modern political community. For Antonius, problematically, a cultural awakening is almost a prerequisite for a political awakening, providing a linguistically specific cultural terrain upon which and through which the nation's aspirations could be articulated (Shalan, 2002).[4] At the same time, this aspiration to establish a cultural terrain struggled to find voice discursively and institutionally at a time of what some authors refer to in terms of 'cultural imperialism' (Reid, 1992).[5]

Such emphases on the cultural are, however, too neglectful of the specificity of the political contained in these founding moments – of resistance and the founding of political community. The drawing up of the 1923 Constitution and indeed the content of this constitution reflected the emergent political society and its basis in mass protest involving Egyptians of all classes, including the peasantry. Members of the elite, and specifically those involved in the nationalist Wafdist Party, were seen as representatives of the nation in their dealings with the colonial power in negotiating independence and in the post-independence period (Botman, 1998). The content of the Constitution was a result of deliberations by a thirty-member constitutional committee, resulting in the establishment of a parliamentary system based on a directly elected house of representatives and a senate composed of three-fifths elected and the rest appointed members. The constitution is seen by both historians and official contemporary Egyptian discourse as having been, according to the latter, 'an advanced step along the course of democracy and representation in Egypt'. However, as is well known, and according to the same source, 'practice was mixed with numerous negative aspects. Political life in the period 1923–1952 varied between tides of limited popular democracy and ebbs due to intervention by occupation forces and the palace, which led to the dissolution of parliament ten times.'[6] While this was indeed an active moment in constitution-making, the persistence of the colonial presence, and a political economy already penetrated by international capital, both contributed to the structuration of class defined inequalities within Egyptian society. Nevertheless, the bourgeois character of the revolutionary leadership does not negate the mass character of the anti-colonial struggle nor its place as a constitutive moment in the emergence of political community, defined not in organic nationalist terms, but in terms of the emergence of political space, and hence the potential for political contestation, including class and religious contestation, within Egyptian society (Mitchell, 1991).

The 1920s are a significant period in the history of the Middle East and the political awakening taking place in that region. What is particularly pertinent to the present discussion is that this period witnessed the emergence of a political society that was not simply based on the nationalist struggle against British and French occupation, though this was both a unifying as well as an over-riding imperative. The diversity of political affiliations, from the liberal to the communist/Marxist, to the Islamic, as well as the feminist,[7] suggests that while the colonial authorities engaged in the suppression of political activity, from the incarceration and exile of political leaders, to assassination, to the use of violence, including the burning of villages, directed at the mass of the population, the political, and more significantly, the carving out of political space continued apace. The call for sovereignty was the defining move, this being expressed in terms of a desire to determine characteristics and limits of political community. No such project could take place as long as foreign occupiers persisted in holding a presence in these societies and their territories, through their militaries, police, and an expatriate European middle class engaged in the dispossession of the colonised.

Writing on the political history of Iraq, one of the foremost historians of political life in the Middle East, Hanna Batatu (1926–2000), looks to the relationship between colonial practices and the formation of social classes and their political consequences in Iraq. Batatu demonstrates the direct link between British practices of control, instantiated through a land policy that empowered the local sheikhs, and an emerging resistance/revolutionary movement that sought, not only the liberation of the country from colonial rule, but political resistance against the increasing socio-economic inequalities that were a direct consequence of British imperial practices, including those that empowered the sheikhs and the merchants. Batatu is especially interested in the development of the Iraqi Communist Party from the 1930s to the 1950s and describes scenes reminiscent of today's moments of resistance in the Middle East. The so-called Great March (al-masira al-Kubra) and the Leap (al Wathba) were as much directed against the increasing powers of the British in Iraq, the monarchy beholden to the British, and the feudal economic structure that the British had put in place and helped sustain.[8] As Batatu highlights, the Iraqi resistance was as much an anti-imperialist as against economic inequalities within Iraqi society. Indeed the Association Against Imperialism, founded in Baghdad in March 1935, aimed its manifesto at both sources of antagonism:

> Today, the English and the ruling class are partners in a compact that aims at perpetuating the oppression and exploitation from which we suffer. The oil and other raw materials of the country have become a preserve for the English and Iraq has been turned into an outlet for their goods and surplus capital and into a war base. The ruling class, for its part, plunders the proceeds of taxes, misappropriates lands, and builds palaces on the shores of the Tigris and the Euphrates. The millions of peasants and workers, in the meantime, continue to starve, and bleed ...[9]

As was the case with Egypt's independence in 1922, while the British Mandate had come to an end in 1932, British presence remained, in military bases and in interference in the appointment of judges and advisors to the king. What is clear in Batatu's detailed analysis of the power struggles that eventually shaped Iraq is a context wherein an emergent political society based both on unity against the colonial order as well as ideological diversity relating to the shape of the future to come gave way to the dictatorship of individuals and cliques mainly as a result, not simply of internal antagonism, but decades of colonial repression aimed at the destruction of politics itself.

The tendency on the part of certain writers on the Middle East generally and on Iraq in particular is to suggest that modern politics was never destined for success in a context replete with interethnic or tribal rivalry. In a statement that reinforces this view and one that illustrates the ways in which ignorance of historical context is no barrier against the proclamation of certainties, Wimmer states,

> Unfortunately enough, Iraq fulfills all conditions for a pervasive and conflictual politicisation of ethnicity. First, it was ethnically too heterogeneous to allow an obvious answer to the question 'who is the people?'. In the year of independence (1932) its population was made up of 21% Sunni Arab speakers, 14% mostly Sunni Kurdish speakers, 53% Shii Arab speakers, 5% non-Muslim Arab speakers, most importantly the Baghdad Jews, and 6% other religious-linguistic groups such as the Sunni Turkmen of Northern Iraq, or the various Christian sects speaking Assyrian.[10]

The author further claims that 'only few modern civil society organizations existed, and none had a trans-ethnic reach'. Again, there is no evidence provided for this statement, when in actuality, the Iraq of the 1920s and beyond was one of vibrant, if repressed (by the colonial authorities) political and cultural activity. Where Batatu's detailed investigations interpret political conflict in socio-political terms, this latter and more recent (in the aftermath of the 2003 invasion of Iraq) interpretation relies on simplistic, though effective as a technology of control, ancient-hatreds ethnic terms. As a contrast to Wimmer, writing the preface to the second edition of his book, republished in the aftermath of the invasion of Iraq, Sluglett (2007: xii) points out that historically 'Iraq had no history of sectarian -based violence' and that, until the fall of Qasim in 1963, '"Sunni rule", which had been accompanied by increasing secularization and the more or less even spread of universal education, was neither particularly fearful nor particularly oppressive'.[11] However, that representations of 'the Arab' have not changed much is reflected in this statement made by one of Her Majesty's representatives in Iraq:

> It is clear that the enlightened and progressive Arab in whom the enthusiasts ask us to believe is a mere fiction as far as Mesopotamia is concerned. Such progressive elements as do exist in the country are not Arabs at all but Jews and Christians. It will be a poor kind of self-determination that places such people at the mercy of an uncontrolled Arab administration.[12]

Such 'ethnic' representations of the Iraqi population bely a more appropriately class-based analysis that indicates cross-ethnic class interests among the various interest groups that constituted Iraqi society at the time of the 'protectorate'.[13]

   How do we isolate what I am calling here 'moments of founding' of political community in the colonial and postcolonial context? As I argue above, a useful approach to this question suggests thinking of a series, not necessarily consecutive, moments of founding, given the circumstances within which these took place, specifically the continued colonial presence in all but name. As we saw above, the 1919 Egyptian revolution was the precursor to the 1923 constitution, which saw the institutionalisation of political community. Iraq witnessed a 'revolution' of its own in 1920, again driven by the impetus towards independence. Unlike Egypt, however, the Iraq revolt ended through the use of phosphorous bombs by the Royal Air Force, under the direction of Winston Churchill. As argued by Sami Zubaida (2002), the 1920 revolution is of prime significance in the constitution of the nationalist anti-colonial struggle in Iraq's history. Over and above the nationalist anti-colonial impetus, what is more significant in relation to the argument presented here is that, like Egypt, the developing political culture in Iraq suggested a recognition of political diversity and the desire for democratic institutions (Dawisha, 2005).

Moments of founding seem also to be moments of revolution. The revolutions highlighted above, the Egyptian in 1919 and the Iraqi in 1920, were distinctly modern revolutions, political in their framing, cross-class, and cross-religious in their affiliational make-up, united in their desire for independence and opposition to colonial rule and occupation, and diverse politically, involving liberal constitutionalists, communists, and nationalists. These were movements that sought new beginnings, even as their discourses and deliberations drew from a rich trajectory of political thought deriving from the region and from Europe, from past and present. Both moments were built on critique, in political thought and political activity, aimed against arbitrary colonial rule and the regimes of oppression and dispossession sustained by the colonial order. While, as we have seen above, there is a genre of writing that rejects this interpretation of political moves in the Middle East, preferring to place emphasis on religious doctrine, ethnic division, and loyalties therein, these readings are largely framed in the 'ancient hatreds' discourse beloved of colonial orders to the present. This does not mean that Islamic thought and practice could simply be placed aside. Indeed Islamic political parties competed for affiliation with other political forces of the time. However, to reduce the socio-political conditions that led to revolt to the primacy of Islam would constitute a misreading, not just of these particular historical moments, but of the trajectory of Islamic thought and practice.[14]

These revolutions, I want to argue, emerged from an age of critique, as I indicate above. The modern period in the Middle East sees the emergence of discourses among journalists, officials, teachers, philosophers, and other writers engaged in learned societies and contributing to journals devoted to the dissemination of literature, especially poetry, and philosophical ideas. Albert Hourani places the emergence of what he calls a 'movement of thought' in the late nineteenth century, first in Turkey, and then in the Arab parts of the Ottoman Empire. The latter, and specifically its members in Egypt, shared an Ottoman Islamic liberalism with an emerging idea of Egyptian territorial nationalism. Indeed the first writer, according to Hourani, who articulated the idea of Egypt as a distinctive political nation was Rifa'a Badawi Rafi' al-Tahtawi, whose writings express the effort to somehow combine traditional Islamic thought with modern, specifically French ideas deriving primarily from Rousseau and Montesquieu. Tahtawi founded the School of Languages and directed translations into Arabic of major works of literature and philosophy and persuaded the Government Press to produce the works of Ibn-Khaldun. Tahtawi as a political theorist was engaged in defining the question of legitimate authority, and this lay not just in divine sanction, but crucially in 'public opinion', in 'good relations between ruler and ruled', and in 'universal political education' enabling citizens to know their rights and duties (Hourani, 1983: 76). Importantly, Tahtawi was not just interested in the virtuous life, but conceived the role of government also in terms of the economic welfare of the population. Education policy was at the heart of Tahtawi's ideas relating to the building of a just society and 'hubb-al-watan', love of country. So, as Hourani maintains, the duty to unite and to obey the law must be combined with the right to freedom, for it is the latter that makes possible the former. For Hourani (1983: 78–79),

> *hubb-al-watan* then has the same meaning as *asabiyya* in the doctrine of Ibn Khaldun – the sense of solidarity which binds together those who live in the same community and is the basis of social strength. But at other times he is using it in a more restricted and a new sense. The emphasis is no longer on the passive duty of the subject to accept authority, it is on the active role of the citizen in building a truly civilized society; it is no longer exclusively on the mutual duties of members of the Islamic *umma*, but also of those who live in the same country. *Hubb-al-watan* thus acquires the specific meaning of territorial patriotism in the modern sense, and the mother-country – la Patrie – becomes the focus of those duties which, for Islamic jurists, bound together members of the *umma* and that natural feeling which, for Ibn Khaldun, existed between men related to each other by blood.

Political community for Tahtawi emerges from a solidarity of rights and duties defining the 'watan' or country conceived not in ethnic Arab terms, but in terms of 'Egypt', the territorial state, as such.

The age of critique was further realised in the Levant, with the emergence of writers, mainly Christian, who sought to emphasise Arabic as a medium of instruction. More significantly in this age of 'enlightenment' was the emergence of journals and newspapers, including one of the first, al-Jawa'ib, covering international as well as local news and translations of diplomatic papers, read across the Arabic speaking world. The emphasis on modern thought, of the merits of Europe, and of Arabic as a source of knowledge and progress was especially emphasised by Butrus al-Bustani (1819–1883), author of an Arabic dictionary and encyclopaedia. In Bustani's case, it is 'Syria' which is appealed to as the 'watan'. This was the defining moment of territorial nationalism, seen as the vehicle through which political community, culture, and progress could be articulated, and used against European colonisation. (Hourani, 1983: 100) This period saw the emergence of another political movement, one that sought to combine pan-Islamism with ideas relating to nationalism. Of primary significance in this period was Jamal al-Din al-Afghani (1839–1897), whose teachings at Al-Azhar were received by Sa'd Zaghlul and Muhammad 'Abduh, both influential thinkers in political Islam.[15] The core message of teaching was opposition to European intervention and the need for unity based on national consciousness, articulated most fully in the 1870s. The age of critique had, with Tahtawi's writings, come to define political aspiration in terms of the territorially defined nation, the *watan*, and through Abduh's writings, encompassed reflection on how Islam could be reconciled with modern thought, so that *umma*, or the community of belief, was not oppositional to *watan*. The age of critique, in Egypt, the Levant, and later Iraq was sustained through published material, from elite publications to newspapers, that acquired mass appeal in the struggle against colonial rule.[16]

The revolutionary moments of 'founding' were hence built upon a discursive edifice that defined the parameters of modern political community. While much writing on the Middle East and other postcolonial regions, Asia and Africa included, emphasise the so-called 'artificiality' of the postcolonial state; that is, that the postcolonial state was by and large a product of colonial boundary drawing,[17] and that conceptions of 'modernity' were purely a product of colonialism,[18] such Eurocentric discourses largely reflect either an ignorance of the intellectual trajectories of these regions and the processes of political mobilisation that were intricately connected to such trajectories, or a reiteration of a colonial discourse that could not, indeed would not, acknowledge the possibility of independent political community enabling of political contestation as constitutive of the populations under colonial occupation and rule. As pointed out by Partha Chatterjee in discussing India, though of equal relevance as we have seen in relation to the Middle East, the colonial form of rule relied on enumerating colonised populations in terms of 'ethnic communities' and 'castes' and their 'natural leaders', as colonial thought

> could not countenance the idea that subject peoples might constitute, in the same way that advanced people did, a singular and true political community such as the nation. At the same time, if 'communities' rather than 'nation' were what characterized this society, those communities had to be singular and substantive entities in themselves, with determinate and impermeable boundaries, so insular in their differences with one another as to be incapable of being merged into larger, more modern political identities.
>
> *(Chatterjee, 1993: 224)*

Such was the colonial discourse of the past and such is the colonial discourse of the present. We have seen that despite such inscriptions and the coercive measures that sustained them, the founding of political community, indeed the claim to politics, could not be attributed to the colonial official, nor indeed could deliberation on modernity and its modes of expression and articulation.

The creation of political community, and one based on deliberative practices focused on a future constitutional trajectory, must hence be seen as the formative backdrop for the postcolonial state. As we have seen, resistance against colonial rule came in the form of mass politics and mass protest, wherein the intellectual discourses of an educated class permeated public discourse through political mobilisation in urban and rural areas, both directly and through the periodical press. The foundational aspect of the political communities being invented were united through the concept of 'watan', the nation, while expressing diverse modes of political affiliation. However, as we will see in the next section, the disjuncture between the promise of anti-colonial liberation and the right to politics suggests a deferral of the moment of founding for the postcolonial political community, a deferral that cannot be fully captured without looking into the role of the postcolonial state, first, in relation to political community and second in relation to the realm of the international. The two contexts, as will be shown below, cannot be treated in isolation, but are, rather, mutually imbricated. The postcolonial subject's right to politics and indeed the distribution of this right globally has historically been subject to the influences of the intersection between the domestic and the international and transformations thereof.

Political community and the postcolonial state

In his film *Al-Ard* (Land), Youssef Chahin, the most significant of Egypt's film directors, depicts a gathering of Egyptian peasants deliberating on the wording of a petition they seek to submit to the authorities in Cairo regarding a new irrigation scheme favouring local landlords and denying the villagers access to land and water. The film was made in 1969 and based on a novel written by Abdel Rahman al-Sharqawi in 1954. The film depicts two generations coming together to resist the expropriation of their land. All the members of the older generation had participated in the independence struggle of 1919 and had, as a consequence, been incarcerated by the British. Abou Swelem is the primary character of this generation. The younger generation is represented by Abou Swelem's daughter Wassifa, her admirers, the educated Mohammed Effendi and the peasant Abdel Hadi, and an array of other characters. There are also the local corrupt mayor, Abdel Ati, and the wealthy Mahmoud Bey, among various policemen, soldiers, and government officials. The issue that creates contention relates to access to water and its imminent diversion away from the peasants' land and towards the wealthy households in the district. When word comes through of the change in irrigation policy, the educated Mohammed Effendi suggests writing a petition to government, while Abdel Hadi wishes to resist by continuing to irrigate his land despite the new edict. The group agrees to pursue the path of the petition and seeks help from Mahmoud Bey, the primary beneficiary of the new policy of expropriation. Mohammed Effendi discovers Mahmoud Bey's agenda when he goes to Cairo to pursue the peasants' case and enlists the help of his uncle Hassouna, a legislator. Hassouna returns to the villlage and calls for unity in resistance against the irrigation policy. On returning, he discovers that most of the peasants have been imprisoned and tortured, released only in the event of protests from the women, led by Wassifa. However, despite all efforts at resistance, and as a result of a combination of coercion and defeat at the hand of soldiers sent to occupy the village, Abu Swelem is ultimately stripped of his land, though he remains the heroic figure willing to loose all in its defence. The film begins with a shot of Swelem's hands clutching his beloved land, so too it ends with him being forcefully dragged from it. This film is about struggle and resistance, and makes intertextual reference to other films, especially to Soviet film-makers of the 1920s and 1930s.[19] The issue of colonial rule is not explicitly stated, though it is clear that the film is set in 1930s Egypt.[20]

Despite the king's police force, his English colonial backers, and the local corrupt officials, the heroic figures are those whose focus is resistance, for it is in relation to these that the continuities with the anti-colonial struggle emerge. Abu Swelem reminds others that his is the generation of the 1919 revolution that sought independence and the end of British colonial rule in Egypt. What is especially pertinent to the discussion in this chapter is that while the struggle is immediately local, its ramifications and implications relate to the land and its constitutive force in relation to political subjectivity. The 'fellaheen' or peasants of the village are depicted as the carriers of a wider struggle against colonial dispossession and its local agents. Significantly, while one interpretation might point to modernisation as the direct cause of the dispossessions to come, another might point to the distinct intellectual spaces given to modernisation on the one hand and independence politics on the other. Herein lie the paradoxes of modernity, enabling on the one hand the very emergence of the political subject, and on the other, the structures enabling of dispossession. The political subject in this case is he who manifests a founding moment wherein action in common is inaugurated. Yet, what is also evident in Chahine's film is that the founding moment for the colonised and the postcolonial subject is all too transient and not so easily located at its most obvious temporal articulation, namely independence. The claim to politics in the postcolonial context comes face to face with the postcolonial state and its capacities to mediate between the articulated expectations of citizens and sectional interests, both local and international.

That the postcolonial state was largely a product of the colonial order has been the subject of much discussion in the postcolonial literature, where the modern state is but the local embodiment of colonial power, reinforced by an elite trained and often nurtured by the coloniser, albeit often in armed struggles against foreign rule. As shown in the last chapter, the very framing of the Subaltern Studies Group relied on a distinction between a seemingly elitist nationalist struggle and the multiform struggles of peasant and indigenous communities against structures of domination and dispossession that persisted into the postcolonial era. However, while this critique of coloniality/modernity is an invaluable situating critique of European domination and what we might refer to as its epistemic extensions, it nevertheless fails to fully grasp the formative, even constitutive role of the postcolonial state in relation to the postcolonial subject and this subject's capacities for claiming the right to politics.

The disenchantment of the postcolonial subject might be traced to an unequal global political economy the rules and institutions of which still overwhelmingly favour the North. We might also refer to inequalities in signifying power, so that 'orientalism' and racism more widely conceived are complicit in the reproduction of hierarchies of worth, of epistemes, of access to material resources and legitimising frameworks. However neither perspective, the material or the discursive, seems capable of grappling with the question of the political in postcoloniality, and specifically the postcolonial subject's capacity to engage in articulations of political agency. For apart from material and signifying inequalities, a foremost inequality relates to political subjectivity and what I have referred to as the right to politics. As Chatterjee highlights above, colonial representational practices denied the colonised exactly this subjectivity and their epistemic violence continues to do so into the present. Furthermore, the suppression of politics was also conducted through the extremes of violence directed at resisting populations and individuals.[21] In the postcolonial context, the context of juridical sovereign statehood, the lens turns on the machinery of the postcolonial state and its practices in the government of populations, including the government of political space and political articulation.[22] The lens focuses on the state as what is at stake for most postcolonial societies is the disjuncture between the promise of liberation from colonial rule and their subsequent dispossession of the right to politics.

If we look to the context of the Middle East and the postcolonial state therein, we find the subject of politics that reveals a most remarkable resilience in the face of overwhelming violence and the perpetuation of fear perpetrated by the security apparatus of the postcolonial state. This is an apparatus that, throughout the twentieth century and into the recent past, has not only had the support of the West, but has indeed been utilised by the West. The primary technology of control used has been incarceration and through this the disciplining of the wider society into submission. The form of 'government' used has hence been largely based on the corporeal vulnerability of the subject of politics, where violence directed at the body is used to perpetuate fear across the wider population, starting from the families of those incarcerated to the wider public. Other technologies of control have focused on the limitation of political spaces, from physical public spaces to the public sphere of the media, both subjected to surveillance practices that penetrate the everyday and the routine. However, the very ferocity of these practices bears testimony to the persistence of the subject of politics and this subject's capacities in articulating contestation and non-conformity to the edicts of sovereign violence. Furthermore, the all-pervasive presence of the state in the lived experience of populations generates a shared knowledge wherein this presence is immediately recognised, so that the state's security apparatus, the infamous 'mukhabarat' (literally meaning the system of informants) are instantly recognised. At the same time, the all-pervasive presence of the state has also led to exile as a method in securing the safety of those left behind and at the potential mercy of the state.[23]

From Weber to present-day discourses on the Middle East, the 'explanation' for what I am describing above is placed at the door of 'culture'. In these discourses, 'Islam' and Arab culture more generally are represented as being hostile to modernity and change. For Weber, as Maxine Rodinson highlights, the systems of patronage that he saw as describing Islamic societies were due to Islamic 'fatalism'.[24] Such orientalist accounts tend to rely on an essentialised understanding of culture, wherein cultural manifestations are seen to 'explain' hostility to a modernising agenda. However, as we have seen above, political contestation in the Middle East and elsewhere during the colonial period and beyond did and continues to use the tropes of modernity to argue against oppressive practices, colonial and postcolonial and finds expression in a diversity of political affiliation, from Marxism to Liberalism, to Islamism and variations therein.

In seeking to locate the subject of politics in postcoloniality the assumption I make is that this subject is situated within different articulations of modernity, including coloniality. The colonial experience should hence not be seen as an 'encounter with modernity', but rather as an encounter of locally articulated modernities – for example, innovations in production practices, in literary and artistic expression, or in new readings of ancient texts – with specifically European modernity. I therefore prefer the idea of an encounter between alternative modernities, including the European version, which emerged as the most coercive and dispossessive while also generating the discourses and ideas drawn upon in the language of anti-colonial struggle. In this sense, while orientalist 'explanations' of forms of rule in the Middle East rely on monolithic interpretations of 'culture' as such, what I am suggesting here is that complexity in political articulation was paralleled by complexity in cultural articulation, one that was and continues to be 'hybrid'.

Explanations of inequalities relating to the right to politics must hence look beyond culture, and one productive avenue for investigation relates to the postcolonial state for it is the case that this state looms large in the lived experience of the postcolonial subject. Partha Chatterjee, writing on the 'national state', provides us with a picture of the structure of the postcolonial state and the economic and political challenges it faced upon independence. Of value in Chatterjee's analysis is the materialist framing within which the postcolonial state is placed, so that we can immediately discern the structural constraints within which the state sought to implement its new social and political programmes. The challenge for the new state was hence the challenge of government, not just the government of ethnic or tribal relations, as most Eurocentric renditions on the postcolonial state would suggest, but primarily the government of populations. The postcolonial state was hence confronted with the immediacy of the problem of 'development' and 'modernisation', not necessarily in a simple mimicry of Western models of development, but through a recognition that the resources of the political community were paramount not simply in relation to the provision of welfare, but in the reconstitution of this community as an independent entity capable of interacting with others in international economic interactions and exchanges. As Chatterjee points out,

> It was in the universal function of 'development' of national society as a whole that the postcolonial state would find its distinctive content. This was to be concretized by the embodiment within itself of a new mechanism of development administration, something the colonial state, because of its alien and extractive character, had never possessed. It was in the administration

of development that the bureaucracy of the postcolonial state was to assert itself as the universal class, satisfying in the service of the state its private interests by working for the universal goals of the nation.

(Chatterjee, 1993: 205)

Where the colonial state had been based on the exploitation and dispossesison of the colonised, the postcolonial state and the nationalist movement that enabled its emergence would be based on a political economy of development, whereby self-government was the necessary first step. To have a political economy of development meant first of all putting in place the administrative machinery that would take charge of planning for the future, a task that required knowledge of existing production practices and the means through which such practices could be transformed into a modern economy. The development ideology propounded by the Congress leadership in India and Nehru in particular had to acquire political legitimacy with the population. There was, and still remains today, in India and elsewhere in the postcolonial world, a disjuncture that had to be negotiated, between the imperatives of a modern and modernising political economy and the demands of political community and its contentions.

The Gramscian analysis that Chatterjee provides of these challenges as they applied to postcolonial India somehow manages to leave the international aside, so that the elements that impact on planning for the future, or the political economy of planning, are largely domestic. The question of the material resources that might be required for planning is not raised. I will return to this question of the international and planning a political economy in postcoloniality later. Suffice it to say for the time being that the 'national state' for Chatterjee is one that becomes fully engaged in the administrative side of planning and the requisite political stakes involved, over legitimacy and the idea that the newly independent state represents the nation as a whole. As Chatterjee highlights:

> The reification of the 'nation' in the body of the state becomes the means for constructing this hegemonic structure, and the extent of control over the new state apparatus becomes a precondition for further capitalist development. It is by means of an interventionist state, directly entering the domain of production as mobilizer and manager of investible 'national' resources, that the foundations are laid for industrialization and the expansion of capital.

At the same time the state constrains capital through a 'constructed hegemony' that seeks to combine 'accumulation with legitimation while avoiding the "unnecessary rigors" of social conflict' (Chatterjee, 1993: 212–213).

Chatterjee's conclusions relate to India as the postcolonial state, where accumulation is accompanied by investment in practices of legitimation, practices that must be read in relation to the specificities of India's political culture and its institutions. However, the interventionist state that Chatterjee highlights is also present in the context of the Middle East. Nazih Ayubi writes about 'over-stating' the Arab state, suggesting two interpretations for this term each of which has relevance for our purposes here. The first, in line with Chatterjee's concept of the 'developmental state', looks to the 'expansion of the state in quantitative terms', manifest across sectors of society from industrialisation, to social welfare, to public sector employment. The term 'over-stating' hence refers to the size of the machinery of the state and its role in economy and society. The second meaning of the term refers to the 'fierce state', relying, as Ayubi highlights, on 'raw coercion' for self-preservation rather than establishing hegemony (in the Gramscian sense of the term) that would enable the emergence, in turn, of a legitimating discourse. For Ayubi (2006: 12), the form of statehood that emerged in the Middle East was a direct consequence of the colonial legacy in the region:

> And as a continuation of this colonial legacy, the military, bureaucratic oligarchy of the independent states has continued to play a mediating role among the competing demands of three owning classes: the landlords, the native capitalists, and metropolitan capital. Inevitably, this gave the state significant power in the economic as well as in the political affairs of the society.

The exaggerated role of the state is attributed in Ayubi to the 'delayed capitalist development of most peripheral countries', so that access to international capital is exactly facilitated by the state, thereby conferring the state primacy in the provision of services and resources, including the compliance of an emergent working class. This mediating role of the state is enabled by a combination of practices that might be 'legitimacy-building', 'violence-applying', or a combination thereof. The fact that the state looms large, as I am suggesting here, suggests that it cannot simply be interpreted as a straightforward reflection of class interests, in that its machinery suggests that it also 'creates' its own 'class' (Ayubi, 2006: 13–14).

Seeking the political subject in postcoloniality is hence related to how we might understand the postcolonial state. While there are, of course, differences in articulations of statehood across the postcolonial world, differences that are clearly related not just to the colonial experience, but also to local conditions relating at one and the same time to structures of political economy as well as political cultural manifestations, what is clear is that the postcolonial state and its machinery of government cannot be extracted from the location of the postcolonial state in relation to the international political economy and therefore the international as such. At the same time, the 'balance' of 'legitimacy-building' and 'violence-applying' practices cannot be reduced to 'external' factors alone, nor to structural factors alone, but derives from the intersection of oligarchical, sectional, as well as international interests. These are, however, not static relationships, so that transformations in the global political economy, for example, the deregulatory imperative of a global neoliberal order, can have manifest impact on local expressions of interest and political contestation. Claiming the right to politics is hence precariously situated in relation to powerful forces, internal and external, that seek to govern politics as such, and specifically the postcolonial subject's access to the terrain of the political. Before I move to the transformations of the global that can impact upon the subject of politics in postcoloniality, the third and final section of the chapter will relocate the postcolonial state in the realm of the international. Specifically, when such a relocation is enacted, we begin to reveal the postcolonial state as subject of resistance in an international political and economic order that does not deliver the promise of liberation.

The postcolonial state, resistance, and the international

For the postcolonial subject, access to the space of the international meant recognition in the sphere of modernity and its institutions; namely, the state and the international political economy. To see the 'international' from the perspective of the 'periphery', the 'South', the postcolonial, is to see a domain dominated by the West, by the former imperial powers and their contemporary counterparts; it is to see international institutions under the control of these very powers, and to see postcolonial structures of domination played out upon the intersections that constitute the discontinuities of geopolitical space, intersections that bring the sovereign state face to face with the international political economy. The dream was always and continues to be the reach of the international, a spatial domain whose temporal manifestation is seen to be modernity itself. What is significant is that postcolonial discourse, specifically related to the decolonisation agenda and questions of racial discrimination, came to reconstitute the international in the post World War II period, so that the remit on the part of the postcolonial state was not simply access to the international in the form of sovereign statehood, but the decolonisation of the international and its structures, including international law and the very concept of sovereignty (Anghie, 2004). It is indeed in the decolonisation of the international that we can see the postcolonial state engaged in resistance, and, through such engagement, reinforcing its legitimating remit 'back home', so to speak. It is in this sense that the international as structure and transformations thereof are implicated in the constitution of postcolonial political community. There is, hence, not just an internal focus in seeking the legitimation of rule, but also one that derives from the enactment and affirmation of sovereignty in relation to the 'outside' world.

To suggest that the international merely represents a location wherein the postcolonial world comes to realise its failed aspiration is far too limited an understanding of postcolonial subjectivity. The postcolonial subject, as argued above, has an aporetic relationship to the international, being on the one hand, the structural manifestation of the colonial legacy, and on the other, constituted in this very structure. However, it is exactly this aporetic relationship that can be seen as being generative of the potential for resistance.[25] Read in this sense, the international can be viewed as a location of limits; limits wherein identities could be forged, juridical access could be reclaimed,[26] resources repossessed, and the political as such reclaimed. The international was hence seen as a space that could confer protections against continued occupation and dispossession; of history, of subjectivity, of self-realisation. However, while access to the 'international' might nominally and symbolically be suggestive of sovereignty, one encompassed by the postcolonial state; the 'reality' of juridical, political, economic, and cultural inequality suggests that the experience of sovereignty for the postcolonial is historically different to that of the European states. The international might then be read as the enduring imperial domain that is always a reflection of the 'colonial encounter'.

However, this perspective does not fully capture the 'meaning' of the international for the postcolonial world. Access to the modern international was the defining force that animated the anti-colonial struggles of the past, so that territorial sovereignty came to be the motor through which political community could be established and consolidated. This is not to reinforce the realist understanding of the international, but rather, to acknowledge the phenomenological, hermeneutic connection between the subject of politics, the national imaginary, and the struggle for recognition. The construction of the national imaginary was clearly a matter of socio-political mobilisation. Of crucial significance here is the idea that relationships to the outside world, the juridical/political space constitutive of the international, was the defining force in limiting political community, in giving this community form, and in distinguishing that which was of the 'nation' as such from collectivities based on other modes of affiliation, including race, ethnicity, or tribe. The self-determination of the formerly colonised could hence only be realised, and recognised, in the form of the sovereign independent state. The meaning conferred to 'sovereignty' was hence not simply limited to the acquisition of juridical personality in international law, vastly significant though this was and continues to be, but related primarily to the definition of the 'national community' as such.[27]

While the postcolonial international is clearly of the colonial, it seems that locating the international in relation to the postcolonial subject raises more fundamental questions about the relationship between this subject and the domain of the international, a relationship that is not totally or fully captured by the colonial structuring of the international. We might, in this second perspective, argue for a mutually constitutive relationship between the postcolonial subject and the international, so that thinking of the reproduction of both necessarily involves reference to, on the one hand, the juridical/political structure of the international and its constituting power in relation to the subjects it encompasses, and on the other hand the postcolonial subject's encounter with the modern international and this encounter's particular reconstituting power in relation to the international. The juridical aspect of the international hence both creates and is itself recreated by the object it creates. The relationship between the international and the postcolonial can be interpreted as, on the one hand, being determined by the enduring effect of the colonial encounter, and on the other hand, being understood in terms of mutual constitution. This latter suggests what Sundhya Pahnja refers to as 'the productive instability' of the juridical framework of the international, and specifically international law. The key concept in this relationship, though certainly not the only concept, is 'sovereignty' (Pahnja, 2005).

Much is written on the attempts of postcolonial states to shape their own destinies, especially in a context defined by the Cold War confrontation between East and West. The Non-Aligned Movement is historically seen as the South's struggle to define a path that was distinct from the influences of either camp and, more significantly, to re-shape the international economic order in ways that would combat 'neo-colonialism', the struggle against which brought much (active) Western hostility,[28] the continued economic domination of the recently decolonised. The aim of this section is not to run over this old diplomatic ground, for there are chroniclers of this episode in international history that have already provided us with analyses of the successes and failures of non-alignment.[29] Rather, the aim here is to focus on particular aspects of 'resistance' that place the postcolonial subject in direct antagonism with what I have referred to as the heteronomy of the international.

In its role in both accumulation and the establishment of legitimacy, the postcolonial state, as we saw in the previous section, is an interventionist state: it seeks to construct a hegemonic structure that functions to legitimise a political economy of development; it builds a state apparatus geared for planning as well as the mobilisation and management of national resources; it negotiates its role as allocator with the demands of a modern sector that seeks its own stakes in the developmental economy. The problem is, however, that each such step, indeed the very definition of the postcolonial state and the limits of its capacities must be considered in relation to the domain of the 'international', its limits, and its constraints. This is where the postcolonial state comes face to face with the colonial structure of the international. The resistance of the postcolonial state as such must hence be measured in terms of how it fulfils its role in relation to the constraints of the international. These constraints are not simply derived from economic inequality within the global political economy, but are also political, juridical, and military, this last presenting the ever-present potential of violent intervention in the face of 'real' resistance; in other words, forms of resistance perceived as threats to the existing order.

Moments of resistance against domination have emerged throughout the history of the postcolonial world. Of interest in this context however is the state itself as a focal point of resistance, as the agent of resistance. As agent, the postcolonial state uses sovereignty as its primary vehicle in building a political economy of development as well as in efforts to re-shape the global order in a direction that favours the postcolonial state as well as those seeking self-determination. Where the first relates primarily to the mobilisation of the apparatus of the state to reclaim national resources in the re-shaping of the political economy, the second utilises the newly acquired access to the sphere of the international to enable the creation of new discourses and institutional alliances in the service, potentially, of the postcolonial world. If the national state was to acquire legitimacy for its actions within, it had to assert its presence internationally, for in the absence of such resistance, the condition of postcoloniality would be rendered meaningless. An indicator of the impact of resistance by particular postcolonial leaders is the response of the powerful, variously the former colonial powers and the United States. Examples of postcolonial state resistance and agency are too many to include here, though some highlights point to the location and content of resistance while being suggestive of the constitutive place of resistance that I have been highlighting. Gamal Abdel-al Nasser and his nationalisation of Suez is perhaps one of the most historically significant moments of resistance that led to the invasion of Egypt and the Suez war; Kwame Nkrumah's efforts to re-design postcolonial Africa, towards political unity in an effort to reclaim what he called 'Africa's riches' and to see the liberation of the whole of Africa from colonial rule, stating in his independence speech that 'the independence of Ghana is meaningless unless it is linked up with the total liberation of the African continent' eventually led, in 1966, to a military coup that was facilitated by the CIA.[30] The list of postcolonial states facing CIA subversions is far too long to recount here. Suffice it to say that each such location bears testimony to effective resistance by the postcolonial state and its leadership.[31]

Most renditions on the postcolonial state include a normative prefix, such that the 'collapsed', the 'failed', the 'quasi', are taken for granted as descriptions which can then be used for the diagnoses of problems particular to the states of the South. However, when these prefixes are acknowledged as inscriptions, then their meaning becomes far more significant in consequence for the postcolonial state, rendering this state deficient in the sovereignty stakes and hence vulnerable to external intervention and control. However, if the postcolonial state constructs its identity in terms of resistance to colonial rule and domination, this construction comes to influence the state's position in relation to interpretations and 'self-images' of political community within and in the state's relationships with other states in the international system.[32] It is indeed at moments of resistance that operations of power and structures of domination are revealed, moments than can potentially be captured in the reconstitution of the international.

This was Nasser's desire when he sought to consolidate Egypt as a postcolonial political community through the modernisation of the political economy, for he recognised, like Nehru, that development could only be meaningful if Egyptian production was taken out of the grip of the colonials and their clients in the private sector, and consolidated through, for example, the nationalisation of land and its equitable distribution, and the nationalisation of Western dominated resources, such as the Suez Canal, so that its vast revenues could at last be used in developing Egypt and its infrastructure.[33] If there is a paradigm moment in postcolonial state resistance it is the nationalisation of the Suez Canal, for in this moment was contained not simply the desire to reclaim a valuable resource for the nation, but to constitute that nation as a viable political community with a right of access to the realm of the international.

The sovereign performance that was the nationalisation of Suez was carried out as Nasser delivered his famous three-hour speech in Alexandria on 26 July 1956. The signal was buried in the speech, broadcast on the airwaves across the country, but specifically awaited by three commando units instructed to carry out the take-over of the offices of the company that owned and ran the canal, the Compagnie

Universelle du Canal Maritime de Suez. Adel Ezzat, a member of the commando unit, recalls the events thus: 'We weren't armed. Our instructions were to carry out the operation peacefully.' On hearing Nasser pronounce the words 'de Lesseps', the group would launch its operation despite the presence of British troops in Ismailia. Despite this, Ezzat states, 'We refused to abandon our plan; history was on the march … The president said "de Lesseps". Then he repeated it a second time, and a third, as if he feared we hadn't heard him.'[34] Nasser's speech both performed the act and announced its implementation, so that the utterance was simultaneously translated into deed, announced the nationalisation of the Canal to the jubilant crowd. For Gamal Abdel Nasser, writing for the journal, *Foreign Affairs*, in 1955,

> For a century and a half the Arab world has been following a negative policy. It has known what it wanted to do away with, but it has not known what it wanted to build. The Western conquest of the Middle East was mental no less than physical.

Overwhelmed and unsettled, Eastern minds lost almost all national values, yet could not absorb Western values … Constitutions framed in the interest of the people of the Middle East became instruments for their exploitation and domination.

For Nasser (1955, 199), such exploitation and domination was both a product of colonial conquest as well as local feudal patterns of production that had, for centuries, exploited the Egyptian people. His analysis is encompassed in the following statement:

> Egypt's story in these years centres upon the effort to free the country from a foreign yoke and to find a policy capable of eradicating the evils accumulated by feudalism and compounded by misuse of governmental power. It was a long and painful search, Egyptians hoped for leaders to champion their cause and defend their interests, but politicians and factions for the most part made themselves subservient to the forces that were ravaging the country – British rulers, corrupt monarchs, feudal overlords, non-Egyptian ruling class and its Egyptian satellites.

British colonial rule had been manifest in a military occupation that remained even after formal independence in 1922, in the control of every government department, and in the economic exploitation of the country through what Nasser refers to as 'chartered monopolies'. Given this total control,

> Egypt had to pass through three revolutions, the Arabi revolution, the revolution of 1919 and the revolution of 1952. Any revolution which fails to realize its basic objectives inevitably lays the seeds for a subsequent uprising. Our national struggle was therefore one continual and unremitting battle, despite intermittent weaknesses. Always there were the two great objectives

– to check despotism and make the nation itself the source of powers, and to put an end to foreign intervention and the usurpation of Egypt's resources.

(Nasser, 1955: 202)

The 'concerns of the revolution' were hence sovereignty and with it the building up of a political economy of development. The Land Reform Bill aimed to 'liberate the bulk of peasants' from feudal control and the 'program for reconstruction' created a Board of Production charged with 'planning national productivity and outlining the new policy of large-scale industrialization,' aided through the financing of emerging industries and the provision of technologies necessary for such a programme (Nasser, 1955: 204).

The nationalisation of Suez must hence be seen as an act of resistance, the ultimate purpose of which was access to the modern international and the modern international political economy. It was the desire for access to the modern, and specifically the modern international as a distinct juridical/political space, and the modern international political economy that raised the ire of the former colonial powers, Britain and France. Eden and Guy Mollet, the French Prime Minister, wanted Nasser 'destroyed', in the words of the former. The detail of how these two conspired, with Israel's help, to retake Suez is not for the context of this book. What is significant, however, is that their actions underscore the point I am making here, namely an understanding of the postcolonial state as one that struggles to gain access to the modern international, first through the anti-colonial struggle that gains its sovereignty, however, more importantly, the subsequent struggle to assert and claim its place in the modern international. It was such a claim that led to the contrived coup against Kwame Nkrumah and that led to the invasion of Egypt in 1956. Even as subsequent histories of the postcolonial state narrate stories of failure and fragmentation, we might say that it is not these that constitute the postcolonial state, but every instance of that state's resistance in the face of continued juridical, political, and economic domination. That the desire to gain access was both an international and an internal fight was clearly recognised by these leaders who, in analyses reminiscent of Fanon, always claimed that the decolonisation process was of the psychological and the material. However, this effort was to be a distinctly modern discourse, one that clearly separated the modern from the traditional, hence Nkrumah's persistant calls for a secular Pan-Africanist ideaology, and Nasser's calls for a secular Pan-Arab ideology. There was no place here for tradition or the 'reactionary religious groups', as the latter labelled the Muslim Brotherhood.[35]

If the defining moment of the postcolonial state was its modernising, developmental imperative, then its point of departure was the design of a state apparatus the remit of which was the mobilisation of resources at once for the service of this imperative and for the establishment of legitimacy, the latter defined in terms of the hegemony of the national project. There was here an intricate negotiation between the modernising/developmental political economy and the building of political community. It is these two elements together, political economy and political community, that must be taken into account when thinking about the postcolonial state as agent of resistance in the modern international. The significance of this dual role of the international as it relates to the postcolonial state is perhaps nowhere more clearly shown than in Deepa Mehta's Hindi film, *Earth*, which depicts Jawaharlal Nehru's independence speech, made at midnight to India's Constituent Assembly, on the eve of India's independence on 14 August 1947. The film shows the main characters listening to the speech on the radio as Hindu-Muslim riots break out after the partition of India, pointing to the paradox of an emergent state, declared in English to the listening world beyond, while communities within burn.[36]

The predominant tendency in international relations, and specifically in realist and liberal thought, is to suggest that the postcolonial world as a whole and the postcolonial state in particular is somehow lagging behind European counterparts. This discourse seems to have no difficulty or even self-reflection on interpellating one of the economically strongest nations, Japan, as 'semi-sovereign',[37] or the vast majority of states in Asia, Africa, and the Middle East as 'failed states'. What is paradoxical, as far as the remit of this book is concerned, is that certain strands of postcolonial thought argue that sovereign statehood remains an alien concept to much of the postcolonial world the experience of which is far from the equalising effects of the Westphalian construct. The problem, however, is that these latter discourses appear to vindicate, if unintentionally, the idea that the non-Western state is somehow lagging behind or somehow not quite the real thing. The point, however, is to focus on how the postcolonial state and postcolonial populations interpret their positionality in relation to the international, and when looked at historically, access to the international affirms the anti-colonial struggle and the founding moment of liberation. What it also does is to impact on subsequent foundational moments, and the struggles towards the form that political community takes.

Does access to the international constitute political community within? Does the declaration of independence and hence the declaration of the founding moment construct the interpretative schema whereby the emergence of the national state onto the terrain of the international is related to another temporality, namely the constitution-making potentialities, the world-making potentialities of a future to come? As must be clear from the orientation of this book, my response to both questions is informed by negativity; the all too significant aporia between the postcolonial and the international is itself generative of potentiality. The notion of potentiality is suggestive of an uncapturable excess to the concepts constitutive of these interpretative schema. The object escapes easy categorisation so that the concept – for example, sovereignty, liberation, community – never manages to capture the object; the state, India, Egypt, Iraq, Ghana, a people, public space, postcolonial bodies, their boundaries and limits. The object is always already imbued with subjectivity, again not quite captured into categories even as our linguistic resources insist on such categories. However, what we do have is a conceptualisation that allows for the emergence of voice, of declaration, of claims made. Claiming the right to politics exceeds somehow the heteronomy of politics, and the heteronomy of the international. It might fall into the interstices of the structural inequalities of a capitalist global political economy and a hierarchically ordained international juridical-political system, inequalities and hierarchies sustained by structures of domination and their agents, with the complicities, often violently expressed, of postcolonial states and local interests. However, the subject of politics re-emerges somehow, claims a right to politics, enunciating the ever unfinished project of liberation. The claim to politics emerges in spaces of governmentality. These spaces might be constructed by the practices and apparatuses of the postcolonial state. They might, on the other hand be constituted by practices that originate elsewhere, through the discourses and institutional frameworks that are global in reach and impact upon the postcolonial state and the postcolonial subject. The 'conduct of conduct', to use Michel Foucault, can hence be directed at both the postcolonial state and at the wider postcolonial publics. Both remain subject to practices of government the origins of which remain outside their control. The aporetic relationship with the international remains so, with the continuities of the colonial legacy reinvigorated in late modernity, as will be seen in the next chapter, and with potentialities too, of forms of resistance that are world-making afresh, as will be shown in the final chapter.

5

GOVERNING OTHERS
War and operations of power in late modernity

> The tradition of the oppressed teaches us that the 'state of emergency' in which
> we live is not the exception but the rule.
>
> Walter Benjamin, *Theses on the Philosophy of History*

There is a powerful sense in which much of the postcolonial world is constructed
in ways that not only reinforce Western hegemony, but also analytically and
interpretatively misconstrue the international politics of non-Western states and
the concerns of their societies. Where realism applies its conceptual schema, from
state interests, to regional balances and the like, to areas of the postcolonial world
such as Asia, expecting particular behaviour patterns that might conform to its
edicts (Kang, 2003), liberalism as a school of thought also seeks to extend its
frameworks, using the assumptions of 'democratic peace theory' again to predict
conforming patterns in the international politics of postcolonial states (Muppidi,
2005). Where the former understands the place of postcolonial states in an
international order premised on the distribution of resources, the latter differentiates
states on the basis of their internal structures of governance. The stronger states in
the former are defined in terms of their regional influence, military superiority, and
reach, while the stronger in the latter are institutionally defined and, like their
realist counterparts, are conferred primacy in ensuring regional and hence
international order. Significantly, the construction of the postcolonial state in both
perspectives is based on conceptual schema that do not derive from local
understandings and local interpretations of what it means to engage in international
politics, in the constitution of international order, or the form that such order
should take. Regardless of their differences, what is of interest to the present
chapter is that both sets of understandings, as systems of knowledge, are implicated,
not just in the construction of the postcolonial world in particular ways, but in
practices that seek to govern the postcolonial world.

As shown in the last chapter, access to the international is constitutive of the
postcolonial subject who, upon such access, is also implicated in the transformation
of the international. The 'declaration of independence' comes to have a dual
constitutive role, in that access to the international is also directed at the constitution

of self, the self-identity of the postcolonial political community. The tropes of the international, from sovereignty to human rights, are used by postcolonial leaders and postcolonial citizens respectively in historic efforts to shape political community within, but also to reshape and transform the international as a distinctive realm of politics. This understanding of the postcolonial departs significantly from interpretations that view the international, and specifically sovereignty, as somehow alien concepts the origins of which lie with other, namely European, epistemes. Far from assuming an oppositional relationship between the postcolonial and the international, therefore, what I want to argue is that here we have an aporetic relationship, one that is at once suggestive of an 'incompatibility' or 'heterogeneity', but that is at the same time generative of future possibilities, relationships, and discourses.[1] In addition, the limits assumed in the structure of the international, limits suggestive of recognition and distinctive agency, are historically drawn upon by postcolonial states and populations in efforts at transforming structures of domination to which and through which they have been subject. Indeed it is the case, as will be highlighted in the next chapter, that postcolonial states and populations may respectively draw upon different discourses, suggesting a role for the international in emerging political contention related to the subject of politics and the reconstitution of postcolonial political community.

The aim in this chapter is to focus the lens on operations of power in late modernity, operations that are not only implicated in the transformation of the international, but have monumental impact on postcolonial polities and specifically those interpellated as resistant or non-conforming to practices of domination scripted elsewhere. What is significant about these operations is that they draw upon war, which then becomes a technology in the control of populations and their redesign as social entities. The corporeality of the other is hence the target and variously through its destruction, injury, distribution, and surveillance, is rendered subject to government. Much of this violence is pedagogically framed, so that those engaged in late modern operations of power over much of the postcolonial world, from states, their militaries, security, and development agencies, to non-governmental organisations, are conferred not just a protectionist role, but also one that is 'pastoral' in character (Foucault, 1982),[2] both elements in a self-legitimising discourse that assumes impunity and seeks to preclude the potential for resistance.

Operations of power in late modernity have a distinctly cosmopolitan character. Their spatial articulation often transcends the boundaries of the state, takes place in what we might refer to as transnational spaces constructed on local terrain, and is manifest through practices conducted by a diverse set of actors related in complex networks of relationships that often obscure the boundary between public and private, the state and market. In this complex 'matrix of war' (Jabri, 2007a), operations may involve state militaries, intelligence, and police forces; however, they may also be franchised to private operators, from security firms, to humanitarian non-governmental organisations, to management consultants. In this cosmopolitan terrain, as will be shown below, violence is interlaced with statebuilding and hence the government of populations. The normative discourse that sustains and legitimises these operations of power is also cosmopolitan in character, framed as it is in terms of human rights and the rescue of populations.

Insurgencies are hence no longer interpreted as being directed primarily against an incumbent government, but as resisting a globally sanctioned order of intervention the remit of which is the protection of humanity at large. Those who resist are hence resisting a globally articulated sovereign power the legitimacy of which is taken as the starting baseline from which categories of judgement and interpellation are derived. That power operates globally, that certain locations of power experience its operations through violence, that is, military force, and that power's claim to legitimacy seeks the domination of global discourses, suggest that forms of resistance to such power also see their remit of operations in global terms. The terrain of the global is hence replete with contestation even as many a liberal or indeed a neoliberal cosmopolitan might claim universal hegemony and hence legitimacy.

This chapter serves as a prelude to the next and hence as a point of anticipation for an exposition of how postcolonial agency, understood here as claiming the right to politics, operates in late modernity. Talk of resistance, as I highlight throughout this book, is a far more complex challenge than the unravelling of power and its operations, though even these, in their multiform articulations in discourses, institutions, and the microcosmic interstices of social and political life, present epistemological and ontological challenges that defy formulaic analysis, or indeed their capture in a framing device such as 'where there is power there is resistance'. The temptation is always to start with locations of resistance, for these would then reveal power and its practices. This is indeed Leila Abu Lughud's (1990) starting point in her ethnographic quest to uncover gendered modes of resistance in an Egyptian village. Here we see the intimate and intricate relationship between gendered subjectivities and articulations of power and resistance where even forms of dress are the materialisations of resistance to a patriarchal order that is sustained by the disciplining of the female's body and its locations, interactions, and modes of communication. The point to draw from Abu Lughud and one that has resonance for our purposes here is that power operates on bodies and in doing so generates modes of corporeal resistance.

I would not wish to stray too far from the Egyptian village and its corporeal ordering when thinking about articulations of resistance in contemporary global politics. For it is exactly through such corporeal ordering, its instantiation in the government of individuals and populations, that manifestations of resistance can be understood today. When considered in global terms, much contemporary discourses on resistance assume dichotomies and oppositions framed in terms of the liberal and the illiberal, the West and Islam, pro-globalisation and anti-globalisation, the technologically driven and the ecologically driven, and so on. There is also a discourse that takes as its starting point biopolitical power and social movements that seek to resist such power. My aim here is to move beyond such representations of power and resistance, as I argued in Chapter 3, and to present a picture of power and its discursive and material articulation that reveals to us the possibility or the potentiality of the subject who escapes capture. This subject emerges in the final chapter to the book, where we see the claim to politics made in the terrain of the late modern cosmopolitan, a form of agency that emerges in spaces of governmentality, but is at the same time creative, world-making. The claim to politics constitutes an imaginary of future potentialities, and significantly in the context of postcoloniality, ones that move the subject beyond the postcolonial.

When power is rendered cosmopolitan

Tracing postcolonial resistance from the anti-colonial struggles that led to decolonisation, to the postcolonial international that saw the postcolonial state emerge as agent of resistance and site of struggle, we see that both were and perhaps continue to be efforts at the building of political community, the constitution of political community, and the bringing it forth, rendered possible in an arena, the international, that must be conceived as the spatial articulation of this potentiality of politics beyond the local and the parochial. To access the international meant for leaders such as Nasser, Nkrumah, and Nehru the possibility of constructing, indeed designing, modern political community. If the ideological push was the developmental state then the struggle was over capturing the national state politically. While the international provided the spatial manifestation of such aspirations, its political economy rendered the all-too-important limits of the state and of political community vulnerable to the workings of transnational power, the practices of which worked at the nexus of the national and the international, the international and the transnational global. The postcolonial state's capacities for resistance, and hence for winning the legitimacy stakes in the building of political community, came face to face with the workings of power on what we might call cosmopolitan terrain.

Within realist discourse, power is predominantly about limiting or constraining the choices that states and their representatives can make in an international system, the dynamics of which are determined by the distribution of capabilities. What is interesting about this particular understanding of power is that the powerful are as subject to the workings of this structural feature of the international as are others, so that the difference, the inequality, within the system is immediately an element in the realist analytic. Liberal discourse, on the other hand, seeks to negate the inequality through a reading of the international wherein the juridical, the legislative force of rules and norms, becomes the great 'civiliser' of all.[3] The empirical fact of inequality is contained through the workings of law and hence a 'domesticated' international subject to the equalising remit of international law and normative structures applicable to all. Under liberalism, the international is not simply an international system of states, but is at the same time an international political economy and a terrain of humanity at large. The question of the international becomes a question of the government of the international, of states and markets, and of populations, their movements and interactions. Where realism places primacy on power, liberal discourse places primacy on regulation.[4] However, if we focus precisely on the question of how power operates through regulation, we begin to unravel the workings of liberal power globally, and specifically the normalising imperative of its discourses and institutions.

The global operations of power and their normalising imperative should not, however, simply be seen in unidirectional terms, for these have often worked through the medium of the postcolonial state. As highlighted in the last chapter, the postcolonial state has a significant presence in the lived experience of postcolonial societies and as such raises questions relating to its disjuncture with the subject of politics in postcoloniality. The capacities of the postcolonial state to establish legitimacy come to rely on the mediating role that the state can play between its developmental imperative and its participation in the international political economy. The problem, however, is that the postcolonial state is already overdetermined structurally, inheriting a powerful administrative/military apparatus that is then used to control and regulate social conflict. For Hamza Alavi, the postcolonial state is distinctly characterisd by the presence of what he refers to as a relatively autonomous bureaucratic-military oligarchy that is largely self-perpetuating and self-sustaining, both economically and politically, and that has a mediating role between international capital and local class interests.[5] We might therefore suggest, in anticipation of the next chapter, that the subject of politics in postcoloniality, the subject who claims the right to politics does so in this context, one that is interlaced with a powerful international and transnational intersection of interests. The bureaucratic-military oligarchy in much of the postcolonial world has indeed served to govern politics as such and raises questions about how it relates to external forces and their complicities in the government of the subject of politics. At the same time, the bureaucratic-military apparatus of the postcolonial state could also be rendered disposable when and if it is seen as no longer servicing global structures of domination and their political economy.

As highlighted earlier in this book and elsewhere, the postcolonial condition and the postcolonial subject emerge from a modernity that is predominantly defined by the colonial project. This project was not simply confined to the occupation and dispossession of the colonised, but was also consistently legitimised by reference to 'civilisation' and its European genesis. But for this 'civilising mission', the non-European world would be confined to barbarism, ignorance, and prejudice.[6] In discourses that clearly have their contemporary articulations, the West is at once both author and legislator of what may count as worthy of recognition, from populations, to languages, to histories, to rights, to political community. The non-West is hence interpellated in discourse as a form of negation suggestive of a perpetual lack that impedes self-definition and self-determination, even in a postcolonial context. Given this all too powerful discursive context, it is not too difficult to see how, in the contemporary period, societies are being re-defined, re-shaped in ways reminiscent of the old colonial order. Modern Iraq could in this sense be bombed back to a medieval sectarian divide based on an ethnic/sectarian division of the population the construction of which had its genesis in the capitals of the invading Western powers and, as seen earlier, in the colonial offices of Britain as the former colonial power in Iraq. The rationality of 'peacebuilding' is similarly based on the premise that while Western-led institutions and organisations possess the capacities, moral and material, to re-shape other societies, those recipient societies themselves are not only lacking in such capacities, but in history, memory, or indeed frameworks of knowledge.[7] This universalising imperative of modern rationality is, when viewed from the perspective of the non-West, a source of subjugation, dispossession, and violent conquest.

When power is rendered cosmopolitan, its technologies of control are drawn from and seek to regulate the discursive and the material terrain of the international and its political economy. As a distinctly modern rationality, its imperative is the government of the socio-political and economic aspects of life and its transformation into a bureaucratic, calculable, and manageable terrain the primary objective of which is the regulation, and through such, the diminution of social conflict. The historical trajectory of the modern European state is hence the model par excellence and indeed comes to define the baseline through which all societies' experience of modernity is measured. How this modernity is articulated institutionally in the postcolonial world, however, differs from the European context. Nevertheless, the imperative of the liberal cosmopolitan project is defined by its capacity to render its modern and modernising rationality universal. This modernising rationality, as we saw in the last chapter, found local articulation in the anti-colonial and postcolonial discourses that sought to emancipate the formerly colonised from structures of domination, political and economic. However, judged according to liberal measures of success and failure, the postcolonial state's conformity with a liberal international political economy, and its capacity to govern social conflict and antagonism, become powerful signifiers of 'emergence'. Consequently, the failure of the modern state postcolonially is a failure that can only be rectified through the introduction of governing practices the genesis of which lies elsewhere.

The distinctive aspect of liberal cosmopolitanism is not, however, confined to the reinstitution of governing capacities to the postcolonial state. For, the constitutive element that renders such universalising power cosmopolitan is that it seeks its legitimacy not from the target population, though this may be an outcome, but the wider global terrain and its institutions. This is a political rationality that is not confined to one particular state, but is a wider apparatus driven by a complex network of institutions that can be national, international, and transnational, and sustained and reinforced by its own normative logic. This apparatus is reproduced not just by a set of discourses that are 'liberal' in orientation, but more crucially, by a material political economy that rewards the agents involved in its operating practices. Understanding liberal cosmopolitanism in this way provides a distinctly different picture to that proffered by liberal constructivists, whose primary message relates to the 'successful' permeation of liberal norms in international relations.[8]

What are the conditions of possibility that render liberal cosmopolitanism hegemonic? The difficulty for any politics of contestation, and especially one that emanates from the postcolonial world and extends outwards, globally, is that the condition of late modernity has come to be defined as the dissolution of limits, so that the emergence of social antagonism is interpreted as an aberration rather than being potentially expressive of grievance. Any discourse suggestive of antagonism is one that is immediately rendered 'radical' and 'exterior' to the rational. Where the leaders of the anti-colonial struggles of the past had, by and large, been informed by a statist, or even a Left political agenda, the political positionality of the postcolonial state in the late modern context could no longer be seen as constituting an alternative political agenda.[9] With the triumph of neoliberalism and globally institutionalised demands for the opening of markets and for deregulation, the legitimacy of the national state was now inextricably defined in terms of its capacities for upholding the welfare of its citizens either against the imperatives of the global marketplace or in adaptation to a neoliberal global order within which the postcolonial state could be a full participant. While such a construction seems to suggest a rather stark choice for postcolonial societies, it nevertheless brings into sharp relief the forces, indeed the structures, within which the national state could manoeuvre its positionality in an international political economy already overdetermined asymmetrically. This positionality is at the same time related to the contingencies of an international political context wherein the decolonising imperative of the postcolonial state and its population come face to face with late modern articulations of a continuing colonial rationality that discursively and materially places its target populations in continued relations of asymmetry.

Despite this asymmetrical positioning, the 'pull' of liberal cosmopolitanism, as a political rationality, does not immediately support a framing that places it in an antagonistic relation with postcolonialism, if the latter is read as a distinctive political rationality rather than as merely a condition. When *post*colonialism is considered as a political rationality, then its defining constitutive feature is its decolonising imperative – that societies of the postcolonial world must be self-determining in a context of an international political order defined by the modern international and modern understandings of the self-determining political community. This self-determination is here conceptualised in terms of political community with defined limits and boundaries, but one nevertheless that is historically contested and not monolithic. The postcolonial rationality could hence also be understood in terms of the contested frameworks of meaning on the question of what constitutes political community as such. Articulations of the political must hence be understood not just in relation to the postcolonial state, but also in relation to the claims of the international political order, the international political economy, and in relation to the transnational terrain of the human. Each of these is a terrain of contestation that can pitch the liberal cosmopolitan rationality in opposition to a postcolonial rationality. We witnessed in the previous chapter how this became manifest in relation to the postcolonial national state and its negotiations of sovereignty over resources, where the international and its political economy were/are implicated. Now in the present, in a late modern context that places in sharp relief the tension between the demands of a transnational terrain of humanity and an international order defined by sovereign statehood, the role of the postcolonial state as mediating force between the international and its citizenry is significantly diminished. Liberal cosmopolitanism as a political rationality seemingly provides the link, according to many a liberal, between the terrain of the human and its constitutive discourses and the terrain of citizenry, especially where the postcolonial state is or indeed becomes, the apparatus that, in the most immediate sense, suppresses the local population through direct violence, incarceration, and widespread practices of exclusion and discrimination.

The hegemony of liberal cosmopolitan discourses and practices derives first and foremost from its discursive framing. The concept that provides us with a picture of how liberal cosmopolitanism operates is 'solidarity'. While this is a widely used concept in the field of international relations,[10] its significance for the analysis of the hegemony of liberal cosmopolitanism has not been investigated. When the concept is used in this field, especially in normative discourse, it is defined as the articulation of support and responsibility towards members of other societies, thereby invoking the tensions that might arise, both theoretically and praxiologically, in operations that lie at the nexus between an international system of states and a transnational realm of humanity that is brought forth, indeed constituted by every articulation of solidarity that transcends state boundaries. Such articulation is built on the assumption that the realm of the international, defined in terms of sovereign statehood, is indeed challenged by another realm, that of the human, and the nexus between the two is the field of operations for liberal cosmopolitanism.

The 'international', as argued earlier in this book, is a distinctly modern construct, historically defined in terms of relations between sovereign states, relations constitutive of an international order the primary juridical-political linchpin of which is sovereignty. Realism and liberal internationalism accept this understanding of the modern international, and both attribute distinctiveness to the international as a juridical-political domain. Indeed regardless of transformations that seek to limit the sovereignty of the state, and regardless of the contested claims around the supposed artifice of sovereignty, nevertheless the concept and what it enables are deeply sedimented and indeed structurated into the discourses and institutional practices of the international, practices that include the inter-state as well as those that transcend the state (Bartelsen, 1995; Walker, 1993, 2010). Practices constitutive of a cosmopolitan terrain are hence always defined in terms of their implications for the international and its ever-shifting limits. If the very definition of the postcolonial as a condition is constitutively meaningful only in relation to the modern international, then any practice that shifts the limits of the international at the same time impinges upon the limits of the postcolonial. How does liberal cosmopolitanism affect the limits of postcoloniality as a condition?

Liberal cosmopolitanism and the government of populations

The profound achievement of the modern period is that it witnesses the consolidation of the international as a distinctive political sphere, albeit one that is inextricably linked to intra-European warfare and ultimately the European colonial project. As a distinctly modern construct, the international comes to be historically defined in terms of relations between sovereign states and the juridical–political practices constitutive of an international order of states. State sovereignty comes to form the linchpin of modern political subjectivity, modern conceptions of political community, the underpinning principal of international law, and aspirations within Europe and beyond towards self-determination based on the secular political nation, aspirations that saw their strongest manifestation in the French and American revolutions,[11] each an instance wherein the subject of politics comes to be defined in terms of the emerging, sovereign, political community. The question for the subject of postcolonial politics is always, as argued by Dipesh Chakrabarty (1992: 20), whether she/he can escape the concepts that both emerge from and constitute modernity, concepts that limit historical discourse and representation. Sovereignty, subjectivity, and indeed modernity frame the limits of the possible so that it is difficult to write a history of the present without always already predetermining that history. For Chakarabarty, the quest to 'provincialise Europe'

> does not call for a simplistic , out-of-hand rejection of modernity, liberal values, universals, science, reason, grand narratives, totalizing explanations, and so on. Frederic Jameson has recently reminded us that the easy equation often made between 'a philosophical conception of totality' and 'a political practice of totalitarianism' is 'baleful'. What intervenes between the two is history – contradictory, plural, and heterogeneous struggles whose outcomes are never predictable, even retrospectively, in accordance with schema that seek to naturalize and domesticate this heterogeneity.

The point, for Chakrabarty, is not to espouse a 'cultural relativism', or the idea that the postcolonial subject might be understood through different conceptual schema that are culturally defined. Rather, it is to locate that which is taken to be 'obvious' in historical contingency.

As foremost political sociologists have shown, the story of European modernity and specifically the modern European state is of the consolidation of the state through the extension of its power over a specified territory and population. War played a major part in the pacification of these populations, in relations between states, and in enabling colonial dispossession (Tilly, 1990; Mann, 1993; Giddens, 1985). The modern period at the same inaugurated a modern conception of humanity and its positive articulation in laws of war and humanitarian law, from the Hague Conventions, to the Geneva Conventions, and later through the Universal Declaration of Human Rights, and conventions against genocide, torture, race and gender discrimination, all forming a discourse of rights and obligations that is now globally acknowledged, though differentially ratified. The modernity of the international and its political economy were now pitched in a tense relationship with the claims of humanity as such, claims that were and continue to be increasingly directed not just at the institutions of the state but also of the modern international. While the domestication of heterogeneity, historically often violent, is associated with the emergence of the modern state – and indeed this finds articulation in the modern postcolonial state – then such practices of domestication also find their violent expression in the context of late modernity. The targets of such practices tend to be located in the postcolonial world, drawing on the trope of 'humanity' in the discourses of legitimisation that sustain and perpetuate such practices. The 'government' of the formerly colonised by others is firmly back on the global political agenda.

The assumption that liberalism bases its ontological foundations on a universally conceived autonomous self belies the historical and cultural specificity of this particular project and its political economy. This historical specificity, when rendered in global terms, comes to assume humanity within its purview of operations, thereby transcending the domestic/international divide, transforming political conflict and antagonism into procedural problems that require resolution or indeed management. The articulation of liberalism as a cosmopolitan project places a distinctly liberal conception of solidarity at the heart of its operations, such that the focus is on the requisite juridical–political–economic structures that enable the realisation of free and equal individuality irrespective of the signifying divide of state or culture. The remit of law, the international political economy, and political institutions are hence no longer subject to the limiting remit of the sovereign state, but extend beyond, into a wider polity of humankind. The binding discursive and juridical thread is a positive conception of rights and its materialisation is in global institutions such as the International Criminal Court and its statute, the European Convention on Human Rights, the Universal Declaration of Human Rights, the UN Convention Against Torture, and a wider body of humanitarian law, all constitutive of a modern conception of humanity as a location of a positive legal and political structure that can call illiberal practices and their perpetrators to account. Thus is Habermas's Cosmopolitan Law brought into force, with every instance of intervention to uphold rights in the name of humanity. In this liberal cosmopolitan worldview, the individual self is no longer subject to the state and its actions, but has this wider legal and political connection constitutive of a machinery of protection and, potentially, of a wider global public sphere that foregrounds local struggles against oppressive and exclusionary practices.[12]

There is much in the liberal cosmopolitan discourse that suggests what Balibar (2002) refers to as an already existing universalism, one that is instantiated through every transnational interaction that is not only manifest in the globalisation of the means of production and exchange, but through discourses that are indeed cosmopolitan in their orientation. Such universalism is not necessarily derived from a Kantian metaphysics, but is materialised through practices and in spaces that are not easily reducible to the local and the national. These spaces are at once both local and global, wherein interactions take place across cultures, languages, aesthetics, currencies, and where affiliations might be transitory, expressive of the distinctiveness of the global city, or of a hybrid subjectivity where the here and the elsewhere are precariously negotiated. As Doreen Massey (2005) highlights, these cosmopolitan spaces are implicated in the production of subjectivities that are not just reflective of 'hybridity', but of a more complex materialised, embodied, subjectivity that is not just constituted in these cosmopolitan social spaces, but is implicated in their reconstitution.

This already existing universalism emanating from the many locales of globalisation does not, however, suggest the triumph of liberal cosmopolitanism as a distinctly political project, nor does it suggest a form of depoliticisation seen by many as the constitutive feature of liberal internationalism as such.[13] As a distinctly political project, the constitutive features of liberal cosmopolitanism do not seek the diminution of the state as such, but rather its reformulation into one the institutions of which cohere with a modern conception of political community based on the rule of law and a free and equal public sphere and situated within a matrix of global juridical regulation that can, in exceptional circumstances, pitch cosmopolitan right against sovereign right. This post-Westphalian ordering, or indeed, re-ordering of the world is emergent from and is constitutive of global articulations of solidarity emanating from social movements, states, and populations, and is hence not easily reducible to the actions of states. How then, can such a seemingly emancipatory project as a framework of thinking and of practice be vulnerable to a postcolonial critique that touches the core of its transformative potential? Is liberal cosmopolitanism a target of resistance or can it be a vehicle through which resistance against tyrannical rule can take place? Both questions go to the heart of the question of what constitute postcolonial political agency in the late modern era where much of this transformation has already taken place and where large tracts of the postcolonial world are already full, albeit not equal, participants.

An alternative reading suggests that what might appear as an emancipatory political project is in fact complicit in the reproduction of structures of domination that perpetuate violence, poverty, and inequality in a global political economy that enriches the few and impoverishes the many. For critics of liberalism, liberal cosmopolitanism is the legitimising arm of a rampant neoliberal order based on the primacy of the global market and the requisite diminution of the state's capacities to regulate the process of production in accordance to local fiscal practices that place priority with local welfare over and above corporate profit margins. For David Harvey, there is a telling correspondence between the emergence of a rights discourse and the primacy of neoliberalism as a global project: 'Human rights issues came to prominence after 1980 and positively boomed after the events in Tiananmen Square and the end of the Cold War in 1989. This corresponds exactly with the trajectory of neoliberalization, and the two movements are deeply implicated in each other' (Harvey, 2007: 176). Just as rights discourses have prevailed with this neoliberal trajectory, according to Harvey, so has the exponential increase in the number of so-called advocacy groups and NGOs claiming to represent the rights of the dispossessed and the excluded where the state has withdrawn social provision. For Harvey, these NGOs

> claim and presume to speak on behalf of those who cannot speak for themselves, even define the interests of those they speak for (as if people are unable to do this for themselves). But the legitimacy of their status is always

open to doubt. When, for example, organizations agitate successfully to ban child labour in production as a matter of universal human rights, they may undermine economies where that labour is fundamental to family survival ... The universality presupposed in 'rights talk' and the dedication of the NGOs and advocacy groups to universal principles sits uneasily with the local particularities and daily practices of political and economic life under the pressures of commodification and neoliberalization.

(Harvey, 2007: 179)

The appeal to rights is hence a dialectical force, emancipatory on the one hand and limiting or even exclusionary on the other. At the same time, and as equally acknowledged by Harvey, neoliberalisation is itself differentially experienced and hence unequal in its realisation and consequences, between regions, states, and certainly within states. When the Indian state, in late modernity, comes to be a fully engaged participant in the global neoliberal marketplace and it seeks to extend the economic potentials to its vast population, it introduces measures that aim to modernise through educational provision. The introduction of a legislative order that seeks to render compulsory educational provision to the age of fourteen might suggest that such modernisation is indeed emancipatory in its inclusive scope. However, according to Ashis Nandy, this same provision means the deprivation of the artisanal class of valuable child labour that ensures the survival of families in deprived localities.[14]

It is not that 'humanism' as such is rejected as being somehow in the providence of the West, for the appeal to humanity is also of other socio-religious and cultural formations wherein concerns are expressed for social justice and the protection of populations. For it is the case that the cosmopolitan worldview is narrated across regions and cultures, from Diogenes in ancient Greece, to Ibn Khaldun in the Near East, to Tagore in South Asia. The idea of the cosmopolitan as a form of being that is at once of the world and of locality is also evocative of an ethos of mutual recognition, inter-connection, and ethical commitment that is found in ancient and modern texts as well as across geographic space in the contemporary era. Seen in this light, cosmopolitanism is largely an ethos, a normative discourse that is worldly in its orientation, expressive of an openness to difference and a hospitality towards the stranger. Cosmopolitanism becomes controversial when it is defined as political project and here the choice appears stark: between a liberal cosmopolitanism premised on the authorship of the liberal West and hence expressive of a colonial rationality articulated and practiced in late modernity, and a 'political cosmopolitanism' of solidarity that does not speak *for* others.[15] Where the first expresses a politics of governmental rationality, the second expresses a politics of solidarity and hence one based on political mobilisation. Liberal cosmopolitanism becomes a problem for the postcolonial world precisely when its defining feature is the government of populations, for it is through such government that, not just the postcolonial state, but postcolonial political community is undermined.

The genealogical background to liberal cosmopolitanism is located in the Enlightenment period and its defining feature, namely the emergence of criticism and opposition to the absolutist state. The Kantian rendition on cosmopolitanism is indeed one that sees cosmopolitan right as a system of security that places limits on the state, both internally in terms of the rights of the individual self and externally in terms that potentially render such rights the responsibility of humanity as a whole. The project of the Enlightenment was hence worldly in its orientation, and as highlighted by Stephen Toulmin, forming the backdrop to a cosmopolitical orientation that sought to 'bind the world' in a political-theological sense, but also in an epistemological sense.[16] This latter aspect of the cosmopolitical reinforced the idea that human progress was built on the rise of science and technology, that knowledge of the world and its resources were within the remit of Europe, indeed that the European subject could not just access the world, but make the world available to the gaze and use of the European. The great exhibitions, highlighted by Timothy Mitchell, provide testimony to this cosmopolitan outlook, one that established the world as the empirical object domain for the European subject.[17] With the dawn of modernity comes an ethos that establishes Europe as sovereign geopolitically and epistemologically, so that a project that came to be defined in terms of Enlightenment at home, the test case of which was the rejection of the absolutist state, came at the same time to project Europe's power outward, into the societies and territories of others.

For postcolonial authors, as has already been highlighted, the liberalism that is assumed to be at the heart of the project of modernity was made possible through practices of dispossession that defined colonial expansion. Indeed the very transformation of power that Michel Foucault attributes to the European context – a shift away from a sovereignty-defined juridical-political articulation of power towards more sophisticated, more modern and scientific modes of government based on calculative rationality – can only be comprehensible when juxtaposed with operations of power by the colonial state and the violence of its military-policing regime. Just as European societies were undergoing the consolidation of democratic and republican socio-political formations, with a defining role for emerging public spheres, the colonial context was being subjected to the curtailment and indeed outright prevention of political expression and the design of political institutions. If colonial domination was to succeed, the emergence of political community authored by the colonised could not take place. The 'dialectic of enlightenment' suggestive of the promise of modernity on the one hand and its consequences in lived experience on the other was clearly felt in class relations in the European context, but it was multiplied in the colonial context where modernisation schemes and projects took place through violent acts of dispossession – of territory, natural resources, labour, history, and the right to politics. This was indeed the context of 'accumulation through dispossession'. Its parallels in the contemporary late modern context are all-too-present.[18]

Can liberal cosmopolitanism be considered a project of solidarity, or is it more appropriately conceived as a project that has discomforting parallels with the colonial legacy, that is indeed dependent on this legacy? With authors who do conceive of this as a project of solidarity, we find inherent hierarchies that differentiate between the liberal self of global reach and the local 'recipient' or target of liberal largess (see Halliwell and Hindess, 2002). The transformation of the juridical structure of the international from one based on the sovereignty of the state to what Habermas refers to as cosmopolitan law, transcendent of the state, and based on the rights of individuals and communities enshrined in human rights law, humanitarian law and the laws of war, is dependent on the practices of states and societies deemed to be in possession of the 'moral resources' to drive progress towards a cosmopolitan order. For Linklater (1998), societies that exhibit such moral resources share three features; namely constitutional modes of governance, democratic accountability, and 'sophisticated' understandings of dialogical communicative practices. This conception of the location of agency for cosmopolitan transformation is present in Habermas on whose 'discourse ethics' Linklater relies. In Habermas, cosmopolitan law comes to be instantiated in every intervention that takes place in the name of human rights and their protection. Such interventions, Kosovo and Sierra Leone are examples, are seen as potentially sanctioned by an international community represented through the UN or, for Habermas, NATO. Such legitimisation is seen to be crucial in a context where intervention might take place in the service of particularistic state or regime interests, as was the case in Iraq.[19] Irrespective of this differentiation, it is evident that while Habermas seeks the equalising force of law as the pacifier of nations, there is nevertheless a hierarchical conception related to the agents of change and their transformative capacity. Where such capacity can be mobilised in the name of rights, and where every protection of such rights, even in situations of militarised intervention, instantiates the forthcoming transformation in law, then the agency of such transformation is located in states that indeed are in possession of global reach, the liberal West and its organisations, both military and non-governmental. As witnessed in cases such as Bosnia and East Timor, such authority might derive from international institutions and/or non-governmental organisations engaged in what is in actually an international civil service that takes charge of governance functions in conflict ridden societies. However, the overwhelming capacity for intervention, and one that Habermas appears to confer constitutive standing in relation to law, is military, and the cases of Kosovo, Iraq, and Afghanistan bear testimony to the military's central role in the disciplining, governance, and ultimately reshaping of these societies. This is the 'liberal way of war' (Dillon and Reid, 2010) and its function is not simply the defeat of an enemy, but the government of populations.

It is exactly this aspect of late modern articulations of power – the government of populations – that comes into full view when considered from the viewpoint of the postcolonial world, for it is this world that has been subject to its operations. In both juridical and governmental terms, cosmopolitanism has profound consequences for societies the emergence of which was based on the modern understanding of sovereignty as political self-determination. The government of populations comes to constitute a legitimate sphere of operations in a politics of protection that confers not just legitimacy but also impunity to the 'protector' and negates the potential of agency in the 'protected' (Jabri, 2007a; Orford, 2003). This hierarchical relationship is at the core of the impunities defining interventionist warfare, as we will see below, but also informs the idea that the agents of liberal cosmopolitan transformation possess the material and epistemological capacities for the government of others.

Such material and epistemological capacities are in turn reinforced by the liberal standpoint which confers to itself the legitimacy to act on behalf of humanity. There is, in other words, an assumed liberal consensus that is drawn upon in the legitimisation of practices of government that have global reach, that seek to permeate the societies of others. Acting on behalf of humanity, the remit of liberal cosmopolitanism is immediately universal, assuming a legitimacy taken to derive from this universal space. If this universal space is taken as being uncontested, then the architect of this space, the liberal self, is by definition the embodiment of humanity as such, and its capacities for progress, civilisation, and justice. The enactment of violence by this liberal subject in the name of humanity is then by definition self-constitutively legitimate. There is no negativity here, no space for contestation, none for the uncapturable, for here is the totality encompassed by the universal, materialised in time and space and through such materialisation enacting a foreclosure of other subjectivities, other discourses and histories, other relationships to time and space. The self-constituting legitimisation is so complete that what can be seen as a wholesale dispossession is perpetually articulated as emancipatory in this liberal cosmopolitan view of things.

Most discourses on liberal cosmopolitanism focus variously on the normative or the juridical aspect of this project. However, when conceived as a practice of government, questions emerge relating to legitimacy: is this the legitimacy of the governed or the legitimacy of the governing? The hierarchical conception of subjectivities highlighted above would suggest the latter as the formative moment in a self-attributed moral authority deriving, as we have seen above, from a combination of institutional and material resources that confer legitimacy to acts that seek to govern others. This is then a discourse of legitimisation that, to use Gayatry Spivak's terms, 'forecloses' the subjectivity of the other; in this case the governed. Let us revisit Spivak's words to underline the extent to which the voice of the governed is simply not a presence in calculations or indeed reflections of legitimacy in the cosmopolitanism of government that I am defining here. Spivak derives the term 'foreclosure' from Lacan, who in turn traces the concept to Freud. She quotes the psychoanalytic 'lexicon', as she puts it, in drawing from Laplanche and Potalis's *The Language of Psycho-analysis*:

> the sense brought to the fore by Lacan ... [is to be found] for instance, in [what] Freud writes ... [about] 'a much more energetic and successful kind of defence. Here the ego rejects (verwirft) the incompatible idea *together with the affect* and behaves as if the idea had never occurred to the ego at all.' ... The work from which Lacan has most readily derived support for his ... idea of foreclosure is the case-history of the 'Wolf-Man'. Foreclosure comes to have an 'inner-outer switch: an internal withdrawal of cathexis ... that becomes a 'disavowal ... of the real external world.'

In Lacan, as highlighted by Spivak, 'what has been foreclosed from the Symbolic reappears in the Real'. Foreclosure comes to encompass two operations, 'introduction into the subject' and 'expulsion from the subject'. Framing this in Lacanian terms, Spivak points out that the 'Real is or carries the mark of that expulsion'. Then in a statement that has much resonance here, she states, 'I think of the "native informant" as a name for that mark of expulsion from the name of Man – a mark crossing out the impossibility of the ethical relation' (Spivak, 1999: 5–6).

This 'mark of expulsion' is the enabling trope that bestows to the cosmopolitanism of government that self-constituting mark of legitimacy that derives from the governing, foreclosing the governed – he/she who is both needed and foreclosed. For Spivak, the 'native informant' as a concept is derived from ethnography. She states:

> In that discipline, the native informant, although denied autobiography as it is understood in the NorthWestern European tradition (codename 'West'), is taken with utmost seriousness. He (and occasionally she) *is* a blank, though generative of a text of cultural identity that only the West (or a Western-model discipline) could inscribe.
>
> *(Spivak, 1999: 6)*

If such foreclosure is the legitimising force enabling the cosmopolitanism of government, its machinery is not confined to the discursive, but is, rather, embodied in an institutionalised, bureaucratised apparatus, both civilian and military, the remit of which is the management of populations primarily through the regulation of their conflicts and, therefore, ultimately their politics.

This machinery of government seeks to regulate the state both internally and externally, and to shape or constitute the state in terms of these limits. The remit is not simply the imposition of juridical limits on dangerous states, but the re-shaping of their polities. How practices are targeted is contingent upon discourses that variously attribute dangerousness to target states and their agencies, or to populations and the dangerous elements contained therein. When cosmopolitanism is understood as a practice of government, it differentiates between the governing and the governed, where the former are conferred the authority to act, while the latter become the recipients of action, or indeed its targets. The terms of reference of such government are no longer limited by the boundaries of the sovereign state or indeed the frameworks of regulation defined by a system of relations between sovereign states. Driven by the imperative of security, its terms of reference are based on distinctions drawn between those who can govern and those who must be subject to government, those who conform to a global liberal order and those who must be trained into conformity with this order (Dean, 1999; Hindess, 2004; Jabri, 2011). The governing and the governed are hierarchically placed, though the latter is always drawn upon in the effort to render 'local' practices the genesis of which lies elsewhere.

The relationship between government and legitimacy, or the self-constituting legitimacy that I highlight here, is hence derived from a foreclosure of the governed, in essence their expulsion from the realm of the political. Such foreclosure is made possible, or is enabled by the hierarchical construction of subjectivities based on a discursive grammar of protection that entails not just a moral positioning that accrues universal agency over progress, civilisation, rights, but also an impunity wherein the governing are not at the same time the sources of injury. Such self-actualisation is further enabled through discourses and practices that interpellate liberal cosmopolitanism as a practice of security, one that is not simply geared towards the security of the state, but of humanity at large. In so ascribing to itself a remit of security, this articulation of government inscribes populations it governs as sources of danger so that the machinery of its technologies come to constitute an apparatus of security that can enact what such apparatuses do – punishment, incarceration, confinement and the rounding-up of populations and individuals, the control of access to pre-defined spaces, the building of barriers through the midst of neighbourhoods, the determination of the distribution of resources and the regulation of movement, the un-trammeled surveillance of households and public spaces, all conducted in other people's countries.

It is hence not too difficult to see this mode of government as being reflective of a colonial rationality of domination and dispossession. While this rationality has been witnessed in recent times, especially in the invasion and occupation of Iraq, the ongoing occupation of Afghanistan, the cosmopolitanism of government has a far wider and deeper remit. Interpreted as an 'art of government', to borrow from Michel Foucault, the cosmopolitanism of government includes within its parameters strategies that seek to shape, and indeed re-shape, not simply the juridical remit of the international, but individuals and populations. The implications are hence not confined to the juridical limits of state sovereignty, but incorporate the shaping of the self and of populations. As Foucault argues, the contours of liberal rule might best be conceived in the form of a 'triangle, sovereignty-discipline-government, which has as its primary target the population and as its essential mechanism the apparatuses of security' (Foucault, 2001a: 219). Cosmopolitanism might hence be conceptualised in terms of strategies that variously target states, individuals, and populations; strategies that are historically conditioned and hence in themselves governed by contingent institutional and discursive formations. These strategies might then be conceived as being constitutive of subjectivity, generating particular identities and indeed working through these identities.

From the postcolonial viewpoint, the security apparatus that reaches deep into the government of postcolonial populations presents a situation wherein the very foundation of their capacity for self-determination comes under threat. While this is at first hand a juridical-political question, it is in fact the historical-sociological aspect of the government of populations that is of even greater consequence, for here we have a condition of dissociation between government and legitimacy. Where the postcolonial national state in the immediate aftermath of independence drew its legitimacy from the anti-colonial struggle, thereby enabling the developmental state a certain manoeuvrability in relation to capital, here in this late modern context where, in many locations of postcoloniality, the state's capacity to govern is supplanted by external others, state and non-state, the nexus between government and legitimacy is broken. As will be shown in the following chapter, this consequence of the liberal interventionism has significance when considering the articulation of resistance in late modernity. Suffice it to argue at the present juncture that the cosmopolitanism of government – interventions aimed at governing others – in its discourses of rescue and protection, seeks to de-politicise others exactly through its focus on the management of populations. Its interventions reduce political contention to technocratic problems of governance thereby extracting the question of legitimacy from the terrain of the postcolonial state and ultimately of the potential of political community based on public deliberation and discourse.

The problem of legitimacy can, according to advocates of liberal cosmopolitanism, be resolved through the emergence or indeed creation of what Habermas (2001) refers to as a 'post-national constellation' or Ann-Marie Slaughter and John Ikenberry refer to as a 'Concert of Democracies'.[20] Both see such constellations as the defining moments of an emergent cosmopolitan law that would underwrite a global order wherein societies would be expected to come to 'PAR' ("Popular, Accountable, and Right-regarding' to use Slaughter and Ikenberry), measured in terms of their record in relation to human rights and democratic governance. This cosmopolitan architecture would be guaranteed and indeed brought into force by states that have the capacities, as seen above, to implement projects of government globally conceived. The question of legitimacy comes up again in relation to the idea of a 'multi-layered citizenship' made by those who aspire towards post-national political community. Where traditionally in liberal political thought, citizenship arises from a social contract authored by the citizens themselves, in the context of cosmopolitan citizenship, it is only the few – those in possession of global capacity – who define the limits and remits of what constitutes universal space. This bifurcation of the world into those conferred the legislative authority to re-configure international space and those not in possession of such authority is superimposed by another hierarchical division that sees the former as sources of security and the latter as distinct sources of threat.[21] Cosmopolitanism as a practice of security can hence draw on coercive/violent as well as pedagogical and juridical tools in its government of populations.

Cosmopolitan re-configurations of international space find expression in both discursive and material terms – discursively in relation to articulations of humanity and the transcendence of territorial sovereignty, and materially in relation to emergent institutionalised frameworks of regulation and government in the name of humanity. The rationality of the cosmopolitan government of other populations is 'protectionist' in its framing, being based variously on the model of policing and pedagogy. From NATO's intervention in Bosnia and the establishment of the Office of the High Representative, to the invasion and occupation of Iraq, to the intervention and military presence in Afghanistan, to a global and transnationally defined security apparatus defining the so-called 'war on terror', to various practices that come under the remit of 'peacebuilding' and 'development aid', all are manifestations of practices of protection wherein populations are divided into those who 'protect' and those that are recipients of such protection. In this world of cosmopolitan government, there is no distinction between war and welfare, so that the bombardment of a village in one instance might be followed, or even accompanied by, the building of a school in another. Both are deemed to be protectionist, and any civilian casualties considered collateral or 'regrettable'.

Violence and the government of populations

Slavoj Zizek (2004: 50–52), writing in the immediate aftermath of the invasion of Iraq, focuses on the question of the reasons for opposing the war, and acknowledges that there were plenty; that the Iraqis should have been left to deal with Saddam's tyranny themselves, that Western values should and could not be imposed on others, that the resources of others should not be plundered, that proclaimed reasons for the war as a counter-terrorist operation would only see terrorism realised as a consequence of war, that Islamic fundamentalism in particular would be reinforced as a political force in the Islamic world. Each is considered, but found wanting as a rallying call against this particular war. He states:

> But, although all this is true, the attack was wrong – and it was *who did it* that made it wrong. The question should be: who are you to do this? The question is not one of war or peace, it is the well-founded 'gut feeling' that there was something terribly wrong with this war, that something will change irretrievably as a result of it.

Borrowing from Lacan, Zizek focuses on the speaker who makes claims; in this case the 'USA' and the Bush Administration. Even if its claims were true, in particular its claim that Saddam held weapons of mass destruction (we now know he did not, but that is not the point here), 'it is still false with regard to the position from which (the claim) is enunciated'. This position was/is about transforming the international into a global order wherein the limits that the 'international' as such constitutes and is constituted by are dissolved or even redrawn. In Zizek's (2004) words, 'Are we aware that we are in the midst of a "soft revolution", in the course of which the unwritten rules determining the most elementary international logic are changing?'

Something had indeed changed irretrievably as a result of the war, more accurately, the invasion of Iraq. From the 'shock and awe' bombardment of the Iraqi population, to the public displays of Iraqi prisoners clad in hoods, hands bound, crouching in lines often several rows deep, to the displays of torture and abuse of Iraqi prisoners at Abu Ghraib, to the public display of Iraqi bodies killed, to the public storming of households, to the use of collective punishment against entire Iraqi towns and villages, to the constructions of road blocks subjecting Iraqis to control edicts at the very least and the occasional shooting at random in the worst cases, to forms of everyday punishment aimed purely at humiliation, to the very intimidatory presence of foreign troops on Iraqi streets. All this and more, for we might list the destruction of Iraq's infrastructure, its electricity grids, its ports, its banks, its waterways, its oil industry. We might list the destruction of society and its deliberate wanton breakdown into medieval rivalries. We might list all these offenses and state that things have changed irretrievably, when we have not even touched on a plethora of others, from Afghanistan, Pakistan, Somalia, and the transnational network of locations of rendition and incarceration. All and every instance of which is conducted with impunity, with the overwhelming assumption that not simply that all such a re-drawing of limits is conducted in the name of humanity, but that it can withstand any resistance that might emerge in opposition, whether such resistance comes in the form of Islamic terror networks, local insurgencies, or even Western publics opposed to such behaviour in their name.

What are the conditions of possibility for such conduct with impunity? Where is the outrage? Can the limits trampled upon be restored even in changed form? Who will restore them? We will return to these latter questions in the chapter to follow. For now, it is the question of the assumed impunity that exercises, for in the absence of understanding this, there is no possibility of understanding the form that resistance has taken. Taken from a Foucaultian angle, we might think of the assumed impunity in several ways, starting with the shock and awe tactics and other open displays of untrammeled power through violence, to the everyday technologies utilised to control populations and their movements. We might understand the politics of impunity through a Marxist lens and focus on the wholesale dispossession of the Iraqi people. We might then seek to understand the assumption of impunity from a Lacanian sense, focussing on 'foreclosure', indeed returning to this concept, and then we might focus on a Freudian informed analysis and draw from Julia Kristeva (1982) the concept of the 'abject'. And then we might look to Hannah Arendt (1963) and focus on the question of 'banalisation', for her, of evil, and for this author, of war as such, of violence against bodies as such, of dispossession as such, of history and subjectivity as such. There is a 'truth' in each of these perspectives. All inform in one way or another this question of how power in late modernity can operate and how it has done so with the assumption of impunity.

The invasion of Iraq was an unashamed display of power, intended as spectacle, not just for the Iraqis – in fact, they in many ways did not count [22] – but for a global gaze. Images of the invasion portrayed the use of overwhelming force through aerial bombardment of a capital city. This is what was meant by 'shock and awe', not simply the defeat of an already defeated enemy, but the open display of an unparalleled military machine the target of which was not just the population below, but the wider public in the Middle East as a political region and the global population as whole. This was sovereign power mobilised not necessarily to kill, but primarily to discipline, to punish, and ultimately to govern (Jabri, 2006). Through rendering its power spectacle, here was a self-constituting act, but it could only be such through the gaze of all who witnessed the act. In providing our gaze to the performance of sovereign violence, we in many ways were complicit in its constitution as a globally articulated sovereignty, one that could indeed act with impunity, for it had already transcended the remits and limits of law, of the logic of the international, of the laws of war. There is no measurable way in which we might determine how such a display of untrammelled power produces certain forms of subjectivisation, except to say that sovereign power emerges, indeed becomes manifest in the performance of the act;[23] that the military machine in all its materiality is there in the possession of the United States, but only becomes manifest as a globally articulated sovereignty when its exposes its kill potential, and through such exposure, self-constitutes and shapes the gaze at one and the same time. Even when the gaze is one of opposition, often of outrage, it is nevertheless one that is ultimately silenced as it is drawn in to the 'field of force of destructive torrents and explosions', to use Walter Benjamin's description of the use of aerial bombardment in the First World War (Benjamin, 1999b: 84).

So the impunity is more than assumed by the perpetrator; it is conferred by us who look on, having known all along that this unleashing of power was indeed a potential possibility. We could say that the awe and wonder was not at the firepower as such, nor its imagery, its starkness against the night sky overlooking Baghdad, but rather at the fact that power had come to realise its potential, that this could indeed be done. The performance of the act hales forth Zizek's question, 'who are you to do this?' Having crossed the threshold, having performed the ultimate sovereign moment, any subsequent acts aimed at the pacification of the Iraqi population and its government through a combination of intimidation and surveillance simply had to pass the test of normalisation; acts of sovereign power permeating the everyday and the routine of the Iraqi population. With such normalisation comes a reinforced impunity, even where the acts incurred, committed, such as the various indiscriminate shootings of Iraqis, revealed in full imagery through Wikileaks, produce outrage anew, and call for some answerability anew. Then we had known such events did take place, could take place, as they had done throughout colonial history. The US military in Iraq had indeed visited the history of British colonial rule in Iraq.

There is a corporeal logic that underpins the military machine, that somehow confers it meaning and that provides the conditions of possibility for its potentiality. The biopolitical aspect of late modern warfare is that its remit is directed at populations, that its technologies blur the boundary between war and welfare, and that its practices are not confined to the battlefield context, but cover a wider spatial and temporal location, manifest on streets and neighbourhoods, during crisis points as well as the routine and the everyday. From militarised checkpoints to the use of biometric identifiers forced upon local populations, to the control of movement and circulation of local inhabitants, the exception, to use Agamben (2005), is constituted as the norm. The most extreme manifestation of this normalisation, and what I am referring here as the banalisation of war, is the use of drones armed with Hellfire missiles as a technology of surveillance and as a killing machine used in extra-judicial assassination, in locations in Afghanistan, Pakistan, Iraq, Yemen. While these might be targeted extra-judicial assassinations, they nevertheless are, for populations on the ground, an unseen source of danger.

The corporeal logic that is the condition of possibility for biopolitical warfare that recognises no limits, juridical, moral, or political, is based on a very specific, distinctive calculation, one that accrues hierarchical worth upon bodies. This is the condition of possibility that Michel Foucault identifies in answer to his own question: how is war possible in a biopolitical age? While Foucault identifies genocidal state racism and colonial wars as exemplars of racialised war, late modern manifestations of war used as a technology of control, a technology of government, are more indicative of the permeation of war into the everyday experience of populations rendered its targets. Calculating hierarchies of worth is in turn based on the assumption that certain bodies are disposable, reduced to what Agamben (1995) refers to as 'bare life'.

The corporeal logic I am suggesting is at the heart of late modern warfare, providing its condition of possibility, is significant for our purposes here for it has implications, as I have already indicated, for international politics and the limits upon which the distinctiveness of the international is based. If war is rendered biopolitical, then the juridical–political limits of modern political community are redundant, not simply in the sense that sovereignty has shifted elsewhere, to a global terrain wherein sovereign performativity can take place in diverse spaces of governmentality, as Butler highlights. More profoundly, that populations of bodies are rendered disposable goes to the heart of our understanding of what it means to be a subject of politics. Biopolitical war, its actuality in certain regions of the world, currently mainly postcolonial, mainly located in South Asia and the Middle East, its actuality when manifest upon postcolonial subjects traversing the world, in streets and neighbourhoods, and the airzones of transnational spaces, and its potentiality elsewhere and upon other subjects, all subjects, suggests we are all made refugees, and hence, in Arendtian sense, all denied the right to politics. Yet the subject of politics emerges despite the odds, however the claim to politics is now beyond the postcolonial, and in being 'beyond' incorporates coloniality and postcoloniality in seeking to capture the moment to come.

In suggesting a temporality that I am referring to as the 'beyond', the argument is that the subject of politics that emerges now in late modernity does so in a historical context wherein the limits constitutive of the postcolonial, limits drawn from the modern international, are rendered disposable. When Balibar (2002: 24) suggests 'We are … at a place where any claim to a right to politics has become risible', his argument is that, given the all pervasive 'globalised accumulation process' sustained by 'the banality of objective cruelty', there is 'practically no possibility for the victims to see themselves and present themselves *in person* as political subjects, capable of emancipating humanity by emancipating themselves'.[24] Yet there is always the potential for the reconstitution of limits, for the insertion of presence in the spaces of the everyday and the routine, where the claim to a right to politics is made even as the spaces wherein such claims can be made continue to be subject to the policing imperative of governmentality, an imperative, as we have seen in this chapter, which derives not just from local forces, but from an apparatus of security that sees the world within the purview of its operations.

The Iraqi artist Adil Abidin recalls returning to his country in 2006, after many years of life in exile from Saddam's Iraq, and being greeted with 'Welcome to

Baghdad' by an American GI at a checkpoint. The surprise was that he was being welcomed back to his own city by the occupier.[25] To know your country is occupied by foreign troops is one thing. To see it manifest in such a way is quite another, for the positions are reversed; it is not the Iraqi who is extending a greeting to the stranger, for his position has been usurped, taken over by this very stranger. This is the moment of displacement, the realisation of dispossession, the moment wherein all agency disappears in that instant when the stranger who has taken over your home welcomes you back to it, rendering you the visitor/stranger, so that the choices available are either to attempt a retrieval of what is yours or to become estranged, to re-enter spaces of exile, for at least in exile there will always be the promise of home.

There has, of course, been much resistance, from the various insurgency groups, to individual acts of resistance, from artists rendering the occupation and local collaborators in satirical form to the seemingly most daring individual, whose shoe-throwing act, aimed at President Bush, has become the iconic gesture of resistance the world over. As another Iraqi artist Halim Al-Karim, explaining his exhibition at the 2011 Venice Biennale, states: 'We will always resist. If we resist you, one day you'll stop doing this.'[26]

6

CREATIVE POLITICS AND POSTCOLONIAL AGENCY

> False praxis is no praxis.
>
> Theodor Adorno, *Marginalia to Theory and Praxis*

The question that continues to occupy postcolonial thought relates to what constitutes postcolonial agency, and specifically how such agency can emerge in the midst of, despite of, and through the matrices of power that continue to reinforce and to reproduce the structures that define global inequality. Any understanding of such agency must somehow provide an understanding of how the postcolonial subject can indeed speak and act when the subject, her speech and action, are already so overdetermined.

I have conceptualised the subject of politics in terms of the claim to the right to politics. This conceptualisation, as shown in Chapter 3, is not premised on a Kantian understanding of the subject, but rather relies on the claim being made, on the words being spoken, and on articulations of presence, discursive and material. The subject of politics comes into being as the subject interjects self into the space of the political, which is in turn constituted by that very interjection. However, this 'self' is a complex being, inscribed with the weight of history, burdened with all its discursive and material bearing. Yet, from this depth of overdetermination emerges potentiality, the imaginary, and the promise of a moment to come. Fanon's refusal of the ontology of the 'white man' was at the same time a declaration of the potentiality of negativity, the ever uncapturable excess that at once problematises the concept that seeks to capture *and* promises 'new' beginnings. Fanon, perhaps more than any other postcolonial thinker, recognised that the moment of the new was always in deferral. The moment of founding in this sense evades capture even as it constitutes the subject of politics.

The aim in this final chapter is to focus on how we might relate this understanding of the postcolonial subject of politics to a late modern context wherein the limits constitutive of the modern international come face to face with biopolitical governmentality, the imperative of which is exactly to govern the space and time of politics. The colonial legacy looms large in the constitution of the subject of politics as does the continuing struggle against coloniality, a struggle articulated in different forms and by different agents, from the postcolonial state to postcolonial individuals and populations. At the same time, this legacy finds its most potent expression in late modern practices of government that view the global within their remit of operations, so that moments of postcolonial resistance can be understood to emerge exactly within this governmentalising global context. Somewhat paradoxically, this context might at once be both enabling and constraining; one wherein solidarities exert a presence and interject discursively and materially, and one that can in turn be subject to government. As will be argued, these solidarities are suggestive of what I want to refer to as a worldly subjectivity, one that comes to constitute a different articulation of the cosmopolitan, one that might be referred to as a cosmopolitanism of politics. Once again the regional reference point is the Middle East, though the discourse does not have to be so confined.

The question of postcolonial agency

As is evident from every formulation presented in this work, Fanon remains the inspirational voice for this author and the many others that I have drawn upon in this work. While this voice is used in a diversity of ways, as indeed should be the case with any iconic thinker, what remains primary are two features that emerge in Fanon: his analytic of colonialism as a structure and phenomenology of domination, and his commitment to the anti-colonial struggle as constitutive of the subject of politics and hence of the potentiality of new beginnings. We saw that this potentiality becomes evident in Fanon's negativity – the subject rendered object of colonial rule is never fully captured by its epistemologies and ontologies. We saw too that the 'constitution-making', to use Arendt, implicated in new beginnings can be conceptualised as the deferred moment, in Fanon, for here we see the postcolonial subject of politics face to face with the lost promise of independence and the founding moment of political community. The heteronomy of the international emerges here, at once both enabling and constraining, both constitutive and constituted by the postcolonial subject's assertion of presence on this terrain of politics.

If we look to other formative voices in the postcolonial literature, voices that I have engaged with throughout this book, the understanding of the postcolonial subject of politics I have defined in this book finds both resonances and contentions. Edward Said's understanding of postcolonial agency, as we have seen, is premised on the formative, constitutive moment of 'independence'. For Said, this independence is distinctly related to the territorial expulsion of the colonial, though he recognises fully the continued struggle against representational practices. What he refers to as 'voyages in' and 'contrapuntal reading' become literary devices expressive of postcolonial agency, and the discourses that emerge here are not external to the inscriptional practices and structures of domination through which the postcolonial subject emerges. Apart from such literary interjections, Said's subject is distinctly a subject of politics; the declaration of independence enables another moment to come, the moment of intersubjective agonistic politics.

We saw in Ranajit Guha an understanding of postcolonial agency that emanates from the 'insurgent', specifically the peasant insurgent who emerges as the 'subaltern' subject. What comes across very powerfully in Guha is that the agency of the insurgent paradoxically becomes evident in the discourses and practices of 'counter-insurgency', a formulation that has much resonance in contemporary locations of 'insurgency' wherein practices constitutive of counter-insurgency come to constitute the insurgent subject as subject of politics. Guha himself is primarily concerned with the inscriptions of the peasant both in official, counter-insurgency discourse, and in historiography, suggesting that the missing element is the consciousness of the peasant, one that is prior to inscription.

For Gayatry Spivak, the very attempt at capturing the consciousness of the subaltern is itself a manifestation of epistemic violence, one that finds expression not just in the colonial discourses and practices of the past, but is revealed to be present in critical discourses, represented for Spivak by thinkers such as Foucault and Deleuze. For Spivak, it is the enactment of 'foreclosure' of the postcolonial subject and the occlusions of imperialism's operations of power that constitute the epistemic violence committed in critical theory. For Spivak, the subaltern cannot speak, for she is always already (mis)represented in the epistemic violence of imperialist framings. However, Spivak's deconstructive efforts also inform her Marxian-inspired appreciation of the structure of capitalist production and exchange and the location of the subject therein. In the combination of Derrida and Marx in Spivak we discern a manifestation of postcolonial agency, one that is 'interruptive', to use Homi Bhabha, of the 'historicities' of race, gender, and class. Spivak's subject of politics is not as clearly framed as Said's in terms of the claim to politics, and yet this claim is evident in the moment of interjection that is assumed when she conceives of agency as 'reversing, displacing and seizing the apparatus of value-coding', a sentence I quote earlier in the book.[1] There is here a recognition of the heteronomy of postcolonial politics, what constitutes, for Spivak, the 'deconstructive predicament of the postcolonial'.

The interruptive, the creative, and the enunciative are all concepts that Homi Bhabha uses in his conceptualisation of postcolonial agency, as already highlighted. Like Spivak and unlike Said, the moment of independence is rather diminished in significance, for the aim in Bhabha is to articulate the potentiality of agency in those intersections of time and space, the modern and the postmodern, the colonial and postcolonial. As Ilan Kapoor (2003: 262–263) highlights, Bhabha takes postcolonial agency 'beyond resistance and towards creativity', where agency finds potentiality in the contingencies of power. As shown earlier, Bhabha's understanding of postcolonial agency derives from Arendt's understanding of politics as presence in the agonistic intersubjective space of the public arena aiming, as Kapoor highlights, towards an 'agonistic cultural pluralism'.

What emerges in these postcolonial writings are understandings of postcolonial agency that locate the subject of such agency in relation to the colonial legacy.

However, this is also a subject that makes a claim, interjects in spaces always already constituted by this legacy. However, in making a claim, in that interruptive moment of interjection, the subject constitutes self as subject of politics, present, to be reckoned with, albeit in the contingent matrices of power that relegate the postcolonial to the subordinate position. At the same time, and apart from Fanon and Said, we somehow lose the specificity of the postcolonial in relation to the international, a specificity that, as shown in Chapters 4 and 5, must form part of the framework of understanding, not just of 'agency', but of the subject of politics in postcoloniality.

The late modern postcolonial

Postcolonial subjects, now in late modernity, are still faced with a colonial rationality which discursively and materially places them in a globally subordinate position. From Frantz Fanon to contemporary postcolonial theory, this construction is understood as the product of a temporal and spatial ordering wherein the subject of Europe is always the point of origin and the universal end. Read in relation to dominant frames of reference in all their epistemic and ontological rendering, the postcolonial subject is never the author of the rules and norms that constitute and transform the international and its discursive and institutional structures, but is always somehow following behind. As indicated earlier in this book, even where certain postcolonial societies are deemed to have 'emerged', their emergence is primarily measured in terms of their co-optation into a global neoliberal order. As shown in the last chapter, where postcolonial societies and states are deemed to be non-conforming, where they are deemed to be sources of danger to the established political and economic order, the imperative is to govern, and as shown, the practices of government, now by definition globally rendered, have ranged from war as a technology of control, to incarceration, to biopolitical initiatives geared to education and welfare provision, to pedagogical exercises aimed at the training of populations and the building of state institutions. Even where war is used as a practice of government, the legitimising discourse is protectionist, framed as it always is in terms of rescue.

It is this protectionist discourse that continues to subordinate the postcolonial subject, postcolonial states and populations, and it is this that confers not just primacy to the dominant, but also impunity. That this discourse draws upon human rights, the welfare of distant populations, that its practices are enacted by state as well as non-state agents, including non-governmental organisations and the private sector, all enable its interpretation as a 'cosmopolitanism of government', geared as its resources and discourses are towards the transformation of other societies. As shown elsewhere (Jabri 2011), this is a 'security apparatus' writ large and its remit is the re-design of populations. The corporeal logic of its practices was highlighted in the last chapter and need not be repeated here. However, what is significant to highlight is that the corporeal logic that underpins colonial rationality renders those at its receiving end always vulnerable to its violence, direct or epistemic. At the same time the material corporeality of the subject is implicated in the subject's claim to politics.

Understanding the subject of politics in late modern postcoloniality, and given the assumptions I have already highlighted, demands a different conceptualisation of the cosmopolitan, one that does not subordinate difference, but rather frames its remit in terms of difference. What I have in the past referred to as a 'cosmopolitanism of politics' might be read in terms of a 'postcolonial rationality', one that places its focus on the idea of 'independence'. As I have shown in Chapter 3 and throughout this book, the 'declaration of independence' is a formative moment in the constitution of the postcolonial subject of politics, even as this subject's lived experience continues to be dominated by and subject to global discursive and material inequalities. The structural context wherein the postcolonial subject is constituted and in turn constitutes – through claims to politics – is the modern international, constructed through the logic of limits (Walker, 2010), and a late modern globalised biopolitical terrain that has a tense relationship with these limits. The postcolonial subject's aporetic relationship with the former, the modern international, is suggestive of a potentiality that derives from the very structure that, despite its colonial roots, confers the postcolonial meaning. As we saw, the assertion of presence onto the terrain of the international is a moment of constitution in relation to postcolonial political community and can also be seen as a moment of transformation of the international as such. Both are moments of politics and are hence replete with contestation. What is important to highlight is that the postcolonial rationality that I want to suggest underpins a 'cosmopolitanism of politics' recognises contestation rather than seeking to govern it.

Claiming the political in late modernity: the Arab Spring

The Arab Spring provides us with a picture wherein the security apparatus that defines a 'cosmopolitanism of government' comes face to face with the postcolonial subject's claim to the right to politics. The events in Tunisia, Egypt, then Yemen and Bahrain, followed by Libya and Syria, initially produced a number of commentaries, ranging from rather banal statements of support for a pro-democracy movement to alarmist calls for caution against the potential of Islamic 'radicalisation', to middle of the road interpretations that suggest if the former fails then the latter will happen. Shared across these discourses is the assumption that what takes place in Egypt and elsewhere in the Arab world has ramifications for Western security concerns.[2] Also shared is a particular discursive framing wherein the Arab and Muslim world is seen to be the source of a problem, namely the problem of violence. While this framing acquired particular resonance in the post September 11th 2001 context, its antecedents, as Edward Said showed, go much further back, to the colonial era and into the postcolonial period.[3] This construction of the Middle East, of Arab societies in particular, as the source of violence is prevalent across the left-right political divide in the Western media, in the practitioner world of foreign policy in the West, and in the academy. Fundamentally in this discursive framing, a framing that is so powerful that to argue otherwise is in itself an act of what Ernesto Laclau (2000: 81) would refer to as 'ethical investment', the Arabs and Muslims more widely conceived geographically are never the victims of a violence that stems from elsewhere, but always its perpetrators.[4] The category of violence in this scheme of things is then conferred an ontological status whereby the very identity/being of the Arab or Muslim is constituted by the term 'violence'. The Middle East and South Asia are seen as the sources of instability and geopolitical danger, their populations 'volatile', and their politics variously feudal, tribal, and tradition-bound – so culturally determined that any semblance of a modern political subjectivity is not part of the equation and when it becomes so is perceived as a distinct threat.

As the uprisings spread, the discursive framing of the Middle East began to change, so that the terms 'Arab Awakening' and then the 'Arab Spring' came into usage. It is as if the revolutions of the Middle East have effected an interjection, not just in their own polities, but into a hegemonic orientalist, demonising Western politics of representation. The central common call made by these various Arab publics was 'Irhul' or 'go', calls aimed at the local dictator and his regime, coupled with demands for democratic transformation, pluralism, and the rule of law. While some of those involved in mass public protests are certainly affiliated to political parties or groups that espouse Islam as a political force – the Muslim Brotherhood in Egypt and the Al-Nahdha Party in Tunisia are two such examples – nevertheless it became quickly apparent that the Arab Spring was primarily about the reclamation of the state and of politics as such. Populations that had, throughout the postcolonial period, been largely subject variously to dictatorial rule, to corrupt official practices, to rigged elections, to the abuse of the judiciary, were now proclaiming their right to have a voice and in doing so, to bring those responsible to account. There is a tendency to focus on the internal grievances; however, these must be seen in conjunction with grievances against local leaders who seemed to place the interests of foreign powers over and above the interests of the population as a whole and the wider concerns of the Arab publics.

It is always a challenge to use simply one term or concept to capture a multitude of events, especially events that have overtaken an entire region. Historians would, of course, be profoundly interested in what happened when and how; the detail of every occurrence set and told in a narrative construction that may be represented in all neutrality and is yet framed within pre-existing judgements and dispositions, discursive formations that are drawn upon, but remain unacknowledged. There is a geopolitics to discursive formations, as emphasised by Gayatry Spivak (1999) when she refers to the 'epistemic violence of imperialism', and as highlighted by Michel Foucault, when he states:

> the formation of discourses, and the genealogy of knowledge need to be analysed, not in terms of types of consciousness, modes of perception and forms of ideology, but in terms of tactics and strategies of power. Tactics and strategies deployed through implantations, distributions, demarcations,

control of territories and organisations of domains which could well make up
a sort of geopolitics …

(Foucault, 1980: 77)

There is, as we will see below, a profound prescience to Spivak's words and to
Foucault's in relation to the capture, conceptual or otherwise, of the events that
have been taking place in the Middle East.

The desire to capture is all too apparent, and in an age of instant communication,
the historian spectator is at once also a participant. What is beyond dispute is that
the historian, philosopher, and political scientist is at one in recognising the events
that have engulfed the Middle East as being of monumental significance, not just
regionally but globally, given the stakes involved. If the events of 11 September
2001 shaped the subsequent decade, its violence and wars, then it is of profound
importance that now at the beginning of a new decade, the region and the
populations most affected had emerged to make their claim to politics.

The construct 'postcolonial agency' appears to suggest a specificity that
recognises the location of such agency in relation to the colonial legacy that is seen
to maintain its constitutive influences on the subject of politics. At the same time,
the agency articulated by the postcolonial subject is premised on the assertion of
'independence' and solidarity with those seeking 'self-determination'. In the
context of late modernity, it might, perhaps, be more appropriate to refer to a
temporal framing that suggests a 'beyond the postcolonial'. This framing is at once
suggestive of continuity and creativity, so that the colonial legacy and the anti-
colonial struggles that led to the founding of the postcolonial polity are as present
as are the creative, 'world-making', to use Arendt, revolutions of the present. The
symbolic moment that is Tahrir Square, and other locations of mass protest
embodies this move I am suggesting – the placing of the temporal 'beyond' into
the materiality of these postcolonial spaces as these spaces are constituted and
reconstituted. That the colonial legacy persists is evidenced by what I suggest is an
imperative towards what can be referred to as the government of revolution, so
that the populations of the region are once again variously denied the right to
politics or steered in directions that might conform to the edicts of global structures
of domination and their agents. Practices I am referring to as the government of
revolution are being enacted as I write this concluding chapter, and the question
of which prevails – revolution or its government, 'world-making' or its government
– is tempting to ask even at this juncture. However, this is not the point of the
chapter, for here, the primary interest lies in providing an understanding of
articulations relating to the claim to politics, their construction, and their implication
for the postcolonial subject of politics. While the question of success or failure
cannot be answered, what remains beyond doubt, at least for this author, is that the
moment of the 'beyond' is also a revolutionary moment and in being so has
instigated, once again, the imperative to govern.

In moving beyond the formulaic representation, where there is power there is
resistance, I have sought to define resistance in terms of the claim to politics, and

specifically the claim to the right to politics. I have argued that such a claim takes place in relation to the heteronomy of the international, one that the postcolonial subject seeks access to, is constituted by, even as this very location of politics is in itself a product of coloniality. The moment of founding for the postcolonial subject incorporates both access to the international and the constitution of political community, and it is the intersection between the two that is of profound interest when it comes to understanding what I have referred to as the overwhelming presence of the postcolonial state in the lived experience of the postcolonial subject. Crucially, this presence was and continues to be expressed in governing practices the imperative of which has been policing, but it has also functioned as a mediating force between a global political economy and local extractive interests, including those of the bureaucratic-military oligarchies that have ruled the Middle East especially throughout the postcolonial period. The revolutions of the region and their government must be read in this light and in relation to this context. The subject of politics makes a claim, interjects self not just in local spaces, but also in global spaces of power, for the latter are always already in the former.

The 2011 uprisings in the Middle East, as show in Chapter Three, prompted Hardt and Negri to argue that these events constitute the realisation of an emergent 'multitude' that is not so much external to 'empire' but imminent to it.[5] I argued that what these events represent is an overwhelming desire to re-capture the political and in doing so to re-capture the (postcolonial) state, not in the name of religion or some premodern form of authority, but in a very distinctly late modern articulation of what we might describe as a worldly subjectivity.[6] This worldly subjectivity at once suggests the constitutive moment of 'world-making', to borrow from Arendt, wherein the interjection of presence creates a public sphere, but is also one that draws on the world while drawing the world in.

How might this conceptualisation work both in terms of understanding and in terms of what the concept of a worldly subjectivity enables? It seems to suggest a cosmopolitan ethos and politics, transcending the state as the primary location wherein the political becomes manifest. However, it can also express a mode of subjectivity that is very much situated in a national discourse, but one that draws its discursive as well as material resources from a domain that is of the world, so to speak, albeit the distribution of which is less than equal. This latter understanding points, for example, to the fact that events on the ground, in all their national, not to mention nationalist evocations – Tahrir means liberation and is the name of many squares in the region's capital cities – were and continue to be communicated to whomsoever out there might be picking up messages, variously on Twitter and Facebook, as well as satellite TV networks such as Al-Jazeera. This worldly subjectivity at the same time is both discursive and material, relying as it does on the precision of words – performatives such as 'yes, we can', or declarations of 'days of rage' – as well as allowing the materiality of protest to gain access to the public sphere, so that banners, bodily presence, photographs of the disappeared, and the coffins of the dead function as artifacts of the revolution, its material founding and realisation.

The worldliness of the protests in the Arab world might also be construed in terms of the reclamation of the state from the excesses of the frames of reference the origins of which were and continue to be outside of the region itself. Deposed leaders as well as those remaining in power seemed to be in service to these outside influences and not to their own populations, so that while it is indeed refreshing that we have not witnessed the burning of the Stars and Stripes, the clients of this symbol of hegemonic power have been the direct targets of protest. Egypt, along with a number of states in the region had, as one protester put it, come to function as 'Torture Inc' for successive US administrations, and had come to service an agenda that was by and large authored elsewhere and in accordance with other states' interests.[7] The suppression and impoverishment of local populations went hand in hand with the enrichment of authoritarian regimes engaged in the plunder and reinvestment of national assets in Western banks, Western property portfolios, and hedge funds, all sanctioned and incorporated into a global security apparatus headed by the West. The prevailing discourse was of a Middle East that was beyond political redemption, a backward location the only politics of which was deemed to be that of force directed at suppressed local populations seen as prime mobilising fodder for Islamist tendencies.

We have witnessed much creativity in these days, starting from January 2011 to the present time of writing (July 2011). However, there had been much by way of creativity preceding these immediate events, manifest not simply on the streets, but in galleries, and in film, not in simple representations of suppression, but in moments of articulation that transcend easy categorisation or predictability. While the West's media, aided by politicians and academic alike, aimed its lenses at the Islamic 'threat', the populations of the Arab world had entered the worldly space of the late modern, had recognised as they had all along that much had been compromised in their name, that the very ground on which they walked had been sold off, and not necessarily to the highest bidder, and that their right to politics, the most important right, had been denied them. Political conflicts and allegiances aside, to visit the region in the recent past meant to witness an unexpected revival, primarily of the intellectual and artistic kind, so that the locals were no longer solely reliant on an exiled community of poets, writers, and artists to be their voice of freedom, but on local expressions of what I am calling here the 'right to politics' (Balibar, 2002). This expression of the right to politics could not be interpreted in some Hegelian 'end of history' formula whereby the region could finally be admitted to a world spirit authored in the West, but rather, this claim to the political has happened in spite of the violence and the asymmetries of power that have characterised this particular world spirit and in whose name the region has been subjected over the years.

There is a certain reluctance on the part of the author to shift the lens away from the protesting peoples of the Middle East, their creativities and innovations in their dealings with their states. My aim is therefore to remain focused on the area as the location of a new mode of political expression, a founding expression of freedom that seeks to reclaim its voice, to reshape its state along constitutional grounds, and to, finally, realise the promise of the anti-colonial struggles of the past. However, there is also much by way of danger that lies ahead, and the primary form that this danger takes is in the potential military intervention in the region proclaimed to be in the name of protection, but the consequences of which would be the deprivation of the region of its own spring, its revolution. Given recent history, it is not too difficult to see that those calling for intervention might exactly seek the wholesale sabotage of these unwanted pro-democracy revolts on oil-rich soil that has been all too cheaply available to the West when local populations remained in the grips of poverty and unemployment. The expressed sentiment 'don't steel our revolution' is understandable given this backdrop.[8]

Who would have predicted that the action of a Tunisian street vendor, Mohammad Bouazizi, would lead to what we now refer to as the Arab Spring? Bouazizi's act of self-immolation, when the police had prevented him from setting up his fruit and vegetable stall, was the spark that led to mass protests across the Arab world, from Tunisia to Egypt, Libya, Algeria, Yemen, Bahrain, the UAE, Iraq, Morocco, and Jordan. The regimes in Tunisia and Egypt were overthrown, Libya descended into a civil war, with one side, the National Transition Council, being supported by NATO no less, Saudi Arabia intervened with tanks in Bahrain, regimes including those in Morocco, Jordan, and Syria promised reform, and the security apparatuses of Bahrain, Yemen, and Syria were unleashed against civilian targets. Across the Arab world, the calls of protest were for an end to oppressive dictatorial rule, democratic transformation, constitutionalism and the rule of law, an end to corrupt practices, the release of political prisoners, and an end to torture.

What is significant about the events unfolding in the Middle East and North Africa for the context of this book is that they are suggestive of a desire for something 'new' and as such another historic moment in the founding of political community. According to Hardt and Negri (2011), writing of the recent events, these might be seen as 'original experiments that open new political possibilities, relevant well beyond the region, for freedom and democracy'. They suggest that the

> Arab world becomes for the next decade what Latin America was for the last – that is, a laboratory for political experimentation between powerful social movements and progressive governments from Argentina to Venezuela, and from Brazil to Bolivia.

This comparison is suggestive of the idea that what connects them is a socio-economic driving force that mobilises a 'multitude' into political action, so that a 'horizontal network that has no single, central leader' comes to be the defining moment of a multitude that can 'organise itself'. Tahrir Square, in this instance, is akin to Seattle, Buenos Aires, and Genoa. What is most significant in Hardt and Negri's immediate analysis of events in the Middle East is their emphasis on a constitutional response, as they put it, 'not aimed at a traditional liberal constitution that merely guarantees the division of powers and a regular electoral dynamic, but rather at a form of democracy adequate to the new forms of expression and the needs of the multitude'. They call for a 'radical constitutional response' that meets not simply demands for employment and the tackling of poverty, but also 'frustrated productive and expressive capacities' as well as a 'common plan to manage natural resources and social production'.[9]

What is significant about Hardt and Negri's intervention relating to the Arab Spring is its conceptualisation of a movement that is at once of locality and globality. These uprisings are not simply about the overthrow of tyrannical regimes, nor are they simply about local grievances relating to basic needs, but are about frustrated creative and productive potentialities that in themselves constitute the networks formative of multitude in a late modern era. For Hardt and Negri, 'A multitude is an irreducible multiplicity; the singular social differences that constitute the multitude must always be expressed and can never be flattened into sameness, unity, identity or indifference'.[10] Local demands for political and economic emancipation are at once also of the global, in that they not only stem from global neoliberal structures that are the root source of local frustrations, but reflect a diversity of demands that become manifest in socio-political struggles that can emerge in different, and at time, unexpected locations.

This idea of the 'universal' location of the Arab uprising is repeated by Slavoj Zizek (2011). As he put it:

> The uprising was universal: it was immediately possible for all of us around the world to identify with it, to recognise what it was about, without any need for cultural analysis of the features of Egyptian society. In contrast to Iran's Khomeini revolution (where leftists had to smuggle their message into the predominantly Islamist frame), here the frame is clearly that of a universal secular call for freedom and justice, so that the Muslim Brotherhood had to adopt the language of secular demands.

This was, furthermore, not the universalism espoused by 'neocons' who condemn multiculturalism 'on behalf of the universal values of freedom and democracy'. For the neocons, according to Zizek are 'uneasy' at the fact that the Egyptian protesters were demanding both freedom and social and economic justice. At the heart of the Egyptian struggle, according to Zizek is a 'will to freedom' and it was this that informed the insistence of the Egyptian public that Mubarak go. There was no room here for negotiation and dialogue, just as there was not 'when the Communist regimes were challenged in the late 1980s'. For Zizek, it was this will to freedom that not only challenged the emergency powers that the Egyptian regime has instituted through decades, but sought to 'reshape the entire state,' so that it made sense 'that so many people on the streets of Cairo claim that they now feel alive for the first time in their lives.'[11] This feeling alive, expressed repeatedly through the claim 'we have overcome our fear', is powerfully suggestive of a reclaimed subjectivity and a sense of agency; it is as if there is an intimacy to the revolt even as this particular revolt is playing out in the public arena.

One significant element that Hardt and Negri as well as Zizek leave out of their analyses is the international and its associated contingencies. These authors place emphasis on the 'new', the desire of Arab populations across the MENA region for freedom, conceived politically and socio-economically. However, the context of the international is also of core significance if we are to fully understand these events as transformative moments wherein the political is reclaimed. For, as I have argued throughout this book, the postcolonial subject is formed in the colonial legacy, in the continuities that define structures of colonial domination and dispossession as well as the promise of independence and the postcolonial era which inaugurated the newly independent national states onto the realm of the international. There is, in these revolts, the overwhelming desire to re-capture the state and in so doing to transform its relationship to the population. At the same time, the wider context of the region, subjected through the postcolonial years to the interests of the West as against the solidarities of the population, was a major factor in the mobilisation of publics against their regimes. This was certainly the case in Egypt, where opposition to the invasion and occupation of Iraq and opposition to the complicities of the Egyptian state in the siege of Gaza, were primary mobilising forces in pre-revolutionary protests.

What I am calling the 'intimacy of revolt', borrowing from Julia Kristeva (2002a), is related to these wider contingencies that redraw the subject and in so doing reconfigure both the subject as political agent and the landscape of revolt that the subject seeks to redefine and reconstitute. This relationship between the psychic element of subjectivity and wider discursive and institutional manifestations of structures of domination and dispossession is best captured by the Palestinian writer and political activist Mustafa Barghouti when, in his analysis of the Arab Spring, he refers to this as the 'revolution of dignity against personal and national degradation'. He writes: 'It was no coincidence that the events in Tunisia and in Egypt were often described as the "dignity revolution".' He locates the sources of degradation to poverty for the working class, the lack of opportunity, the theft of elections, corrupt practices, the abuse of rights and the incarceration of opponents, as well as the violations of the 'national dignity of every Arab nation' relating to Palestine, the blockade of Gaza, the various invasions of Lebanon, and the invasion of Iraq.[12] As Noam Chomsky so correctly states,

> A common refrain among pundits is that fear of radical Islam requires reluctant opposition to democracy on pragmatic grounds. While not without some merit, the formulation is misleading. The general threat has always been independence. The US and its allies have regularly supported radical Islamists, sometimes to prevent the threat of secular nationalism.[13]

It is indeed the idea of 'independence' in the postcolonial world and of the Middle East in particular that has always been feared by the West. The examples that stand out most forcefully relate to Iran in 1951 and Egypt in 1956. The former saw the UK threaten war against the nationalist Mossadegh regime in Iran following

Mossadegh's threat to nationalise Iran's oil reserves, then under the control of the British.[14] Again relating to independence and the sovereign right over national resources,[15] Nasser's nationalisation of the Suez Canal, as we saw in Chapter 4, led to the invasion of Egypt by the UK, France, and Israel. These locations of resistance were both moments which I have referred to as 'declarations of independence', postcolonial moments that sought the founding and affirmation of postcolonial political community. Responses to them, in different ways, sought to govern political developments for the future.

Much has been written about political change and political contestation in the Middle East and elsewhere in the postcolonial world. In relation to the former specifically, the tendency is to provide analyses of state-civil society relations, where 'change' is closely governed by local authoritarian regimes. Writing on the Gulf states in particular, though applicable to much of the region, Anoushiravan Ehteshami and Steven Wright (2007, 914) state:

> Historically, power has been held firmly by the elites and their control over civil society in effect means that top-down reform is the only viable course. The tendency is for ruling elites, wishing to retain their traditional hold on power over the long term, to liberalize rather than implement substantive reforms challenging the patriarchal power structure. However, liberalization can be seen as an intermediate stage of enfranchisement in which power shifts to civil society (and an associated emergent national bourgeoisie), enabling reform led from below to take place.

As these authors indicate, the ruling elites use restrictive measures to curtail public demonstrations and enact exclusionary measures in recruitment strategies to ensure loyalty in the security and armed services of the state. However, the drive for legitimacy in the face of changing local and external forces is seen as influencing the dynamic of reform in the region. The imperative for local regimes and their external backers, however, is to control change through discourses of fear that seek to construct 'political and societal insecurity', so that repressive practices are combined with a self-inflicted caution and sense of unease within civil society.

While the internal imperative to govern change is indeed significant, at the same time, the external dynamic in the government of change is perhaps best represented by US funded programmes, such as the Middle East Partnership Initiative (MEPI) which, as Ehteshami and Wright highlight, 'offers selective funding for democracy and reform promotion initiatives.'[16] For these authors, this particular programme is not determining of social change, but is nevertheless 'influential'. Of interest for our purposes in this book however is how MEPI uses technologies of governmentality, primarily pedagogical, in not simply influencing change, but in its government. This distinction is important, for while influence is suggestive of a linear dynamic, 'government', understood as it is throughout this book in Foucaultian terms, refers to the shaping of societies and their management. The US State Department describes the role of MEPI thus:

The Middle East Partnership Initiative (MEPI) is a regional program that helps citizens in the Middle East and North Africa develop more pluralistic, participatory, and prosperous societies. From within the Near Eastern Affairs Bureau at the State Department, MEPI advances U.S. foreign policy goals by supporting citizens' efforts at economic, social, and political empowerment, expanding opportunities for women and youth, and helping communities work alongside governments in shaping their own futures. MEPI's activities underscore President Obama and Secretary Clinton's commitment to democracy and civil society in the region, and follow the approach the President laid out in his Cairo speech: engaging with peoples as well as governments, in a spirit of mutual respect and rooted in a commitment to universal values.[17]

The programme is run, according to the State Department, by offices in the region, through US embassies, and in association with NGOs, academic institutions, as well as governments.[18] From engaging 'social entrepreneurs' in civic development projects to the provision of seed funding to young 'business entrepreneurs' in Egypt, Tunisia, and elsewhere, to a variety of women's projects, to IT training, to the provision of grants to local businesses geared towards economic development, MEPI is the example par excellence of a programme premised on government through pedagogy.

Elsewhere and in another place (Jabri, 2011) I make the distinction, as I indicate at the outset, between a 'cosmopolitanism of government' and a 'cosmopolitanism of politics'. I define the former in Foucaultian terms; that power and its operations seek the government of populations and their management, that the very life processes of a population, its welfare, its conflicts and internal relations, can be subject to intervention and through interventionary technologies, be subject to shaping and re-shaping. This government of populations as mass and as categories is at the same time built upon the disciplining of bodies, technologies geared to the shaping and re-shaping of individuals, in their comportment, their relations with others, and their discursive formations. Such is the picture that Michel Foucault provides of European liberal government from the eighteenth century and into the twentieth. To render Foucault's analytics international is to suggest that such 'governmentality' and its technologies are not confined to the internal citizenry of the liberal state, but extend outwards, into the societies and citizenry of other states, constituting interventions into the lives of others, interventions that have drawn upon a range of technologies, from the hardware of military machines, to the use of incarceration, to welfare programmes relating to health, education, and basic needs provision, and indeed the government of politics. The cosmopolitanism of government is hence liberalism's security apparatus writ large, its remit extending into the terrain of others, and its practices enacted by military and civilian agencies. I want to argue that these practices are at once of both cosmopolitanism and of government; the re-design of other populations in accordance with a script authored by the liberal West and its institutions, wherein the governing and the governed remain hierarchically constituted. The expressed fears about the uprisings in the various Arab states can hence be read as a product, indeed a consequence, of the potential of un-governed spaces; spaces that declare, or have the potential to declare, independence.

Representations of recent events in the Middle East have overwhelmingly suggested the primacy of cyberspace as the mover and enabler of dissent and resistance; that satellite TV such as Al-Jazeera enabled the mobilisation process and helped in the realisation of the 'domino effect' that spread resistance across the Arab world. It is as if the ideas behind the revolt simply came from elsewhere; in this case the virtual space that connected the youth of the region to a (Western) world outside. However, there is a local theorisation of culture and politics that has fed into movements of dissent and resistance, and moreover, these discourses are framed in relation to wider discourses that constitute the hybridity of postcolonial space.

The neglect of Arab critical thought derives from the prevalent idea that cultural production is simply absent in the Arab and wider Muslim world. The assumption of a youth indebted to Western ideas derives primarily from the notion, as highlighted by Chakrabarty, that only Europe can be known theoretically, so that the rest of the world is merely its empirical testing ground. There is, as a consequence, a hierarchy of legitimacy in the sphere of cultural production that so permeates and is so powerful in its hegemonic standing that even local intellectuals are complicit in this framing of intellectual worth. However, intellectual production is also a product of the intersection of East and West historically, and as shown in Chapter 4, this 'hybridity' is indeed present in the writings of intellectuals in the nineteenth and early twentieth centuries, where political thought is replete with reference to Western liberal or Marxist discourses. These local articulations of primarily Western ideological frameworks have, historically, played a significant part in discourses of resistance, both in relation to the nationalist struggles of the past and in opposition to the postcolonial state and its practices.

The hybridity of cultural and political production is evident in writings that might be referred to as constitutive of an emerging age of 'critique' in the Arab world. The very presence of such production, its articulation despite the violence of the state, itself constitutes a moment of interjection, one the discourses of which are suggestive of the desire to capture afresh the postcolonial moment of independence and the promise of political community in postcoloniality. For Fatima Mernissi,[19] who writes on the subject of democracy and Islam, and who herself is a highly significant voice in this age of critique, political thought in the Arab world is framed by a discourse of nationalism that has as its reference points, pan-Arabism, the national state, and Islam. The agonism of politics we witness in the Middle East can only be understood in relation to the contestation that these frames of reference suggest. What is evident in reading Mernissi and others is that this moment of 'awakening' derives from an intellectual trajectory wherein the critique of these frames of reference is foregrounded.[20]

It would hence be appropriate to trace a longer historical background to the present context, one that sees the development of the concept of 'critique' as a formative moment in any conception of resistance to hegemonic domination, whether of the colonial past or the postcolonial present. That critique, as Kosseleck (1988) reminds us, emerges in opposition to the absolutist state in Europe, and indeed comes to be crucial in the eighteenth century conception of 'revolution', is an idea that has its parallels in the context of the colonies and the postcolonial state. Just as the context of the eighteenth-century European state was one of crisis and rupture, so too we might suggest that such crisis and rupture formed the context within which ideas relating to critique began to emerge and fed into the anti-colonial struggle.

The tendency in the recent past has been to foreground Islam as the primary mobilising forcefield that would transform the region. This discourse has especially acquired primacy since the events of September 11, contextualised in a vast industry of terrorism and security studies that currently dominates the intellectual agenda, especially in the social sciences. Despite the diversities of cultural and political production in the region, Western representation of political discourse in the region continue to frame subjectivities in terms of modernity and tradition, a binary that comes at the expense of greater complexity. It is the negations, or absences, in Western representations of political discourses in the Middle East and Asia that are of paramount significance.

One such negation could be said to be related exactly to the emergence of the concept of 'critique' and its directionality at the colonial state and its absolutism, first and foremost, and then against the absolutism of the postcolonial state in more recent times. Understood through the concept of 'critique', the various strands of political thought in the region can be interpreted not as manifestations of a reified culture that remains unquestioned, but rather, of a new era where the social dynamics of transformation, specifically the impact of globalisation on local practices of economic and cultural production, the local implications of geopolitical events, including the invasion of Iraq and the continuing issue of Palestine, increasing cross-cultural interaction and inter-Arab communication through the new media, all conspire to generate a critical discourse that engages not just the state and its failings, but also the political discourses that constitute the points of reference for public deliberation. The point to emphasise is that the heterogeneity of political discourses in the region and beyond was, in the representations of the West, being reduced to a single narrative based on Islam. So singular was this representation that it has largely framed the reception of recent protests, much to the consternation of those immediately involved. Furthermore, to point to the heterogeneity of political discourse is not to deny the significance or otherwise of the Islamist component of this heterogeneity.

The claim I want to make in this section is that one very powerful form of postcolonial resistance is the project of 'writing back'. This idea is, following Edward Said's *Orientalism*, indebted to a deconstructive move wherein the target remains the representational practices that inscribe the non-Western other as inferior, usually through the racialisation of the other and the assumption that the West represents the universal while the non-West is of the cultural particular. This notion of 'writing back' is also assumed in discourses that seek the continuing project of 'the decolonisation of knowledge' in the era of postcoloniality, emphasising continuities between the colonial and the postcolonial eras. This aspect of 'writing back' has, at certain points in the era of the postcolonial, in the aftermath of independence, been largely directed by the postcolonial state, but has also been harnessed by local intellectuals, historians and artists, as we will see. However there are other targets to the project of 'writing back', and it is in this context that the concept of 'critique' becomes significant.

A cosmopolitanism of politics

Tracing the postcolonial subject through spaces of governmentality, we might, following Partha Chatterjee (2004), point to the emergence of what Chatterjee refers to as 'political society' in spaces of governmentality – that categories created by technologies of governmentality emerge as sites of agency wherein populations affected come to acquire a relationship with the modern state. However, this is not a relationship of civil rights, but one of the right of access to the welfare provisions, or lack thereof, of the state. In the context of practices I am referring to as the cosmopolitanism of government, and by extension from Chatterjee, we might argue that this relationship between the governed and the state is defined by others, thereby impacting upon the very emergence of 'political society' and its directionality. Tracing the postcolonial subject is hence meaningful not just in relation to the postcolonial state, and postcolonial political community, but also, now in late modernity, this biopolitical realm of cosmopolitan government. Conceptualised thus, we might argue that the postcolonial subject has a reflexive relationship with the postcolonial state and with the apparatus of cosmopolitan government. The crucial question, however, is how these relationships translate or indeed come to constitute the basis from which articulations of politics might arise.

The postcolonial subject might also be traced in relation to a different form of cosmopolitan articulation, namely that of solidarity. This 'cosmopolitanism of politics' (Jabri, 2011) is not based on the assumption of a hierarchy between the liberal self of global reach and the other of this self, the mass of populations deemed in need of rescue, pedagogy, and protection. When cosmopolitanism is expressed in terms of the government of others and such government serves the imperative of security, the consequence is not that such practices depoliticise others, but rather that they circumscribe access to politics and political mobilisation; what I am referring to in this book as the right to politics. The paradoxical consequence is that elements the cosmopolitanism of government deems 'dangerous' come to acquire the political agency that its practices seek to govern. The 'object' of government, in this sense, always exceeds the inscriptive determinations of the epistemic subject of liberal governmentality. NATO's intervention in Libya is not an expression of a depoliticisation, but rather a political intervention that seeks to govern the time and place of revolt, and its modes of articulation in all their diversity.[21]

The parallel with Libya is Afghanistan, where the political is so circumscribed that the only choices in town are between the Taliban and a regime co-opted as partner in efforts to govern through security, and this despite the plurality of political expression in Afghan society. Indeed, Malalai Joya, the youngest woman to be elected to the Afghan Parliament in 2005, provides a glimpse of how target societies interpret such practices of government:

> Unfortunately the Afghan people are not yet strong enough to drive out the US, overthrow the mafia government of Karzai and bring an end to the crimes of the Taliban and other fundamentalists. Our history proves that this resistance to occupation will continue until we have won our freedom. Until both the US and the fundamentalists – of both the Northern Alliance and Taliban brands – are driven out of power in Afghanistan, we cannot see a bright future ... The only change that can make us hopeful is the strengthening of a national anti-fundamentalist and democracy-loving movement. Such a movement can be built only by Afghans. And while we want the world's support and solidarity, we neither need nor want Nato's occupying forces.[22]

'Resistance to occupation' is here a prerequisite to freedom and the call of the colonised across the ages. NATO and the US are not perceived as liberators but as being complicit, with the Taliban and the Karzai regime, in impeding this freedom.

The subject of politics in late modern postcoloniality is hence located at the intersection between two articulations of cosmopolitanism; where one seeks to govern, the other expresses solidarity, where the former is framed as a hierarchy (the directionality of resource provision is unidirectional), the latter locates agency and authorship of choices to the other. While the former might proclaim itself to be an apparatus of solidarity, its practices are suggestive of an apparatus of security. The asymmetries of power that constitute the relationship between provider and recipient, protector and protected, suggests that this is not just an unequal pedagogic relationship, but one that can also be extractive. However, as Chatterjee has shown, practices of governmentality can generate, indeed produce, spaces for politics in the midst of governmentality and its operating practices. Thus, to use an illustrative example, if India's census is based on the categorisation of the population into the various castes, including the so-called 'backward' and 'less backward' castes, then these categorisations and their inscriptions can then be drawn upon in the constitution of political categories open to mobilisation and potential conflict with others.[23] The cosmopolitanism of government can similarly produce political categories, and these might be intended. However, they might also be unintended.

The postcolonial context within which cosmopolitanism as a practice of government is being articulated provides a setting wherein investigating the political subject is already limited by a modern vocabulary that subsumes this subject into its own categories, thereby differentiating populations into elements that might be contained within this vocabulary and elements that are excluded discursively. The circumscription of political subjectivity can therefore be as much a product of the government of populations through security as through expressions of solidarity. What emerges is a binary representation of the political subject in postcolonial modernity – one represented by the idea of modern citizenship in the context of the modern postcolonial state, and the other somehow excluded from the institutions of modernity and the various modes of articulation that such institutions take.[24]

Chatterjee's 'politics of the governed' places emphasis on the dynamics involved in the emergence of political subjectivity in the postcolonial context that is late modernity. That this collective effort constitutive of political society takes place on the terrain of governmentality is suggestive of a moment of interjection and a politics of presence, reclaiming as it does the very discourses and categories utilised in its government. So, for example, when populations are governed through security, are interpellated as 'dangerous', then these very tropes might be used to mobilise, to make claims, and more significantly still, to redefine the very concepts through which they are governed. While Chatterjee does not engage directly with what I am referring to here as the cosmopolitanism of government, nevertheless his categories provide a way in which we might begin to think about the question of how within this context, now globally rendered, political subjectivity emerges and how it is articulated. While Chatterjee's conception of political society is limited to the territorial state, we know that spaces of government through security are not so limited or confined. We might then extrapolate the concept of political society to rethink its significance in relation to cosmopolitanism and its articulations in the government of populations and in the politics of solidarity.

Cosmopolitan space might be seen as contested space and practices constitutive of this space can have the government of others as their imperative. However, the cosmopolitan is also suggestive of solidarity. A cosmopolitanism of politics recognises the agency of the other as paramount and seeks to extend solidarity where this is invited and mobilised. The extension of solidarity assumes, therefore, mutual recognition on the part of those involved, retaining rather than subsuming difference, recognising in turn the limits and boundaries constitutive of 'independent' and self-determining political subjectivity. Far from subsuming the subjectivity of the other into globally instituted practices of government, the political subject, indeed the 'political' emerges, is articulated and performed, in moments of interjection and assertions of presence.[25] Such interjections might take place in taken-for-granted realms of meaning, the discursive formations that typify, constrain, and intimidate at one and the same time. They might also take place in unexpected material spaces, reclaiming the everyday – the street, the art gallery, the church and mosque, the market-place, the university square – for politics.

Tracing the postcolonial subject in cosmopolitan space is immediately suggestive of hybridity, not simply in the sense of what Homi Bhabha refers to as the 'in-between' of culture, but in the sense of the 'worldly subjectivity' I refer to above, where the situatedness of the nation, its political capture, or indeed re-capture, is enabled by drawing upon the discursive and material resources that a globalised arena can provide. The hybrid condition does not then mean the diminution of a nationally defined postcolonial political community, but rather its use as a distinct space of mobilisation and articulation, a location wherein expressions of solidarity might take place transnationally without diminishing the idea of a modern situated political community. This form of subjectivity, the postcolonial subject in cosmopolitan space, does not, therefore, suggest an inward-looking political subjectivity, though this too is a potentiality that can emerge in certain contingencies, but rather a subject formed in complex local and transnational discursive and institutional matrixes within which and through which interactions take place, articulations of identity come to take shape and shift, and interpretations of events come to be shared and their contestations aired.[26] Such a complex terrain of intersubjectivity plays out not simply locally, but can be instantly available to a global audience which is then rendered a terrain for solidarities, mobilisations, and pedagogic cross-fertilisations. The subject of politics in late modernity is precariously located not simply in the in-between of culture, but more seriously at the intersection between a cosmopolitanism of government and a cosmopolitanism of politics.

How does a worldly subjectivity translate into agency? While the temptation is to suggest a linear relationship between the subject and agency, no such linearity is assumed here. The call, as declared by Arjun Appadurai (1993), to 'think ourselves beyond the nation' can be articulated in a number of transnational discourses, all in one way or another possessing a 'worldly' or 'outward' focus. The thinking of self beyond the nation might invoke post-national, religious, or cultural forms of identity across the boundaries of the state, just as it might involve struggles over global inequalities based on class or gender. Political struggle comes to be articulated by looking beyond the state, a looking beyond that brings into force a transnational terrain utilised in political mobilisation. For some authors, this transnational rendering of the political is suggestive of an emergent global public sphere, cosmopolitan in its constitution, and deliberative in its forms of expression, though it may also be confrontational (Buck-Morss, 2003; Fraser, 2007). These authors seek to reclaim a global public space that in some way re-politicises a terrain governed largely by the interests of capital and its hegemonic state backers.

The cosmopolitanism of politics that I am defining here, however, does not assume a shared 'post-national' global public sphere, or one that is defined by the activities of largely Western-dominated social movements. Rather, the 'worldliness' of the subject of politics I am tracing here places the lens firmly on the *emergence* of political subjectivity and the assertion of presence in the midst of contested spaces where the overwhelming imperative is to regulate, to domesticate, and hence to pacify. Spaces of politics are hence constituted through practices, and these may be articulated in streets and neighbourhoods just as they might take place on the high seas in convoys that seek to defy the siege of populations.[27] Claiming the right to politics has a materiality of presence and being such seeks to occupy spaces, not in an effort to undo the state, but in the recognition that the state and its machinery is already undone in relation to politics.

A cosmopolitanism, the remit of which is the government of other populations, draws upon the discursive tropes of liberalism – human rights, the pedagogic training of society and its institutions in ideas relating to the rule of law, for example – in governing through security as the defining imperative. As liberal societies and their institutions engage in what can be seen as a colonial rationality, they instantiate subjectivities that have deep roots both within liberalism and the target societies that it seeks to govern. Taking place in a postcolonial context, a liberal cosmopolitan re-configuration of the international produces two forms of subject; on the one hand, the liberal self of global reach, the citizen whose claims are articulated in terms of rights in relation to the state and other global institutions, and whose capacities constitute a global civil and military machine geared for the government of populations, and on the other hand, the mass of the governed, conceived as categories of population inhabiting a transnational terrain of humanity, utilised in the productive capacities of the global market, and subject to practices that seek to render populations governable. Expressions of political subjectivity, the articulation of presence, and interjection into spaces configured as governable, come to be constructed as threats to a terrain of regulation now globally defined. However, such articulations of presence constitute interjections onto the discursive and spatial manifestation of power so that the assertion of presence, therefore, can be conceived as an act of creating as well as reclaiming political space within and across the boundaries of state, culture, and more significantly, government.

The temptation is to capture the subject in concepts, and the concept that draws the epistemic subject of critical thought most profoundly is resistance. However, the subject of resistance escapes capture at every instance of objectification, as we learn from Frantz Fanon. The subject of resistance is at the same time object, materialised in embodied being and yet defiant of the inscriptive fixities of 'identity' or 'identification'. For Theodor Adorno, as we saw in Chapter 3, epistemology understood as the claim to knowledge must be 'materialist', for it must be motivated by the fact of corporeal human suffering: 'The need to let suffering speak is a condition of all truth. For suffering is objectivity that weighs upon the subject ...'[28] Critical thought for Adorno aims to reveal the history that resides in objects and not to dispossess them of this history. The postcolonial world, past and in the present, has been subsumed in discourses that assume identity between subject and object, thereby accruing constitutive primacy to the epistemic subject. What Spivak refers to as the 'epistemic violence of imperialism' can only be understood thus, in Adorno's terms, the negation of the 'non-identity' of the object – in this context the colonised and the postcolonial.

NOTES

Introduction

1 There is, as will be revealed in the first chapter, an extensive literature on postcolonial social and political theory and postcolonial approaches in International Relations. In anticipation of the discussion to follow, I must highlight Frantz Fanon's *Wretched of the Earth* (1967) as holding iconic status in its influence on subsequent postcolonial theory. Major influential, if somewhat diverse voices, include Edward Said (especially 1978 and 1993); Homi Bhabha (1994); Gayatry Spivak (especially 1988 and 1999); Dipesh Chakrabarty (2000); and Partha Chatterjee (1986 and 1993).

2 Michel Foucault's analytics of war can be found in his published books and lecture notes now published in book format. See especially Foucault (1977) which provides an understanding of war as permeating the microcosmic workings of society, and focuses mainly on the idea of power as disciplinarity. Foucault (1978) begins to discuss war in biopolitical terms, a theme that is developed in his lecture series, *Society Must Be Defended* see Foucault (2003).

3 Throughout the book, the term 'government' or 'governmentality' is used in Foucaultian terms to refer to the control and management of individuals and populations. It is important to stress from the outset that Foucault's understanding of 'government' is suggestive of both disciplinary and biopolitical power, the first directed at individual bodies and the second at populations. However, these modes of power do not 'replace' 'sovereign power'. As he states: 'in reality one has a triangle, sovereignty-discipline-government, which has as its primary target the population and as its essential mechanism the apparatus of security'. See Foucault (2001a: 219–220).

4 I use the term 'liberal cosmopolitanism' to highlight the extension of liberal principles to the realm of 'humanity' at large, thereby transcending the domestic/international divide, and hence articulating a moral, political, and juridical project that has global aspirations. For this definition of liberal cosmopolitanism, see Jabri (2007c). For advocates of a distinctly liberal understanding of cosmopolitanism, one that frames its discourse in terms of a post-Westphalian understanding of the international, see, for example, Linklater (1998), Bobbio (1995), and Held (1995).

5 Burgess and Owen (2004) refer to the 'malleability' of 'human security' as the basis of its 'attraction' as a concept.

6 Linklater (1998) suggests that societies that exhibit constitutional modes of governance, democratic accountability, and sophisticated understandings of 'dialogical communicative

practices' hold the 'moral resources' to drive progress towards a cosmopolitan global order. Habermas (1994) refers specifically to existing democracies as having this particular responsibility.

7 For critiques of liberal cosmopolitanism, see especially Douzinas (2007), Duffield (2007), Grovogui (2006), Jabri (2007a) and Walker (2010).

8 See note 3 above. Foucault develops his understanding of liberal governmentality as an 'apparatus of security' in Foucault (2001a) and more extensively in (2007). For applications of Foucault's notion of 'dispositif de securite', see Dillon and Reid (2009) and Dillon and Lobo-Guerrero (2008).

9 Two stories that have emerged recently place the past of Kenya in the present of Iraq. While the details differ, the structure of the colonial encounter remains the same, the first of modernity/coloniality and the second of a late modern form of colonisation. The stories are told in their present manifestations. The Kenyan story relates to four elderly Kenyans seeking the right to sue the British government for atrocities committed during the Mau Mau insurgency in colonial Kenya. British governments have, over the years, somewhat bizarrely, but pertinently for the discussions to follow, claimed that answerability for abuses committed during the colonial era had passed on to the Kenyan government. The context of the abuses committed, as revealed by the archives, relates to the state of emergency imposed during the uprising, abuses including the forced removal of an estimated million of the Kikuyu and their incarceration in compounds for the mass and detention camps for insurgents, who were then subjected to torture, castration, sexual abuse, and murder. This past has emerged in a present wherein other cases of abuse, from Iraq, have begun to appear in British courts. However, this is not the past of colonial era Iraq, the violence of which is well documented. This is the Iraq of the 2003 invasion and subsequent occupation. The particular case that I want to highlight here in this Introduction stands out for it took place on the same day that the elderly Kenyans were granted leave to sue the British government. This is of the decision by the Ministry of Defence to compensate an Iraqi family with the sum of £100,000 for the drowning of their teenage son, Saeed Shabram. The MOD did not admit liability, but made an out-of-court settlement. Shabram and his cousin, Menem Akaili, had been forced at gunpoint by British soldiers into the Shat Al-Arab river as part of the practice known as 'wetting' used for petty crime against the local youth in southern Iraq. While Akaili was pulled out by onlookers, Shabram drowned and his body was later recovered. This being a formal practice of the occupying forces, the soldiers involved have not been charged. See *The Guardian*, 22 July 2011.

Chapter 1

1 David Harvey (2005), in Marxist perspective, uses the formulation, 'accumulation by dispossession', while Derek Gregory (2004), in reference to the interventions in Iraq and Afghanistan, and to the situation of the Palestinians, refers, in his poststructuralist account, to 'the colonial present'.

2 This is what is referred to as the 'liberal peace project'. For critical engagements, see, for example, Richmond (2005), Duffield (2007), and Chandler (2008).

3 See especially Inayatullah and Blaney (2004) in the context of international relations, in the context of sociology, McLennan (2003); and in the context of literary studies, see various in Lazarus (2004).

4 For a powerful critique of the historical and philosophical underpinning of what I am referring to here as the politics of anamnesis, see Beate Jahn (2000). Jahn reveals the place of the colonial encounter in liberal political philosophy. For a discussion of Hobbes, his corporate colonial experience of Bermuda and Virginia, and his configurations of the 'state of nature' and of 'sovereignty', see Srinivas Aravamurdan (2009).

5 For critical engagements with poststructural theory from a postcolonial angle, see, for example, Sajed (2011) and Jabri (2007b). Sajed provides an insightful critique of

poststructural thought, and specifically Derrida, Lyotard, and Cixous, suggesting, through an investigation of their representations of the Algerian war of independence, that these tend to idealise the 'marginalised' in place of engaging with their agency. Jabri provides a critique of Foucault's engagement with the Iranian Revolution, suggesting, again from a postcolonial perspective, that he presented an idealised version of this particular event and its place in relation to resistance.

6 Jackson (1993), who uses the term 'quasi states', is perhaps the exemplar of this literature. For alternative postcolonial readings, see Grovogui (2002) and Ahluwalia (2001).

7 For this constitutive perspective on postcolonial agency in global politics, see especially Muppidi (2005) and Barkawi and Laffey (2006). For a discussion of how postcolonial agency draws upon the discourses 'human rights' in gaining transformations of the international, see Reus-Smit (2011).

8 On 'non-Western' international political theory, see Chan, Mandaville, and Bleiker (2001); and Shilliam (2011). For the implications of 'diversity' in international relations, and the dangers of 'normalisation', see Pasha (2011).

9 Just as these examples represent the diversity of sites and meanings of postcolonial agency, so too there is diversity in postcolonial discourses seeking to capture such agency in global politics. In relation to violence and security studies, see Ayoob (1995) and Barkawi (2006); in relation to India's foreign policy and its tense negotiations with global institutions, see Muppidi (2004), and Krishna (1999); on the postcolonial and globalised resistance, see Krishna (2009); on postcolonial resistance in local spaces wherein international politics finds expression, see Agathangelou and Ling (2009).

10 I borrow the formulation, 'the aftermath of sovereignty', from Scott (1996).

11 There is much debate in political theory that focuses on the question of 'political community' and its boundaries. This debate is often framed in terms of the communitarian/cosmopolitan divide, where the former, primarily associated with thinkers such as Charles Taylor and Alisdair MacIntyre, is opposed to the latter, associated with John Rawls, and Will Kymlycka, among others. For useful discussions of this debate and its implications for international relations, see Hutchings (1999). For a distinctly cosmopolitan approach to the question of political community in international relations, and that argues for a 'post-Westphalian' international order, see Linklater (1998).

12 For a most significant rendition of this choice, for international relations, see Walker (2010). For its implications in relation to war, see Joas (2003).

13 While the Kelsen-Schmitt debate in international relations focuses on a conception of 'sovereignty' as command, centring as it has done in recent times on the question of the 'exception', another conceptualisation relates the concept of 'sovereignty' to 'democracy', thereby focusing attention on what Kalyvas (2008) refers to as 'new popular beginnings'. In his focus on the 'extraordinary' in relation to democratic founding, Kalyvas's very useful discussion places Schmitt's understanding of 'constituent power' between Max Weber on the one hand and Hannah Arendt on the other. See also Kalyvas (2005).

14 Especially significant for my purposes here, and as will be seen in Chapter 3, is Arendt (1977), first published in 1963, and Arendt (1958).

15 As I will elaborate later, I want to assert that 'independence' is constitutively related to the postcolonial subject of politics, while acknowledging powerful critiques of the 'national' project in relation to the postcolonial. See especially Chatterjee (1993) as an exemplar of such critiques.

16 Bhabha (1994) points to this 'negation' in Michel Foucault's 'What is Enlightenment'. See Foucault (1984: 43–44).

17 Foucault, 'The Shah is a hundred years behind the times', Corriere della sera 1978, reproduced in Afary and Anderson (2005: 195–197), quoted in Jabri (2007b).

18 See especially Shapiro (1997 and 2007) for this understanding of what I understand to be the nexus between the cartographic and the experiential.

19 I am thinking here especially of Kant's 'Idea for a universal history with a cosmopolitan purpose', in Kant (1970).
20 This Hegelian historical imagination, as Hannah Arendt points out, is always suggestive of the excluded, racialised, other. See Arendt (1968).
21 For Edward Said, this 'implied applicability' is also present in 'critical' discourses. See his *Culture and Imperialism* (1993), p. 336.
22 As Chakrabarty highlights, much subaltern histories are written in terms of 'historical transition' – 'a tendency to read Indian history in terms of a lack, an absence, or an incompleteness'. See Chakrabarty (1989). See also Mignolo (2000 and 2005).
23 Chakrabarty (1992) is here quoting Marx (1975) in 'On the Jewish question', in (Marx, 1975), pp. 215–222.
24 Pratab Bhanu Mehta, Director of the Delhi based Centre for Policy research, proclaimed, in an interview with the author, that it was 'India's destiny' to be a permanent member of the United Nations Security Council.
25 Jameson (2003: 712). Jameson is here using, or drawing on Karl Heinz Bohrer (1994) *Suddenness: On the Moment of Aesthetic Appearance* (New York: Columbia University Press).
26 See his Afterward to the 1994 edition of Orientalism. Quoted in Mishra and Hodge (2005, p. 375).
27 See Dirlik (1994), for a powerful critique of 'postcolonial theory'.
28 Jean-Paul Sartre (1964) 'Colonialism is a system', reprinted in Sartre (2006).
29 Foucault, 'Space, knowledge, and power', see Foucault (1984b).

Chapter 2

1 Qabbani's poem, 'We are accused of terrorism', is reproduced in Tariq Ali (2003).
2 For one of the most powerful revelations of the violence constitutive of European modernity, see Enrique Dussel (1998). See also Walter Mignolo (2005).
3 The idea of the paradoxes of modernity is perhaps best captured by the critical theorists of the Frankfurt School. The interdisciplinary perspective that informed the intellectual productions of the School, from sociology to psychoanalysis, from the Marxist to the Freudian, provided a conception of the subject striving for emancipation, but one whose desire is always already situated in and constituted by the formative (and hence constraining) continuities of social and political life. This is the paradox of modernity, and indeed of the modern subject, and it is perhaps best captured in Theodor Adorno and Max Horkheimer's *Dialectic of Enlightenment* (1979).
4 To authors of Middle Eastern origin, the 'capture' and attribution of the 'modern' to the European is always interpreted as yet another form of dispossession. The preferred concept is always modernities in the plural, the European being only one form. Chakrabarty's provincialising of European modernity is all too resonant here. On the intersection of philosophy and science in Arab history, see Jim Al-Khalili (2010).
5 The story is told in Yunan Labib Rizk, *Al-Ahram Weekly*, 29 April–5 May 1999; accessed 25 May 2011.
6 See the National Gallery of Modern Art, Delhi, India, at http://ngmaindia.gov.in/sh-bengal.asp (accessed 6 March 2012).
7 See especially Mitter (1994).
8 I am especially grateful to the following sources on modern Arabic poetry and Al-Sayyab in particular: Boullata (1970, 1983); Terri DeYoung (1998); and an article on Al-Sayyab that appeared in Al-Ahram in the aftermath of the invasion and occupation of Iraq, authored by Mursi Saad El-Din (2004). See note 10 below for this last reference.
9 Nazik Al-Mala'ka (1923–2007) is another celebrated (female) modern poet from Iraq.
10 Al-Sayyab, *Rain Song*, Translated by Mursi Saad El-Din, in *Al-Ahram* weekly, 24 March 2004 at http://www.weekly.ahram.org.eg/2004/682/bo7.htm (accessed 4 March 2012).
11 Badr Shakir al-Sayyab, *Asatir* (Najaf, 1950), p. 8, quoted in Issa Boullata (1970), p. 255.

12 See Kristeva (2002b). As Cecelia Sjoholm (2005: 110) points out in relation to Kristeva, 'The intimate is a sphere of singularity, irreducible to the private.'

13 Kwame Anthony Appiah presents a comparable (to Said) analysis of African writing, using the term 'stages' to point to the first stage as constituting 'national', anti-colonial writing, and a second, 'postcolonial' stage, one representing disillusionment with the national state. See Appiah (1997).

14 Edward Said (1997) spent much of his later writings on representations of Islam in US political circles and the media. For an analysis of the emergence of Islamic transnational and state-based political movements and their representations in the West, see especially Peter Mandaville (2001 and 2007). What is apparent from Mandaville's work is the complexity of Islamic politics as opposed to the simplifications of its representations in Western discourses.

15 For authors using 'culture' as an unquestioned form of interpellation, see, for example, Bernard Lewis (2004), Samuel Huntington (1997).

16 A label currently applied to India, China and Brazil.

17 I am using the term 'govern' to suggest the control and management of conduct, borrowing from Michel Foucault's understanding of 'governmentality'. See Foucault (2001a).

18 I develop this argument in Jabri (2009).

19 For an insightful discussion of 'toleration' and the inequalities assumed by the concept, see Asad (1997).

20 See, for example, Butler (2006) and Jabri (2007a).

21 The play was staged by the National Theatre of Wales in August 2010.

22 Charlotte Higgins, 'The National Theatre of Wales does battle with Aeschylus's *The Persians*', *The Guardian, Review*, 14 August 2010, p. 14.

23 Quoted in Higgins, *The Guardian, Review*, 14 August 2010, p. 15.

24 BBC Radio 4, Today, 19 August 2010.

25 For details of the Chilcot (Iraq) Inquiry, including the full witness statements, see Chilcot Inquiry, http://www.iraqinquiry.org.uk (accessed 6 March 2012).

26 Green Zones are constructed both discursively and materially as 'safe zones', containing as they do Western militaries of occupation, private security firms, and open to other 'visiting' personnel, from NGO workers, to academics, to journalists. What distinguishes the Green Zone is that it is barricaded against the 'others' in whose countries these spaces are constructed. For a revealing insight into the Green Zone in occupied Baghdad, see Chandrasekaran (2006).

27 See also Hughes (2009) for another account of British counter-insurgency methods in Palestine.

28 Norris quotes a Private Bellows who states in a letter found at the archives of the Imperial War Museum, 'It was a dirty trick, but we enjoyed it.' And another, 'If the prisoner survived a day, the driver would swerve the vehicle suddenly, the poor wog on the front would roll off onto the deck. Well if he was lucky he'd get away with a broken leg, but if he was unlucky the truck behind would hit him. But nobody bothered to go and pick the bits up.' Norris (2008: 34).

29 A term used by the High Commissioner in Palestine, Harold MacMichael, to justify the destruction of the village of Kawkab Abu Haija. Quoted in Norris (2008: 38).

30 For a history of the term 'counter-insurgency', a term that came to replace 'imperial policing', see Ian Beckett (1990).

31 From the Colonial Office of the colonial past to defence ministries of the present, the tendency is to respond to claims of atrocity through a variety of methods, from denial to the attribution of guilt to the enemy and its population, to the construction of complaints as propagandist and politically motivated, to the charge, more recent and in the context of counter-terrorism, of claiming 'moral equivalence' between the violence of insurgents, or 'terrorists', and the violence of counter-insurgents.

32 For colonial atrocities and their cultures of impunity, see David Anderson (2004) and Caroline Elkins (2005).

33 Halim Al-Karim's work was included in a 2007 exhibition of Middle Eastern contemporary art at the Saatchi Gallery in London. For examples of his work, see Saatchi Gallery (2007).

34 Such is the case in the example of the young female Israeli soldier, whose Facebook image shows her seated in front a number of blindfolded Palestinian prisoners while sending text messages claiming sexual attraction to the prisoners shown in her snaps. So too the violence of US troops at Iraqi checkpoints, a violence often unleashed in a hail of gun fire directed at families.

35 NATO's 'Female Engagement Teams' are a case in point. See http://www.nato.int (accessed 6 March 2012).

Chapter 3

1 Apart from Arendt's own books, I owe much of my understanding of this complex thinker to readings of Arendt that exactly highlight these philosophical and conceptual controversies in political theory. Primary among these are: Calhoun and McGowan (1997); Calhoun (2002); Honig (1988, 1991, 1995, 2007); Ingram (2008); Kalyvas (2005, 2008). Among engagements with Arendt in international relations, see especially Owens (2007).

2 See Lefebvre (1991) for one of the most influential critiques of and shift away from the Kantian understanding of space as a 'tool of knowledge'. On the materiality of space and its constitutive potential, see Diana Coole (2010); Diana Coole and Samantha Frost (2010); Doreen Massey (2005).

3 Homi Bhabha's discussion of Fanon makes reference to the 'negativity' in Fanon's thought and has been most informative in my interpretation of Fanon. See Bhabha (1994).

4 Michel Foucault makes the distinction between the 'philosophical-juridical discourse of law and sovereignty' and the 'historico-political discourse of war', to elaborate on the shift in articulations of power, from sovereignty to biopolitics. See Foucault (2003).

5 See Introduction and Chapter 1.

6 Reus-Smit (2011), for example, suggests that the transformation of the international in the aftermath of the Second World War was due to the colonised claiming human rights in the face of oppressive colonial practices. The problem with this formulation is that Europe remains the authorial voice.

7 In relation to Indian independence, see for example, Partha Chatterjee (1986 and 1993).

8 So all-encompassing is the apparatus of the state taken to be that Mbembe refers to the 'zombification' of the 'dominant and those apparently dominated' (2001: 104).

9 Independence speech, Jawaharlal Nehru (1889–1964).

10 Many Indian commentators refer to India's 'Founding Fathers' in discussions of the aspirations of independence and contemporary discourses on 'emergence'.

11 See, for example, Elizabeth Frazer and Kimberly Hutchings (2008).

12 There is much philosophical controversy around Kant's use of the concepts of autonomy and heteronomy. Of use in the present context is Howard Caygill's understanding of these concepts. See Caygill (1995: 88–89; 223–224).

13 See, for example, Ahmad (1992); Dirlik (1994); Kapoor (2002).

14 For one of the most useful and insightful discussions of 'negativity', see Coole (2000).

15 The very emergence of the 'G20' as a forum for negotiation where the 'sovereign funds' of the formerly colonised are sought to ameliorate the 'sovereign debts' of Europe and the United States bears early testimony to this potential structural shift in the global political economy.

16 See essays in Jones (2006).

17 A discourse that also frames the dependency school, represented especially by Andre Gunder Frank.

18 See Kapoor (2002) for an excellent discussion of this opposition.

19 Spivak is here quoting from Foucault's lecture, 14 January 1976, reproduced in Foucault (1980), p. 104.

20 For Young (2004: 23), the present fragmentation of the African state into civil war and forms of 'localism' have shifted the terrain of politics away from the immediate aftermath of the anti-colonial struggles. He states that where the 'achievement of independence was a defining historical moment', the 'erosion of the stateness of many African polities by the 1990s limited the scope for effective reform and opened the door for a complex web of novel civil conflicts' together with 'a renewed saliency of informal politics, as local societies adapted to diminished state presence'. He suggests that 'perhaps the post-colonial moment has passed'.

Chapter 4

1 This discussion of Egyptian history draws primarily from Ayubi (2006). Other sources that highlight the historiographic contests relating to Arab nationalism include Dawn (1991); Khalidi (1991); Dawisha (2003); Choueiri (2003). These underscore the point I make later in the chapter on the difficulties of isolating 'founding moments' in the constitution of political community.

2 See the following for invaluable accounts of this period of Egypt's history: Vatikiotis (1992) and Mitchell (1991). For a vivid New York Times account of the 1919 events and one that is evocative for its contemporary parallels, see '800 Natives Dead in Egypt's Rising; 1,600 Wounded', go to http://select.nytimes.com/gst/abstract.html?res=F10B 17F83D5C147A93C7AB178CD85F4D8185F9&scp=1&sq=800%20natives&st=cse (accessed 7 March 2012).

3 The 1923 Constitution, widely interpreted as hailing Egypt's liberal turn, was drafted by a 30-member multiparty legislative committee. The history of constitution-making in Egypt is long and reveals the parameters of the contemporary constitutional contestations in Egypt.

4 See George Antonius (1946), quoted in Shalan (2002). Shalan uses the novels, by Muhammad Husayn Haykal, *Zeinab* (1913), and Tawfiq al-Hakim, *'Awdat al-Ruh* (Return of the Spirit)(1933), constituting the 'first phase of cultural nationalism' in Egypt and the Arab world.

5 See here Khalidi *et al.* (1991); Dawisha (2003); Choueiri (2003).

6 Egypt State Information Service, available online at http://www.sis.gov.eg/en/Story. aspx?sid=353 (accessed 26 June 2011).

7 On the emergent women's movement in Iraq of the 1920s, see Saeid N. Neshat (1993) 'A look into the women's movement in Iraq', *Farzaneh*, 6(11), available online at www.iiav.nl/ezines/web/Farzaneh/1993/Vol1Nr1/farzanehjournal/ar. Feminist journals such as *Leila,* established in the 1920s, sought equal rights in education and employment. Journals in the 1930s included *Modern Woman* and *Arab Woman.*

8 Peter Sluglett, review of Hanna Batatu (2004), available online at www.dissentmagazine. org/democratiya/article_pdf/d4Sluglett.pdf (accessed 26 June 2011).

9 From Batatu, quoted in Bob Feldman, 'A people's history of Iraq', available online at http:// www.towardfreedom.com/middle-east/516-a-peoples-history (accessed 6 March 2012).

10 Andreas Wimmer, 'Democracy and ethno-religious conflict in Iraq' (Centre on Democracy, Development and the Rule of Law, Stanford, 2003). Available online at http://iis-db. stanford.edu/pubs/20214/wimmer.pdf (accessed 6 March 2012). This paper was presented at Stanford in 2003, clearly in the wake of the invasion of Iraq and the subsequent political turmoil whereby Iraq's ethnic diversity was used as a technology of control.

11 For other useful sources on Iraq's modern history, and written from different perspectives, see Al-Jabbar (1995), Marr (2007), Tripp (2002) and Dodge (2003).

12 Quoted in Sluglett (2007), p. 23.

13 Hanna Batatu's monumental work on Iraq uniquely provides a class-based investigation of political forces in that country.

14 Some would argue against the perspective I am applying here to the Middle East context on the basis that Islamic political thinkers would place the moment of founding that I

am describing here with the Caliphate and suggest that any other arrangement, juridical and political, that emerged subsequently could not compare to the ideals of the past. However, according to this perspective, as argued by Albert Hourani (1983: 8), 'History could have no more lessons to teach, if there was change it could only be for the worse, and the worse could only be cured, not by creating something new but by renewing something that had once existed.' As Hourani and others, including Talal Assad more recently, have shown, Islamic thought and practice is largely dialogical rather than monolithic, responsive to historic challenges emanating variously from Greek philosophy, to Byzantium, and into the modern period.

15 While much intellectual discourse at this time was heavily influenced by French Enlightenment ideas, German romanticism was also drawn upon in the evolution of ideas relating to identity, national and religious. See Ayubi (2006).

16 One newspaper, *al-Jarida*, was edited by another important critic who came to influence nationalist thought, Ahmed Lutfi al-Sayyid (1872–1963), whose writings targeted the absolutism of British rule in Egypt. See Hourani (1983: 178).

17 Gertrude Bell, for example, is credited with 'inventing' Iraq.

18 See Ferguson (2003) for a discourse that celebrates the impact of colonisation on modernising the East. This form of discourse, articulated from a not-so-celebratory angle, is provided by Nandy (1983), who calls for the constitution, or re-constitution, of India based on its local traditions.

19 See Michael Dembrow, http://spot.pcc.edu/~mdembrow/the_land.htm (accessed 15 June 2011).

20 For an excellent critical analysis of Egyptian cinema, including Chahin's films, see Kiernan (1995).

21 The treatment of the Mau Mau rebels in Kenya and of the Palestinians in colonial Palestine are but two examples of the extremes of violence used against resistance movements and populations.

22 See, for example, Mbembe (2001) and other postcolonial authors on postcolonial leaderships.

23 Iraq's exiled community stood at least at 4 million during the reign of the Baath regime.

24 Rodinson (1974) quoted in Nafissi (1998), the latter providing an excellent critical account of Weber's orientalism.

25 See my discussion in Chapter 3. For the generativity of 'aporia', see Jacques Derrida's use of the term as discussed in Beardsworth (1996). See also Bernstein (2006).

26 I use the term reclaim here to point to the fact that in pre-colonial times, juridical equality enabled treaty-making among Western and non-Western entities that was later lost in the hierarchical relations borne of the colonial order. For an insightful discussion of this transformation, see Keen (2007).

27 See, in the context of India, for example, Kaviraj (1997). On the complex intersection of the modern and the 'traditional' in the national movement's mobilisation effort, see Chatterjee (1993) and Chakrabarty (2000).

28 For the significance of the Non-Aligned Movement for postcolonial national leaders, see Nehru (1961).

29 See, for example, Willetts (1978).

30 For Kwame Nkrumah, the decolonisation process had to encompass not just the institutions of the state, but the political economy and African consciousness itself. Western hostility towards Nkrumah was exactly directed at disrupting his efforts to combat what he called 'neo-colonialism', his support for liberation struggles across the continent and globally, and his proposal, according to David Birmingham (1998), to allow the establishment of a Soviet airbase in Ghana. Indeed in 1999, the Historian's Office of the US State Department published declassified intelligence reports relating to American activities in Africa, including plans for the overthrow of Nkrumah. In a case reminiscent of the overthrow of Mossadeq in Iran and the reinstatement of the Shah and the Pahlavi dynasty in 1952, an event instilled in the Iranian mind, the 8-point 'proposed Action Programme for Ghana', drawn up by William Trimble, the Director of the

Office of West African Affairs in February 1964, stated: 'Intensive efforts should be made through psychological warfare and other means to diminish support for Nkrumah within Ghana and nurture the conviction among the Ghanaian people that their country's welfare and independence necessitate his removal.' The US Secretary of State at the time, Dean Rusk, along with CIA Director John McCone, explored the potential of particular generals in the Ghana military as authors of an envisaged coup d'état that would overthrow Nkrumah, and this coming in parallel with considerations of ending US support for large scale infrastructural projects in Ghana initiated during the Kennedy Administration. See full discussion of these papers in Issaka K. Souare (2006).

31 See, for example, William Blum (2003).
32 See Muppidi's (2005) discussion of India's foreign policy and constructions of identity.
33 One of the motivations for the nationalisation of the Suez Canal was the financing of the Aswan Damn.
34 For an account of events surrounding the nationalisation of Suez, see Joelle Bassoul, 'The day Nasser nationalized the Suez Canal', *Daily News Egypt*, 26 July 2006. Available online at http://www.dailynewsegypt.com (accessed 16 December 2010).
35 Gamal Abdel Nasser, 'The Egyptian Revolution', *Foreign Affairs*, 33 (1955): 209.
36 See International Movie Database: *Earth* (1998). See www.imdb.com (accessed 6 March 2012).
37 See Kang (2003) for a powerful critique of realist discourses on Asia.

Chapter 5

1 See my discussion of the concept of aporia in the last chapter. This relies on Jacque Derrida's use of the concept in his discussion of 'forgiveness'. See Richard Bernstein (2006).
2 For Michel Foucault (1982: 783), 'pastoral power' suggests 'salvation'. The 'modern state', according to Foucault is premised on 'pastoral power', for it is a 'sophisticated structure, in which individuals can be integrated, under one condition: that this individuality would be shaped in a new form and submitted to a set of very specific patterns.' I am contending that this pastoral power has a global articulation in contemporary times.
3 See Koskenniemi (2005) for a critique of liberal assumptions relating to international law.
4 Liberal arguments focus on the workings of international rules and norms as products of the practices of agents and as constitutive of the identities and preferences of those agents. Their understanding of what is referred to here as 'regulation' is hence not based on the 'repressive model', to use Michel Foucault, but rather on a model of law and norms as productive. See, for example, Finnemore and Toope (2001).
5 Alavi (1972) suggests that the presence of the bureaucratic-military oligarchy differentiates the postcolonial state from the 'state as analysed in classical Marxist theory'.
6 For a discussion of the 'civilising mission' that underpins 'modernisation' and war, see Joas (2003)
7 For an excellent account of how this colonial rationality operated in occupied Iraq, and written from the perspective of a post-invasion government minister (defence and finance), see Alawi (2007).
8 As Fiona Adamson (2005) points out, there is a 'liberal bias' in the constructivist literature in international relations, so that liberal norms are conferred constitutive power in relations to the international, while other norms (Adamson is concerned in this context with Islamic frameworks) are not so conferred. For an illustration of Adamson's argument, see Finnemore (2003). For international relations' difficulties in incorporating other frames of reference, see Mustapha Kamal Pasha (2011).
9 Some authors have argued for the different model of 'emergence' provided by 'new' Latin American leaders such as Hugo Chavez and Evo Morales. On the promise of Latin America, see Oscar Guardiola-Rivera (2010).
10 See, for example, Wheeler (2002) and Caney (2005).

11 Writing a critique of attributions of human rights to the West, Siba Grovogui writes that his essay 'takes it for granted that the revolutions in America and France encoded historical conceptions of political subjectivity, personal liberties, and political freedom. The established legislation – the American Declaration of Independence and Bill of Rights and the French Declaration of the Rights of Man and Citizen – contributed to opening the possibility of the universalization of the concept of human rights.' See Grovogui (2006).

12 See Jabri (2007a) for a detailed and critical engagement with Habermas and his advocacy of 'cosmopolitan law'.

13 The more appropriate designation here might refer to the politics of depoliticisation. Read in the context of liberalism's 'turn to law' in response to conflict, see Dillon (1998).

14 In conversation with Ashis Nandy, April 2010, Delhi. While Nandy's comments point to the dialectic of every modernising move, nevertheless, it must be pointed out that The Children's Right to Free and Compulsory Education Act in India also received much endorsement in India's press as it specifically made elementary education a fundamental right. Nandy's interpretation of this latest 'developmental' 'modernising' move must be placed in the context of his wider, and earlier, critique of the national state as inheritor of the colonial regime. See especially Nandy (1983).

15 I make this distinction in Jabri (2007c). See also Dallmayr (2003).

16 For a historical treatment of the emergence of the modern international, see Toulmin (1990).

17 See Tim Mitchell (1991) for a discussion of The Great Exhibition of the Works of Industry of all Nations, or The Great Exhibition of 1851, aimed to showcase Victorian Britain not simply as an industrial power, but one that had a global remit.

18 The almost immediate privatisation of Iraq's oil industry after the 2003 invasion bears testimony to the dispossessive drive of this particular late modern practice of colonisation. Ali Alawi provides a first hand account of how the Provisional Authority excluded Iraqi contractors from reconstruction projects, awarding these almost exclusively to American companies. See Alawi (2007).

19 However, the invasion of Iraq was effectively legitimised, despite its illegality, through the sanction conferred to the 'Coalition Provisional Authority' to oversee Iraq's revenues. Security Council Resolution 1483 is especially significant in this case. Authored by the United States and passed on 23 May 2003, it created the Development Fund for Iraq, enabling the CPA to make decisions relating to Iraq's oil revenues and the distribution of contracts relating to the reconstruction of the infrastructure destroyed in the invasion shock and awe tactics. In the event of practices of legitimisation, it is difficult to argue against the case that, for example, both Kosovo and Iraq constituted practices of exception. For the argument that differentiates between the two interventions, again based on the differentiation of legality and legitimacy, see Richard Falk (2005).

20 See The Princeton Project on National Security (2006), Woodrow Wilson School of Public and International Affairs. Available online at http://www.princeton.edu/~ppns/report.html (accessed 6 March 2012).

21 The Princeton Project on National Security provides a clear indication of what it sees as constituting 'major threats and challenges that confront the United States and the wider world'. These are: 'the collapse of order in the Middle East, global terror networks, the proliferation and transfer of nuclear weapons, the rise of China and order in East Asia, global pandemics, energy, and the need for a protective infrastructure within and around the United States.' Ikenberry and Slaughter (2006: 33). See Note 20.

22 In both senses of the word 'count'. As uncounted bodies, see the Iraq Body Count, at www.iraqbodycount.org, and its effort to exactly count the dead. On the politics of counting the dead, see Maja Zehfuss (2011).

23 On the performativity of sovereign power, see primarily Michel Foucault (1977). In the context of international relations and poststructural understandings of sovereignty, see for example Bartelsen (1995); Edkins and Pin-Fat (1999); and Weber (1995).

24 See Balibar (2002), p. 24.
25 Interviewed by Alan Yentob, BBC 1, 26 July 2011.
26 Ibid.

Chapter 6

1 See Chapter 3. Spivak is here quoted in Bhabha (1994: 183).
2 See, for example, A.H. Cordesman, 'Symposium: The Arab Uprisings and US Policy: What is the American National Interest?', Middle East Policy, Vol. 18, No. 2 (2011), pp. 1-28 and in the same issue, C. W. Freeman, 'The Arab Reawakening: Strategic Implications'.
3 For Said, the discursive formation that he describes as the 'structure of cultural domination' of the Arab and Islamic world wherein this world's own cultural and epistemic productions tend to be relegated to the margins in preference for what are deemed to be 'social scientific facts' relating to regional 'attitudes' or 'trends'. See Edward Said, 'In the Shadow of the West' (Said, 1978: 251). See also various essays in Said (2004).
4 This is, of course, always surprising to anyone either from the region or in possession of a certain reflexivity relating to the bodycount. If we consider Iraq alone, then the pre-war sanctions regime + the war dead takes us well beyond the million mark. There is, of course, politics involved in the numbers and their re-counting, as the responses to the Lancet report on Iraqi civilian casualties showed, some of them framed in a 'scientific' language. See Burnham et al. (2006) for the Johns Hopkins report on Iraq 'mortality' rates. Iraq Body Count provides an ongoing (since the invasion of 2003) survey of violent deaths (see www.iraqbodycount.org). We might also reflect on other locations subject to high technology bombardment. These are so evident that listing them seems somehow to push the point.
5 See Hardt and Negri (2004) for their understanding of the constitutive forces that generate the 'multitude' of singularities.
6 This does not mean that identities and the historic discourses that constitute them do not play a part. In a region replete with historic deliberation on exactly the meaning of community in the midst of diversity, from the Abbasid renaissance in ancient Baghdad to the multicultural world of the Ottomans to contemporary contestations, the form and content of representational practices have always been at issue, at stake. See especially Fatima Mernissi (1993).
7 The practice of 'extraordinary rendition' as part of the so-called 'war on terrorism' and conducted by the United States, with the material help of its allies (in the provision of landing spaces for flights used in the transport of the incarcerated and the 'rendered'), would not have been possible without the complicity of Arab regimes in the torture of 'suspects'.
8 This event is the 'huge event of the twenty-first century', proclaimed Bernard Henri Levi on Al Jazeera (10 March 2011), and this new event is seductive not just for the writer who seeks to capture in concepts, but for forces that seek to govern the uncertain, the unpredictable, and the undesirable. The military intervention in Libya, conducted by NATO and sanctioned by the UN, took place shortly after Henri Levi's statement.
9 Michael Hardt and Antonio Negri (2011) 'Arabs are Democracy's new Pioneers: The leaderless Middle East uprisings can inspire freedom movements as Latin America did before', The Guardian, Thursday 24 February. Available online at http://www.guardian.co.uk/commentisfree/2011/feb/24/arabs-democracy-latin-america?INTCMP=SRCH (accessed 6 March 2012).
10 Hardt and Negri are here arguing against the dichotomy relating to the question of 'class' and its conceptual framing as either unitary or plural. See Hardt and Negri (2004: 105).
11 Slavoj Zizek (2011) 'What We Are Witnessing is the Miracle of Tahrir Square', The Guardian, Friday 11 February, p. 38.

12 Mustafa Barghouti (2011) 'Lessons from the Egyptian revolution', *Al Ahram Weekly*, 3–9 March 2011. See http://weekly.ahram.or.eg/print/2011/1037/op181.htm (accessed 10 August 2011).

13 Noam Chomsky (2011) 'Radical Islam doesn't worry the US. Independence does', *The Guardian*, 5 February.

14 The overthrow of Iran's elected Prime Minister, Mohammed Mossadegh, in 1953 is deemed the CIA's 'first successful overthrow of a foreign government'. As James Risen of the New York Times states on reading the CIA document relating to this event: 'The document, which remains classified, discloses the pivotal role British intelligence officials played in initiating and planning the coup, and it shows that Washington and London shared an interest in maintaining the West's control over Iranian oil.' See James Risen (2000) 'Secrets of History: The C.I.A. in Iran – A Special Report; How a Plot Convulsed Iran in '53 (and in '79)', The New York Times, 16 April. Available online at http://web4.uwindsor.ca/users/w/winter/Winters.nsf/0/dd2d7252bba29965852570b50052c48f/$FILE/Iran_CIA_Coup_NYT.pdf (accessed 6 March 2012).

15 For one of the best readings of postcolonial states' contests with former colonial powers in the framework of international law, contests that have predominantly concerned sovereign rights over natural resources, see Anthony Anghie (2004).

16 On the MEPI programme, see Thomas Carothers (2003) 'A better way to support Middle East Reform', *Policy Brief*, February; and Tamara Cofman, 'The promise of Arab liberalism', *Policy Review*, 125, June to July: 1–3. Both quoted in Ehteshami and Wright (2007). For a piece seeking reflection on Western foreign policy towards the Middle East, see Joshi (2011).

17 See The Middle East Partnership Initiative at http://mepi.state.gov/about-us.html (accessed 6 March 2012).

18 MEPI provides funding opportunities for local actors involved in the 'transition' processes in the various Arab states. One such initiative covers Tunisia and aims to support local civil society groups, enhance the role of an independent media, 'strengthening the rule of law, and developing the electoral process.

19 For Mernissi (1993: 38), one of the most influential political thinkers for the youth of the Middle East, and especially North Africa, is Moroccan philosopher, Muhammad al-Jabiri. As she states, Al-Jabiri 'has reconciled millions of Arab young people to modernity.'

20 Apart from Fatima Mernissi and Al-Jabiri, other intellectuals of influence, and interestingly all at the University of Rabat in Morocco, include Sa'id Binsa'id, Kamal 'Abd al-Latif, 'Abdallah Sa'if. For a comprehensive discussion of ideas relating to democracy and civil society in the Middle East, see Ayubi (1993), Browers (2006).

21 For an analysis of NATO's intervention in Libya, and one that places particular emphasis on the discursive constructions geared to its legitimisation, what the author refers to as 'mystifications', see Hugh Roberts, 'Who Said Gaddafi Had to Go?', *London Review of Books*, 17 November 2011. What is especially interesting about this notion of mystification is that, as the author highlights, the discourses of intervention can be used by 'rebels' on the ground exactly to manufacture the space for intervention.

22 Malalai Joya (2010) 'Any hope I had in the ballot box bringing change is gone', *The Guardian*, 2 November, p. 28. There is, unfortunately, not enough space in this particular book to engage more fully with the voices of women in the Middle East and the wider Islamic region. Malalai Joya is one such voice. See her *Raising My Voice* (2009).

23 See, in relation to India, Pandey (2006).

24 For a postcolonial author such as Partha Chatterjee (2004), a way of dealing with the above paradox is to suggest a binary that distinguishes between civil society and the domain of 'political society'. Where the former is representative of what might be recognised as the liberal self, largely self-governing, a member of civil society, the latter is more reflective of a heterogeneous humanity whose relationship to the state is not based on the citizenship of the individual rights holder, but on categories of population whose mobilisation comes to be based on what he refers to as 'demographic categories of governmentality'.

25 As I have argued in Chapter 3, this is a distinctly Arendtian reading of politics. For this Arendtian understanding of 'world-making' set within the context of a critique of what I would refer to as 'liberal' cosmopolitanism, see Craig Calhoun (2002).

26 Bleiker (2000) refers to 'transversal' politics as a mode of articulation that is not nationally based, but finds articulation in spaces that transcend boundaries. Bleiker's case-study is based in the East German protest movement.

27 I am here referring to the humanitarian convoys of mainly Turkish-registered vessels that sought to challenge the blockade of Gaza in May 2010.

28 See Adorno (1973: 17).

BIBLIOGRAPHY

Abdel Nasser, G. (1955) 'The Egyptian revolution', *Foreign Affairs*, 33: 199–211.

Abu Lughud, L. (1990) 'The romance of resistance: tracing transformations of power through Bedouin women', *American Ethnologist*, 17(1): 41–55.

Adamson, F. (2005) 'Global liberalism versus political Islam: frameworks in international politics', *International Studies Review*, 7(4): 547–569.

Adorno, T.W. (1973) *Negative Dialectics,* trans. E.B. Ashton (New York: Continuum).

Adorno, T.W. (1998) 'Marginalia to theory and praxis', in *Critical Models: Interventions and Catchwords*, trans. H.W. Pickford (New York: Columbia University Press).

Adorno, T.W. and M. Horkheimer (1979) *Dialectic of Enlightenment* (London and New York: Verso).

Afary, J. and K.B. Anderson (2005) *Foucault and the Iranian Revolution* (Chicago and London: University of Chicago Press).

Agamben, G. (1995) *Homo Sacer: Sovereign Power and Bare Life*, trans. D. Heller-Roazen (Stanford, CA: Stanford University Press).

Agamben, G. (2005) *State of Exception* (Chicago, Ill: University of Chicago Press)

Agathangelou, A. M. and L. H. M. Ling (2009) *Transforming World Politics: From Empire to Multiple Worlds* (London and New York: Routledge).

Ahluwalia, P. (2001) *Politics and Post-Colonial Theory: African Inflections* (London and New York: Routledge).

Ahmad, A. (1992) *In Theory: Classes, Nations, Literatures* (London: Verso).

Al-Jabbar, F.A. (1995) *The State, Civil Society and the Democratic Transition in Iraq* (Cairo: Ibn Khaldun Centre).

Al-Khalili, J. (2010) *Pathfinders: The Golden Age of Arabic Science* (London: Allen Lane).

Al-Mattar, H. (2011) *Anatomy of a Disappearance* (London: Penguin).

Alawi, A. (2007) *The Occupation of Iraq: Winning the War, Losing the Peace* (New Haven, CT: Yale University Press).

Ali, T. (2003) *Bush in Babylon: The Recolonisation of Iraq* (London: Verso).

Almond, I. (2004) 'The madness of Islam: Foucault's Occident and the revolution in Iran', *Radical Philosophy*, 128: 12–22.

Amin, S. (2011) *Maldevelopment: Anatomy of a Global Failure* (Cape Town, Nairobi, and Oxford: Pambazuka Press).

Anderson, D. (2004) *Histories of the Hanged* (London: Weidenfeld and Nicolson).

Anghie, A. (2004) *Imperialism, Sovereignty and the Making of International Law* (Cambridge: Cambridge University Press).

Antonius, G. (1946) *The Arab Awakening: The Story of the Arab National Movement* (New York: Capricorn Books).

Appadurai, A. (1993) 'Patriotism and its futures', *Public Culture*, 5(3): 411–429.

Appiah, K.A. (1997) 'Is the "post" in postcolonial the same as the "post" in postmodern?', in A. McLintock, A. Mufti, and E. Shohat (eds) *Dangerous Liaisons: Gender, Nation, and Postcolonial Perspectives* (Minneapolis: University of Minnesota Press).

Aravamudan, S. (2009) 'Hobbes and Amercia', in D. Carey and L. Festa (eds) *Postcolonial Enlightenment* (Oxford and New York: Oxford University Press).

Archibugi, D. (2008) *The Global Commonwealth of Citizens: Toward Cosmopolitan Democracy* (Princeton, NJ: Princeton University Press).

Arendt, H. (1958) *The Human Condition* (Chicago: University of Chicago Press).

Arendt, H. (1963) *Eichmann in Jerusalem: A report on the banality of evil* (New York: Viking).

Arendt, H. (1968a) *Men in Dark Times* (New York and London: Harcourt, Brace and Company).

Arendt, H. (1968b) *The Origins of Totalitarianism* (San Diego, New York, and London: Harcourt Inc.).

Arendt, H. (1977) *On Revolution* (London and New York: Penguin).

Asad, T. (1997) 'Europe against Islam, Islam in Europe', *The Muslim World*, 87(2): 183–195.

Asad, T. (2003) *Formations of the Secular: Christianity, Islam, Modernity* (Stanford, CA: Stanford University Press).

Ayoob, M. (1995) *The Third World Security Predicament: State-making, Regional Conflict, and the International System* (Boulder, Co: Lynne Rienner).

Ayubi, N. (1993) *Political Islam: Religion and Politics in the Arab World* (New York, NY: Routledge).

Ayubi, N. (2006) *Over-stating the Arab State: Politics and Society in the Middle East* (London: IB Tauris).

Balibar, E. (2002) *Politics and the Other Scene* (London: Verso).

Banerji, D. (2009) *The Alternate Nation of Abanindrabath Tagore* (London and New Delhi: Sage).

Barkawi, T. (2006) *Globalization and War* (Lanham, MD: Rowman and Littlefield).

Barkawi, T. and M. Laffey (2006) 'The postcolonial moment in security studies', *Review of International Studies*, 32: 329–352.

Bartelsen, J. (1995) *A Genealogy of Sovereignty* (Cambridge: Cambridge University Press).

Batatu, H. (2004) *The Old Social Classes and the Revolutionary Movements of Iraq* (London: Saqi Books, 2004).

Bauman, Z. (2000) *Liquid Modernity* (Cambridge: Polity).

Bayat, A. (1998) 'Revolution without movement, movement without revolution: comparing Islamic activism in Iran and Egypt', *Comparative Studies in Society and History*, 40: 136–169.

Beardsworth, R. (1996) *Derrida and the Political* (London and New York, Routledge).

Beckett, I. (1990), 'The study of counter-insurgency: a British perspective', *Small Wars and Insurgencies*, 1(1): 47–53.

Ben Jelloun, T. (2002) *The Blinding Absence of Light* (New York: The New Press).

Benjamin, W. (1999a) 'Theses on the philosophy of history', in *Illuminations*, edited with an Introduction by Hannah Arendt, trans. H. Zorn (London: Pimlico).

Benjamin, W. (1999b) 'The storyteller', in *Illuminations*, edited with an Introduction by Hannah Arendt, trans. H. Zorn (London: Pimlico).

Bernstein, R. (2006) 'Derrida: the aporia of forgiveness', *Constellations*, 13(3): 394–406.

Bhabha, H. (1994) *The Location of Culture* (London and New York: Routledge).

Birmingham, D. (1998) *Kwame Nkrumah: The Father of African Nationalism* (Athens: Ohio University Press).

Bleiker, R. (2000) *Popular Dissent, Human Agency and Global Politics* (Cambridge: Cambridge University Press).

Blum, W. (2003) *Killing Hope: US Military and CIA Interventions since World War II* (London: Zed Books).

Bobbio, N. (1995), 'Democracy and the international system', in D. Archibugi and D. Held (eds) *Cosmopolitan Democracy* (Cambridge: Polity Press).

Bohrer, K.M. (1994) *Suddenness: On the Moment of Aesthetic Appearance* (New York: Columbia University Press).

Botman, S. (1998) 'The Liberal age, 1923–1952', in M.W. Daly, *The Cambridge History of Egypt*, vol. 2 (Cambridge: Cambridge University Press).

Boullata, I.J. (1970) 'Badr Shakir al-Sayyab and the free verse movement', *International Journal of Middle East Studies*, 1, 3: 248–258.

Browers, M. (2006) *Democracy and Civil Society in Arab Political Thought: Transcultural Possibilities* (Syracuse, NY: Syracuse University Press).

Buck-Morss, S. (2003) *Thinking Past Terror: Islamism and Critical Theory on the Left* (London: Verso).

Burgess, P.J. and T. Owen (2004), 'Editors' note', Special Section, *Security Dialogue*, 35(3): 345–346.

Burnham, G., R. Lafta, S. Doocy, and L. Roberts (2006) 'Mortality after the 2003 invasion of Iraq: a cross-sectional cluster sample survey', *The Lancet*, 368(9545): 1421–1428.

Butler, J. (2004) *Precarious Life: The Powers of Mourning and Violence* (London and New York: Verso).

Calhoun, C. (2002) 'Imagining solidarity: cosmopolitanism, constitutional patriotism, and the public sphere', *Public Culture*, 14(1): 147–171.

Calhoun, C. and J. McGowan (1997) 'Introduction: Hannah Arendt and the meaning of politics', in C. Calhoun and C. McGowan (eds) *Hannah Arendt and the Meaning of Politics* (Minneapolis, MN: University of Minnesota Press).

Caney, S. (2005) *Justice Beyond Borders: A Global Political Theory* (Oxford: Oxford University Press, 2005).

Canovan, M. (1992) *Hannah Arendt: A Reinterpretation of Her Political Thought* (Cambridge: Cambridge University Press).

Caygill, H. (1995) *A Kant Dictionary* (Oxford: Blackwell).

Chakrabarty, D. (1989) *Rethinking Working Class History: Bengal 1890–1940* (Princeton, NJ: Princeton University Press).

Chakrabarty, D. (1992) 'Postcoloniality and the artifice of history: who speaks for "Indian" pasts', *Representations*, 37: 1–26.

Chakrabarty, D. (2000) *Provincialising Europe: Postcolonial Thought and Historical Difference* (Princeton, NJ: Princeton University Press).

Chan, S. (2007) *Grasping Africa: A Tale of Tragedy and Achievement* (London: I.B. Tauris).

Chan, S., P. Mandaville, and R. Bleiker (eds) (2001) *The Zen of International Relations* (London and New York: Palgrave Macmillan).

Chandler, D. (2006) *Empire in Denial: the Politics of Statebuilding* (London: Pluto).

Chandler, D. (2008) *Statebuilding and Intervention: Policies, Practices, and Paradigms* (London and New York, Routledge).

Chandrasekaran, R. (2006) *Imperial Life in the Emerald City: Inside Baghdad's Green Zone* (London: Bloomsbury).

Chatterjee, P. (1986) *Nationalist Thought and the Colonial World* (London: Zed Books).

Chatterjee, P. (1993) *The Nation and its Fragments: Colonial and Postcolonial Histories* (Princeton, NJ: Princeton University Press).

Chatterjee, P. (2004) *The Politics of the Governed: Reflections on Popular Politics in Most of the World* (New York, NY: Columbia University Press).

Choueiri, Y.M. (2003) *Modern Arab Historiography: Historical Discourse and the Nation-State* (London and New York: Routledge).

Coole, D. (2000) *Negativity and Politics: Dionysus and Dialectics from Kant to Poststructuralism* (London and New York: Routledge).

Coole, D. (2010) 'The inertia of matter and the generativity of flesh', in D. Coole and S. Frost (eds) *New Materialisms: Ontology, Agency and Politics* (Duke University Press).

Coole, D. and S. Frost (2010) 'Introducing the new materialism', in D. Coole and S. Frost (eds) *New Materialisms: Ontology, Agency and Politics* (Duke University Press).

Dallmayr, F. (2003), 'Cosmopolitanism: moral and political', *Political Theory*, 31(3): 421–442.

Dawisha, A. (2003) *Arab Nationalism in the Twentieth Century: From Triumph to Despair* (Princeton, NJ: Princeton University Press).

Dawisha, A. (2005) 'Democratic attitudes and practices in Iraq 1921–1958', *The Middle East Journal*, 59(1): 11–30.

Dawn, C.E. (1991) 'The Origins of Arab Nationalism', in R. Khalidi, L. Anderson, M. Muslih, R.S. Simon (eds) *The Origins of Arab Nationalism* (New York, NY: Columbia University Press).

Dean, M. (1999) *Governmentality: Power and Rule in Modern Society* (London: Sage).

Desai, K. (2006) *The Inheritance of Loss* (London: Hamish Hamilton).

DeYoung, T. (1998) *Placing the Poet: Badr Shakir al-Sayyab and Postcolonial Iraq* (Albany, NY: State University of New York Press).

Dillon, M. (1998) 'Criminalising social and political violence internationally', *Millennium: Journal of International Studies*, 27(3): 543–69.

Dillon, M. and L. Lobo-Guerrero (2008), 'Biopolitics of security in the 21st century: an introduction', *Review of International Studies*, 34(2): 265–292.

Dillon, M. and J. Reid (2009) *The Liberal Way of War* (London and New York: Routledge).

Dirlik, A. (1994) 'The postcolonial aura: third world criticism in the age of global capitalism', *Critical Inquiry*, 20(2): 328–356.

Dodge, T. (2003) *Inventing Iraq* (New York: Columbia University Press).

Douzinas, C. (2007) *Human Rights and Empire: The Political Philosophy of Cosmopolitanism* (London and New York: Routledge).

Duffield, M. (2007) *Development, Security and Unending War: Governing the World of Peoples* (Cambridge: Polity).

Dussel, E. (1998) *The Underside of Modernity* (New York: Humanity Books).

Edkins, J. (1999) *Poststructuralism and International Relations: Bringing the Political Back in* (Boulder, CO: Lynne Rienner).

Edkins, J. and V. Pin-Fat (1999) 'The subject of the political', in J. Edkins, N. Persram, and V. Pin-Fat (eds), *Sovereignty and Subjectivity* (Boulder, CO: Lynne Rienner).

Ehteshami, A. and S. Wright (2007) 'Political change in the Arab oil monarchies: from liberalization to enfranchisement', *International Affairs*, 83(5): 913–932

Elkins, C. (2005) *Britain's Gulag: The Brutal End of Empire in Kenya* (London: Cape).

Falk, R. (2005). 'Legality and legitimacy: the quest for principled flexibility and restraint', review of *International Studies*, 31: 33–50.

Fanon, F. (1986) Black Skin, White Masks, trans. C.L. Markmann (London: Pluto Press).

Fanon, F. (1967) *The Wretched of the Earth*, trans. C. Farrington (Harmondsworth: Penguin).

Ferguson, N. (2003) *Empire: How Britain Made the Modern World* (London: Allen Lane).

Findlay, R. and K. O'Rourke (2007) *Power and Plenty: Trade, War, and the World Economy in the Second Millennium* (Princeton, NJ: Princeton University Press).

Finnemore, M. (2003) *The Purpose of Intervention: Changing Beliefs about the Use of Force* (Cornell University Press).

Finnemore, M. and S. Toope (2001) 'Alternatives to legalisation: richer views of law and politics', *International Organisation*, 55: 743–758.

Foucault, M. (1970) *The Order of Things* (London: Routledge).

Foucault, M. (1977) *Discipline and Punish*, trans. A. Sheridan (London: Penguin).

Foucault, M. (1978) *The Will to Knowledge, History of Sexuality*, vol. 1, trans R. Hurley (London: Penguin).

Foucault, M. (1980) *Power/Knowledge*, ed. Colin Gordon (New York and London: Prentice Hall).

Foucault, M. (1980) 'Questions of geography', in M. Foucault, *Power/Knowledge*, ed. Colin Gordon (New York and London: Prentice Hall).

Foucault, M. (1982) 'The subject and power', *Critical Inquiry*, 8(4): 777–795.

Foucault, M. (1984a) 'What is Enlightenment?', in P. Rabinow (ed.) *The Foucault Reader* (London: Penguin).

Foucault, M. (1984b) 'Space, knowledge, and power', in P. Rabinow (ed.) *The Foucault Reader* (London: Penguin), pp. 239–256.

Foucault, M (2001a) 'Governmentality', in *Power: The Essential Works*, vol. 3, ed. J.D. Faubion (London: Allen Lane).

Foucault, M. (2001b) 'The subject and power' in *Power: The Essential Works*, vol. 3, ed. J.D. Faubion (London: Allen Lane).

Foucault, M. (2003) *Society Must Be Defended*, trans. D. Macey (London: Allen Lane).

Foucault, M. (2006) *History of Madness* (London and New York: Routledge).

Foucault, M. (2007) *Security, Territory, Population*, trans. G. Burchell (London and New York: Palgrave Macmillan).

Fraser, N. (2007) 'Transnationalizing the public sphere: on the legitimacy and efficacy of public opinion in a postWestphalian world', in S. Benhabib, I. Shapiro, and D. Petranovich (eds) *Identities, Affiliations and Allegiances* (Cambridge: Cambridge University Press).

Frazer, E. and K. Hutchings (2008), 'On politics and violence: Arendt contra Fanon', *Contemporary Political Theory*, 7: 90–108.

Giddens, A. (1985) *The Nation-State and Violence* (Cambridge: Polity).

Giddens, A. (1991) *Modernity and Self-Identity: Self and Society in the Late Modern Age* (Cambridge: Polity).

Goldberg, E. (1992) 'Peasants in revolt – Egypt 1919', *International Journal of Middle East Studies*, 24(2): 261–280.

Gregory, D. (2004) *The Colonial Present* (Oxford: Blackwell).

Grovogui, S. (1996) *Sovereigns, Quasi Sovereigns, and Africans: Race and Self-Determination in International Law* (Minneapolis, MN: University of Minnesota Press).

Grovogui, S. (2002) 'Regimes of sovereignty: international morality and the African condition', *European Journal of International Relations*, 8(3): 315–338.

Grovogui, S. (2006) 'Mind, body, and gut! Elements of a postcolonial human rights discourse', in B.G. Jones (ed.) *Decolonising International Relations* (Lanham, MD: Rowman and Littlefield).

Guardiola-Rivera, O. (2010) *What if Latin America Rules the World?* (London: Bloomsbury).

Guha, R. (1994) 'The prose of counterinsurgency', in N. B. Dirks, G. Eley, and S. B. Ortner (eds), *Culture/Power A Reader in Contemporary Social Theory* (Princeton, NJ: Princeton University Press).

Guha, R. (1997) 'Not at home in Empire', *Critical Inquiry*, 23, 3: 482–493.

Habermas, J. (1994) *The Past as Future*, interviewed by M. Haller, trans. and ed. M. Pensky (Cambridge: Polity).

Habermas, J. (1997) 'Kant's idea of perpetual peace, with the benefit of two hundred years' hindsight', in J. Bohman and M. Lutz-Bachmann (eds) *Perpetual Peace: Essays on Kant's Cosmopolitan Ideal* (Cambridge, MA, and London: The MIT Press).

Habermas, J. (2001) *The Postnational Constellation: Political Essays* (Cambridge, Mass: MIT Press).

Hall, S. (1996), 'When was the post-colonial'? in I. Chambers and L. Curtis (eds), *The Post-colonial Question: Common Skies, Divided Horizons* (London and New York: Routledge).

Halliwell, C. and B. Hindess (2002) 'The empire of uniformity and the government of subject peoples', *Cultural Values*, 6(1–2): 139–152.

Hardt, M. and A. Negri (2001) *Empire* (Cambridge, MA: Harvard University Press).

Hardt, M. and A. Negri (2004) *Multitude* (New York: Penguin).

Hardt, M. and A. Negri (2011) 'Arabs are democracy's new pioneers', *The Guardian*, 25th February 2011: 34.

Harvey, D. (2005) *The New Imperialism* (Oxford: Oxford University Press).

Harvey, D. (2007) *A Brief History of Neoliberalism* (Oxford: Oxford University Press.

Held, D. (1995) *Democracy and the Global Order: From the Modern State to Cosmopolitan Governance* (Stanford, CA: Stanford University Press).

Held, D. (2010) *Cosmopolitanism: Ideals and Realities* (Cambridge: Polity).

Hindess, B. (2004) 'Liberalism - what's in a name', in W. Larner and W. Walters (eds) *Global Governmentality: Governing International Spaces* (London and New York: Routledge).

Honig, B. (1988) 'Arendt, identity, and difference', *Political Theory*, 16(1): 77–98.

Honig, B. (1991) 'Declarations of independence: Arendt and Derrida on the problem of founding a republic', *American Political Science Review*, 85(1): 97–113.

Honig, B. (1995) 'Introduction: the Arendt question in feminism', in B. Honig (ed.) *Feminist Interpretations of Hannah Arendt* (University Park, PA: Pennsylvania State University Press).

Honig, B. (2007), 'Between decision and deliberation: political paradox in democratic theory', *American Political Science Review*, 101(1): 1–17.

Hourani, A. (1983) *Arabic Thought in the Liberal Age 1798–1939* (Cambridge: Cambridge University Press).

Hughes, M. (2009) 'The practice and theory of British counter-insurgency: the histories of the atrocities at the Palestinian villages of Al-Bassa and Halhul, 1938–1939', *Small Wars and Insurgencies*, 20(3–4): 528–550.

Huntington, S.P. (1997) *The Clash of Civilisations and the Remaking of World Order* (New York, NY: Simon and Schuster).

Hutchings, K. (1999) *International Political Theory: Rethinking Ethics in a Global Era* (London: Sage).

Inayatullah, N. and D. Blaney (2004) *International Relations and the Problem of Difference* (London and New York: Routledge).

Ingram, J.D. (2008) 'What is a "right to have rights"? Three images of the politics of human rights', *American Political Science Review*, 102(4): 401–416.

Jabri, V. (2006) 'Shock and awe: power and the resistance of art', *Millennium: Journal of International Studies*, 34(3): 819–839.

Jabri, V. (2007a) *War and the Transformation of Global Politics* (London and New York, Palgrave Macmillan).

Jabri, V. (2007b) 'Michel Foucault's analytics of war: the social, the international, and the racial', *International Political Sociology*, 1(1): 67–81.

Jabri, V. (2007c) 'Solidarity and spheres of culture: the cosmopolitan and the postcolonial', *Review of International Studies*, 33: 715–728.

Jabri, V. (2009) 'Security, multiculturalism, and the cosmopolis', in A. Closs Stephens and N. Vaughan-Williams (eds) *Terrorism and the Politics of Response* (London: Routledge).

Jabri, V. (2011) 'Cosmopolitan politics, security, political subjectivity', *European Journal of International Relations*, published online first, at http://ejt.sagepub.com/content/early/20 11/04/22/1354066110397218.

Jackson, R.H. (1993) *Quasi-states, Sovereignty, International Relations and the Third World* (Cambridge: Cambridge University Press).

Jahn, B. (2000) *The Cultural Construction of International Relations: The Invention of the State of Nature* (London: Palgrave Macmillan).

James's, C.L.R. (1938) *The Black Jacobins* (London: Penguin).

Jameson, F. (2003) 'The end of temporality', *Critical Inquiry*, 29, 4: 695–718.

Joas, H. (2003) *War and Modernity* (Cambridge: Polity Press).

Jones, B.G. (ed) (2006) *Decolonising International Relations* (Lanham, MD: Rowman and Littlefield).

Joya, M. (2009) *Raising My Voice: The Extraordinary Story of the Afghan Woman Who Dares to Speak Out* (New York: Rider, Random House).

Kalyvas, A. (2005) 'Popular sovereignty, democracy, and the constituent power', *Constellations*, 12(2): 223–244.

Kalyvas, A. (2008) *Democracy and the Politics of the Extraordinary* (Cambridge: Cambridge University Press).

Kang, D.C. (2003) 'Getting Asia wrong: the need for new analytical frameworks', *International Security*, 27(4): 57–85.

Kant, I. (1970) *Political Writings*, ed. H. Riess, trans. H.B. Nisbet (Cambridge: Cambridge University Press).

Kapoor, I. (2002) 'Capitalism, culture, agency: dependency versus postcolonial theory', *Third World Quarterly*, 23(4): 647–664.

Kapoor, I. (2003) 'Acting in a tight spot: Homi Bhabha's postcolonial politics', *New Political Science*, 25(4): 561–577.

Kaviraj, S. (1997) 'Religion and identity in India', *Ethnic and Racial Studies*, Vol. 20(2): 325–344.

Keen, E. (2007) 'A case-study of the construction of international hierarchy: British treaty-making against the slave trade in the early nineteenth century', *International Organisation*, 61: 311–339.

Khalidi, R. (1991) 'Ottomanism and Arabism in Syria before 1914: a reassessment', in R. Khalidi, L. Anderson, M. Muslih, R.S. Simon (eds) *The Origins of Arab Nationalism* (New York, NY: Columbia University Press).

Kiernan, M. (1995) 'Cultural hegemony and national film language', *Alif: Journal of Comparative Poetics*, 15: 130–152.

Koskenniemi, M. (2005) *From Apology to Utopia: The Structure of International Legal Argument* (Cambridge: Cambridge University Press).

Koselleck, R. (1988) *Critique and Crisis: Enlightenment and the Pathogenesis of Modern Society* (Cambridge, MA: MIT Press).

Krishna, S. (1999) *Postcolonial Insecurities: India, Sri Lanka, and the Question of Nationhood* (Minneapolis, MN: University of Minnesota Press).

Krishna, S. (2009) *Globalization and Postcolonialism: Hegemony and Resistance in the Twenty-First Century* (Lanham, MD: Rowman and Littlefield).

Kristeva, J. (1982) *Powers of Horror: An Essay on Abjection* (New York: Columbia University Press).

Kristeva, J. (2000) *Crisis of the European Subject*, trans. S. Fairfield (New York: Other Press).

Kristeva, J. (2002a) *Revolt, She Said*, interviewed by P. Petit, trans. B. O'Keeffe, ed. S. Lotringer (Cambridge, Mass: The MIT Press).

Kristeva, J. (2002b) *The Intimate Revolt*, trans. J. Herman (New York, NY: Columbia University Press).

Laclau, E. (2000), 'Identity and hegemony: the role of universality in the constitution of political logics', in J. Butler, E. Laclau, and S. Zizek (2000) *Contingency, Hegemony, Universality* (London: Verso).

Lazarus, N. (ed.) (2004) *The Cambridge Companion to Postcolonial Literary Studies* (Cambridge: Cambridge University Press).

Lefebvre, H. (1991) *The Production of Space*, trans. D. Nicholson-Smith (Oxford, Blackwell).

Lewis, B. (2004) *The Crisis of Islam: Holy War and Unholy Terror* (New York: Random House).

Linklater, A. (1998) *The Transformation of Political Community* (Cambridge: Polity Press).

Loomba, A. (1993) 'Dead women tell no tales: issues of female subjectivity, subaltern agency and tradition in colonial and postcolonial writings on widow immolation in India', *History Workshop Journal*, 36: 209–227.

Mahfouz, N. (1991) *Palace Walk, The Cairo Trilogy*, vol. I, trans. W.M. Hutchins and O.E. Kenny (London and New York: Doubleday).

Mamdani, M (1996) *Citizen and Subject: Contemporary Africa and the Legacy of Late Colonialism* (Princeton, NJ: Princeton University Press).

Mandaville, P. (2001) *Transnational Muslim Politics: Reimagining the Umma* (London and New York: Routledge).

Mandaville, P. (2007) *Global Political Islam* (London and New York: Routledge).

Mann, M. (1993) *The Sources of Social Power*, Vol II (Cambridge: Cambridge University Press).

Marr, P. (2007) 'The development of a nationalist ideology in Iraq, 1920–41', *The Muslim World*, 75(2): 85–101.

Marx, K. (1975) *Early Writings* (Harmondsorth: Penguin).

Massey, D. (2005) *For Space* (London: Sage).

Mbembe, A. (1992) 'Provisional notes on the postcolony', *Africa*, 62(1): 3–37.

Mbembe, A. (2001) *On the Postcolony* (Berkeley, CA: University of California Press)

McLennan, G. (2003) 'Sociology, Eurocentrism and postcolonial theory', *European Journal of Social Theory*, 6(1): pp. 69–86.

Memi, A. (1967) *Coloniser and Colonised* (Boston: Beacon Press).

Memi, A. (2006) *Decolonization and Decolonized* (Minneapolis, MN: University of Minnesota Press).

Mernissi, F. (1993) *Islam and Democracy: Fear of the Modern World* (London: Virago).

Mignolo, W. (2000) *Local Histories/Global Designs: Coloniality, Subaltern Knowledges, and Border Thinking* (Princeton, NJ: Princeton University Press).

Mignolo, W. (2005) *The Idea of Latin America* (Oxford: Blackwell).

Mignolo, W.D. and M.V. Tlostanova (2006), 'Theorizing from the borders: shifting to geo- and body-politics of knowledge', *European Journal of Social Theory*, Vol 9 (2): 205–221.

Mishra, V. and B. Hodge (2005), 'What Was Postcolonialism?', *New Literary History*, Vol. 36, pp. 375–402.

Mitchell, T. (1991) *Colonising Egypt* (Berkeley, CA: University of California Press).

Mitter, P. (1994) *Art and Nationalism in Colonial India 1850–1922* (Cambridge, Cambridge University Press).

Mouffe, C. (2000) *The Democratic Paradox* (London: Verso).

Muppidi, H. (2004) *The Politics of the Global* (Minneapolis, MN: University of Minnesota Press).

Muppidi, H. (2005) 'Colonial and postcolonial global governance', in M.N. Barnett and R. Duvall (eds) *Power in Global Governance* (Cambridge and New York: Cambridge University Press).

Nafissi, M.R. (1998) 'Reframing Orientalism: Weber and Islam', *Economy and Society*, 27(1): 97–118.

Nandy, A. (1983) *The Intimate Enemy: Loss and Recovery of Self under Colonialism* (Oxford: Oxford University Press).

Nehru, J. (1961) India's foreign policy: selected speeches (Bombay: Ministry of Information and Broadcasting).

Neruda, P. (1976) *Fully Empowered*, trans. A. Reid (London: Souvenir Press).

Nkrumah, K. (1965) *Neocolonialism: The Highest Stage of Imperialism* (London: Heinemann).

Norris, J. (2008) 'Repression and rebellion: Britain's response to the Arab Revolt in Palestine of 1936–39', *The Journal of Imperial and Commonwealth History*, 36 (1): 25–45.

Nussbaum, M (2006) *Frontiers of Justice: Disability, Nationality, Species Membership* (Cambridge, Mass: Harvard University Press).

O'Hanlon, R. (1988) '*Recovering the Subject*: Subaltern studies and *Histories of Resistance in Colonial South Asia*', *Modern Asian Studies*, Vol. 22, No. 1, pp. 189–224.

Okri, B. (1999) *Stars of the New Curfew* (London: Vintage).

Orford, A. (2003) *Reading Humanitarian Intervention: Human Rights and the Use of Force in International Law* (Cambridge: Cambridge University Press).

Owens, P. (2007) *Between War and Politics: International Relations and the Thought of Hannah Arendt* (Oxford: Oxford University Press).

Pahnja, S. (2005) 'The postcoloniality of international law', *Harvard International Law Journal*, 46(2): 459–469.

Pandey, G. (2006) *Routine Violence: Nations, Fragments, Histories* (Stanford, NJ: Stanford University Press).

Pasha, M.K. (2011) 'Western nihilism and dialogue: prelude to an uncanny encounter in international relations', *Millennium – Journal of International Studies*, 39(3): 683–699.

Reid, D.M. (1992) 'Cultural imperialism and nationalism: the struggle to define and control the heritage of Arab art in Egypt', *International Journal of Middle East Studies*, 24: 57–76.

Reus-Smit, C. (2011) 'Struggles for individual rights and the expansion of the international system', *International Organisation*, 65(2): 207–242.

Richmond, O. (2005) *The Transformation of Peace* (London and New York: Palgrave).

Rodinson, M. (1974) *Islam and Capitalism* (London: Penguin).

Roy, P. (1998) *Indian Traffic: Identities in Question in Colonial and Postcolonial India* (Berkeley and Los Angeles, CA, and London: University of California Press).

Russell, M. (2001) 'Competing, overlapping, and contradictory agendas: Egyptian education under British occupation, 1882–1922', *Comparative Studies of South Asia, Africa, and the Middle East*, 22, 1 and 2: 50–60.

Saachi Gallery (2007) *Unveiled: New Art from the Middle East* (London: Booth Clibborn).

Said, E. (1978) *Orientalism: Western Conceptions of the Orient* (London: Penguin).

Said, E. (1993) *Culture and Imperialism* (London: Chatto and Windus).

Said, E. (1997) *Covering Islam: How the Media and the Experts Determine How We See the Rest of the World* (London: Vintage).

Said, E. (2004), *Power, Politics, and Culture: Interviews with Edward W. Said*, ed. G. Viswanathan (London: Bloomsbury).

Sajed, A. (2012) 'The post always rings twice? The Algerian war, poststructuralism, and the postcolonial in IR theory', *Review of International Studies*, 38(1): 141–163.

Sartre, J-P (2006) *Colonialism and Neocolonialism*, trans. A. Haddour and T. McWilliams (London and New York: Routledge, 2006).

Sassen, S. (2006) *Territory, Authority, Rights: From Medieval to Global Assemblages* (Princeton, NJ: Princeton University Press).

Scott, D (1996) 'The aftermaths of sovereignty: postcolonial criticism and the claims of political modernity', *Social Text 48*, 14(3): 1–26.

Shalan, J. (2002) 'Writing the nation: the emergence of Egypt in the modern Arabic novel', *Journal of Arabic Literature*, 33(3): 211–247.

Shapiro, M.J. (1997) *Violent Cartographies: Mapping Cultures of War* (Minneapolis, MN: University of Minnesota Press).

Shapiro, M.J. (2007) 'The new violent cartography', *Security Dialogue*, 38(3): 291–313.

Shilliam, R. (2011) 'The perilous but unavoidable terrain of the non-West', in R. Shilliam (ed) *International Relations and Non-Western Thought: Imperialism, Colonialism and Investigations of Global Modernity* (London and New York: Routledge).

Sjoholm, C. (2005) *Kristeva and the Political* (London and New York: Routledge).

Sluglett, P. (2007) *Britain in Iraq: Contriving King and Country*, 2nd edn (New York: Columbia University Press).

Souare, I.K. (2006), 'Kwame Nkrumah: still remembered 34 years on' *African Renaissance*, 3(3) May/June: 110–116.

Spivak, G.C. (1988) 'Can the subaltern speak?', in C. Nelson and L. Grossberg (eds) *Marxism and the Interpretation of Culture* (London: Macmillan).

Spivak, G.C. (1999) *A Critique of Postcolonial Reason: Toward a History of the Vanishing Present* (Cambridge, MA, and London: Harvard University Press).

Sylvester, C. (1994) *Feminist Theory and International Relations in a Postmodern Era* (Cambridge: Cambridge University Press).

Tilly, C. (1990) *Coercion, Capital, and European States AD 990-1990* (Oxford: Blackwell).

Toulmin, S. (1990) *Cosmopolis: The Hidden Agenda of Modernity* (Chicago, Ill: Chicago University Press).

Tripp, C. (2002) *A History of Iraq* (Cambridge: Cambridge University Press).

Vatikiotis, P.J. (1992) *The History of Modern Egypt*, 4th edn (Baltimore, MD: Johns Hopkins University).

Walker, R.B.J. (1993) *Inside/Outside: International Relations as Political Theory* (Cambridge: Cambridge University Press).

Walker, R.B.J. (2010) *After the Globe Before the World* (London and New York, Routledge).

Weber, C. (1995) *Simulating Sovereignties* (Cambridge: Cambridge University Press).

Wheeler, N. (2002) *Saving Strangers: Humanitarian Intervention in International Society* (Oxford: Oxford University Press).

Willetts, P. (1978) *The Non-Aligned Movement: The Origins of a Third World Alliance* (London and New York: Francis Pinter).

Young, C. (2004) 'The end of the post-colonial state in Africa? Reflections on changing African political dynamics', *African Affairs*, 103(410): 23–49.

Zehfuss, M. (2011) 'Targetting: precision and the production of ethics', *European Journal of International Relations*, 17(3): 543–566.

Zizek, S. (2004) *Iraq: The Borrowed Kettle* (London: Verso).

Zizek, S. (2011) 'What we are witnessing is the Miracle of Tahrir Square', *The Guardian*, Friday 11 February, p. 38.

Zubaida, S. (2002) 'The fragments imagine the nation: the case of Iraq', *International Journal of Middle East Studies*, 34: 205–215.

INDEX

Lightning Source UK Ltd.
Milton Keynes UK
UKOW030730100413

208995UK00001B/44/P